USE YOUR WORDS

Word Power Quizzes and Quotable Quotes
from America's Most Popular Magazine

New York / Montreal

A READER'S DIGEST BOOK

© 2021 Trusted Media Brands, Inc.

All rights reserved. Unauthorized reproduction,
in any manner, is prohibited.

Reader's Digest is a registered trademark of
Trusted Media Brands, Inc.

ISBN 978-1-62145-571-4

We are committed to both the quality of our products and the service we provide to
our customers. We value your comments, so please feel free to contact us.

Reader's Digest Adult Trade Publishing
44 South Broadway
White Plains, NY 10601

For more Reader's Digest products and information, visit our website:
www.rd.com

Printed in China

1 3 5 7 9 10 8 6 4 2

FOR VOLUME 1:
Illustrations copyright ©
Jill Calder, pp. 9, 10, 15, 16, 95, 96, 123, 124, 173, 174
Luc Melanson, pp. 37, 38, 69, 70, 73, 74, 91, 92, 99, 100, 119, 120, 127, 128, 149, 150, 201, 202
Edwin Fotheringham, pp. 39, 40, 43, 44, 65, 66, 141, 142, 197, 198
Ingo Fast, pp. 115, 116, 145, 146, 153, 154, 167, 168, 177, 178 193, 194

Word Power Quiz copyright © by Emily Cox and Henry Rathvon, except
"In Words We Trust," © by Paul Silverman (p. 37); "Words of Yesteryear," © by Alison Ramsey (p. 73); "Decorating Tips," © by Alison Ramsey (p. 119); "Solar Powered," © by Joan Page McKenna (p. 201)

FOR VOLUME 2:
Illustrations copyright ©
Jill Calder, pp. 37, 38, 49, 50, 67, 68, 125, 126, 153, 154, 199, 200
Matthew Cohen, pp. 40, 90, 101, 102
Ingo Fast, pp. 17, 18, 21, 22, 73, 74, 119, 120, 171, 172, 193, 194
Edwin Fotheringham, pp. 45, 46, 123, 124, 195, 196, 197, 198
Hal Mayforth, pp. 63, 64, 91, 92, 127, 128, 167, 168, 175, 176, 179, 180, 203, 204
Luc Melanson, pp. 9, 10, 95, 96, 97, 98, 121, 122, 141, 142, 147, 148, 151, 152
Sirichai Puangsuwan/Shutterstock, pp. 20

Word Power Quiz copyright © by Emily Cox and Henry Rathvon except:
"Morning Papers," p. 9 and "Going Places," p. 141, copyright © by Rub Lutes; "English Cousins," p. 39 and "All That Glitters," p. 93 copyright © by Sarah Chasse; "Perchance to Dream," p. 147, copyright © by Monique Riedel

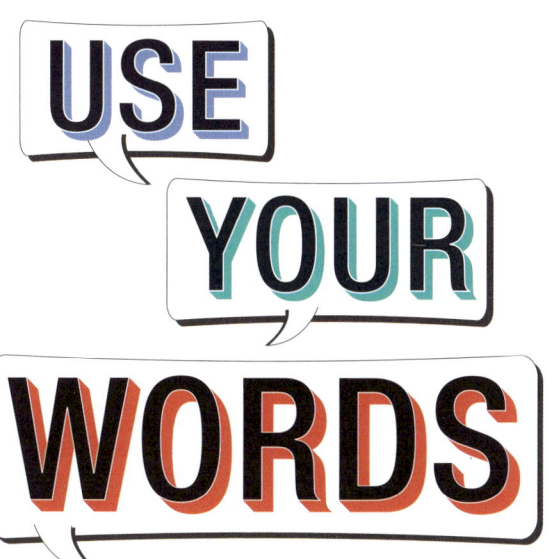

CONTENTS

Introduction
vi

The American Dream
1

Patriotic & Proud
27

Aging Gracefully
55

Love & Marriage
81

Family & Friends
107

Life Is Good
133

A Laugh a Minute
159

Words of Wisdom
185

You'll never have any mental muscle if you don't have any heavy stuff to pick up.

—DIANE LANE

Words matter more than ever in today's world, and we at *Reader's Digest* have a long history of sharing words and their meanings with our readers. Two beloved features of our magazine, Quotable Quotes and Word Power, are brought together for the first time in this unique package so that we can continue to share with you effective and entertaining ways to use your words.

Whether you are looking for the perfect quote for a special occasion or you are simply working on building your vocabulary to impress people at your next social event, you'll find the ideal words right here in these pages. We've combed the archives to pull the funniest and pithiest quotes for all occasions—from family gatherings to political speeches to celebrations of personal milestones—so you'll always feel that you have just the right words at your fingertips. Drawn from books, interviews, speeches, and television shows, these words of wisdom from actors, politicians, scientists, and other thought leaders reflect the diversity of our world and yet ultimately highlight the ways in which we are tied together by profound, humorous, and universal sentiments. Whether we are laughing at the ways children upend our routines, commiserating about heartbreak, or striving to find ways to age gracefully, we find common ground in words that reflect the human experience.

And while we are inspired by words from those we think are more eloquent than we are, we also know that our readers enjoy the challenge of testing their own ways with words. So we've gathered some of our best Word Power quizzes to give you the opportunity to enrich your own vocabulary. With more than fifty quizzes that have challenged readers over the years, we'll help you discover the meaning of unfamiliar words, add new or unusual words to your vocabulary, and help you stay up to date on new words entering the lexicon. Just ask fans of the hit musical *Hamilton* how inimitable it feels to be complicit in the success of a show about manumission, and you'll be on your way to becoming a Word Power expert (see p. 45).

We hope you'll love this unique blend of wit and wisdom to stretch your heart plus fun quizzes to strengthen your brain. As Margaret Atwood said, "A word after a word after a word is power." Use your words, find your power, and amuse yourself one-upping friends and family along the way.

The Editors of *Reader's Digest*

I'm not a businessman.
I'm a business, man.
—JAY-Z

THE AMERICAN DREAM

Though we author our own destinies, we find inspiration in the success stories of others. By listening to the wisdom they have accrued, we can build the next steps into the future.

MAKING IT

Do or do not. There is no try.
—**YODA**

"

Don't just stand there; make something happen.
—**LEE IACOCCA**

"

Every success is usually an admission ticket
to a new set of decisions.
—**HENRY KISSINGER**

"

The key to success?
Work hard, stay focused, and marry a Kennedy.
—**ARNOLD SCHWARZENEGGER**

"

Success is a lot like a bright, white tuxedo. You feel terrific when you get it, but then you're desperately afraid of getting it dirty, of spoiling it in any way.
—**CONAN O'BRIEN**

"

You only have to do a very few things right in your life—
so long as you don't do too many things wrong.
—**WARREN BUFFETT**

Anybody who's really successful has doubts.
—JERRY BRUCKHEIMER

"

There's a ball. There's a hoop. You put the ball through the hoop. That's success.
—KAREEM ABDUL-JABBAR

"

Success is falling nine times and getting up ten.
—JON BON JOVI

"

Success is more permanent when you achieve it without destroying your principles.
—WALTER CRONKITE

"

If you want to be successful, just meditate, man. God will tell you what people need.
—CARLOS SANTANA

"

There is no point at which you can say, "Well, I'm successful now. I might as well take a nap."
—CARRIE FISHER

"

Winning depends on where you put your priorities. It's usually best to put them over the fence.
—JASON GIAMBI

If you're willing to fail interestingly,
you tend to succeed interestingly.

—EDWARD ALBEE

"

Celebrate what you've accomplished,
but raise the bar a little higher
each time you succeed.

—MIA HAMM

"

To succeed in life, you need three things:
a wishbone, a backbone, and a funnybone.

—REBA MCENTIRE

"

You have to dream big, wish hard,
and chase after your goals because
no one is going to do it for you.

—CEELO GREEN

Success is a lousy teacher. It seduces people into thinking they can't lose.

—BILL GATES

THE RIGHT ATTITUDE

Do not allow people to dim your shine because they are blinded. Tell them to put on some sunglasses.
—**LADY GAGA**

"

Fearlessness is the mother of reinvention.
—**ARIANNA HUFFINGTON**

"

If you have the choice between humble and cocky, go with cocky. There's always time to be humble later, once you've been proven horrendously, irrevocably wrong.
—**KINKY FRIEDMAN**

"

It is our responsibilities, not ourselves, that we should take seriously.
—**PETER USTINOV**

"

When you're out of willpower, you can call on stubbornness.
—**HENRI MATISSE**

🐦 QUOTABLE TWEETS

@Tawni3469 Here is what is important. As women we need to support one another not tear each other down. Let's lift each other up.
@SUZEORMANSHOW

❝

When in doubt, look intelligent.
—GARRISON KEILLOR

❝

I go into every game thinking I'm going to be the hero. I have to, or I wouldn't enjoy it.
—DEREK JETER

❝

If you make every game a life-and-death proposition, you're going to have problems. For one thing, you'll be dead a lot.
—DEAN SMITH

❝

One of the secrets of life is to make stepping stones out of stumbling blocks.
—JACK PENN

❝

I know for sure that what we dwell on is who we become.
—OPRAH

MONEY

What's money? A man is a success if he
gets up in the morning and goes to bed at night
and in between does what he wants to do.
—**BOB DYLAN**

"

Success should be worn like a t-shirt, not a tuxedo.
—**PRIYANKA CHOPRA**

"

I don't care how much money you have,
free stuff is always a good thing.
—**QUEEN LATIFAH**

"

They say everybody gets 15 minutes. I hope I'm just inside
the first minute and the next 14 go really slow.
—**TERRENCE HOWARD**

 **QUOTABLE TWEETS**

The greatest commodity to own
is land. It is finite. God is not
making any more of it.
@REALDONALDTRUMP

The American Dream   **7**

THE PERFECT WORDS FOR
COVER LETTERS

Real success is finding your lifework
in the work that you love.
—DAVID MCCULLOUGH

"

The work praises the man.
—IRISH PROVERB

"

Just as there are no little people or
unimportant lives, there is no insignificant work.
—ELENA BONNER

"

One of the greatest sources of energy
is pride in what you are doing.
—UNKNOWN

"

The more I want to get something done,
the less I call it work.
—RICHARD BACH

"

Pleasure in the job puts perfection in the work.
—ARISTOTLE

WORDS AT WORK

Roll up your sleeves and punch in for this quiz of on-the-job vocabulary. If the grind wears you down, turn the page for answers.

1. **oeuvre** ('oo-vruh) *n.*—A: job opening. B: body of work. C: French chef.

2. **arduous** ('ar-je-wus) *adj.*—A: passionate. B: cheap. C: difficult.

3. **bum's rush** (bumz rush) *n.*—A: mass retail markdown. B: five o'clock traffic. C: forcible eviction or firing.

4. **functionary** ('funk-sheh-nar-ee) *n.*—A: jack-of-all-trades. B: number cruncher. C: one who works in a specified capacity or as a government official.

5. **remunerate** (ri-'myu-neh-rayt) *v.*—A: pay for work. B: do the same job repeatedly. C: break a contract.

6. **proletariat** (proh-leh-'ter-ee-et) *n.*— A: working class. B: head honcho. C: cowboy skilled with a lasso.

7. **indolent** ('in-doh-lent) *adj.*—A: unpaid. B: averse to work, lazy. C: migratory.

8. **Luddite** ('luh-diyt) *n.*—A: one who opposes technological change. B: freelancer. C: bigwig.

9. **on spec** (on spek) *adv.*—A: with no assurance of payment. B: exactly as planned. C: in a supervisor's role.

10. **trouper** ('troo-per) *n.*—A: traveling theater actor. B: infantry soldier. C: temp-agency worker.

11. **sinecure** ('siy-nih-kyur) *n.*—A: herbal healer. B: math faculty. C: cushy job.

12. **métier** ('met-yay) *n.*—A: fee for services. B: oath of office. C: area of expertise.

13. **sedentary** ('se-den-ter-ee) *adj.*—A: multitasking. B: mindlessly obedient. C: not physically active.

14. **garnishment** ('gar-nish-ment) *n.*—A: extra pay. B: withholding of wages. C: job in name only.

15. **indentured** (in-'den-sherd) *adj.*—A: having perks. B: bound to work. C: illegally employed.

The American Dream

"Words at Work" Answers

1. oeuvre—[B] body of work. A*nnie Hall* is my favorite movie in Woody Allen's *oeuvre*.

2. arduous—[C] difficult. Rounding up all 400 guests proved a tad *arduous* for the groom.

3. bum's rush—[C] forcible eviction or firing. Whoever built these wobbly chairs should be given the *bum's rush*.

4. functionary—[C] one who works in a specified capacity or as a government official. A local *functionary* for 20 years, Tyler plans to run for a federal post in 2014.

5. remunerate—[A] pay for work. Which office *remunerates* us for these long-distance deliveries?

6. proletariat—[A] working class. Claire is clearly too aristocratic for the rank-and-file *proletariat*.

7. indolent—[B] averse to work, lazy. Santa is furious with this new generation of *indolent* elves.

8. Luddite—[A] one who opposes technological change. Etymology note: *Luddite* refers originally to 19th-century workmen who destroyed machinery as a protest (they took their name from folkloric rebel Ned Ludd).

9. on spec—[A] with no assurance of payment. Despite the lousy market, we agreed to build the house on *spec*.

10. trouper—[A] traveling theater actor. Darla's first paid gig was as a *trouper* with the national cast of *Annie*.

11. sinecure—[C] cushy job. Carol's uncle is the boss, so she's got a *sinecure* as a paper shuffler.

12. métier—[C] area of expertise. They pay her to sing, but Margot's true *métier* is astrophysics.

13. sedentary—[C] not physically active. Studies warn that your body was not meant to be *sedentary* all day.

14. garnishment—[B] withholding of wages. Half of Troy's salary is in *garnishment* for alimony.

15. indentured—[B] bound to work. Hey, I'm not your *indentured* serv*ant*—I quit!

USE YOUR WORDS

PROGRESS

When springtime buds gallop toward the summer growing season, we look at words related to forward movement and progress. See how much headway you can make, then proceed to the next page for answers.

1. expedite ('ek-spuh-dite) *v.*—A: speed along. B: diversify. C: transport.

2. catalyst ('ka-tuh-lihst) *n.*—A: great leap. B: milestone. C: agent of change.

3. anabasis (uh-'na-buh-sis) *n.*—A: military advance. B: groundbreaking idea. C: executive decision.

4. fructify ('fruhk-tuh-fie) *v.*—A: branch out. B: skyrocket. C: bear fruit.

5. instigate ('in-stih-gayt) *v.*—A: incite. B: set goals. C: enact as law.

6. synergy ('sih-ner-jee) *n.*—A: enthusiasm for change. B: combined action. C: lack of drive.

7. watershed ('wah-ter-shed) *n.*—A: sudden loss. B: turning point. C: reserve of strength.

8. precipitately (prih-'sih-puh-tayt-lee) *adv.*—A: very cautiously. B: sequentially. C: with reckless haste.

9. entrepreneur (ahn-truh-preh-'nyoor) *n.*—A: gatekeeper. B: business starter. C: social climber.

10. stratagem ('stra-tuh-jem) *n.*—A: level of success. B: smooth move. C: clever plan.

11. aggrandize (uh-'gran-dize) *v.*—A: enlarge. B: inspire with words. C: replace.

12. vaticinate (vuh-'tih-sih-nayt) *v.*—A: steer to completion. B: predict. C: become holier.

13. avant-garde (ah-vahnt-'gard) *adj.*—A: fearless. B: on the leading edge. C: well-planned.

14. incremental (ihn-kruh-'mehn-tuhl) *adj.*—A: time-saving. B: step-by-step. C: using brain waves.

15. propagate ('prah-puh-gayt) *v.*—A: support. B: prosper. C: spread.

The American Dream

"Progress" Answers

1. expedite—[A] speed along. Would a note with Mr. Hamilton's likeness *expedite* the delivery?

2. catalyst—[C] agent of change. The ambassador's speech was the main *catalyst* for this peace agreement.

3. anabasis—[A] military advance. The general's brilliantly planned *anabasis* forced the enemies to retreat.

4. fructify—[C] bear fruit. "Our efforts will *fructify*," said Holmes to Watson, "if we trace these footprints."

5. instigate—[A] incite. My sister is the most argumentative person I know—she's always *instigating* a fight.

6. synergy—[B] combined action. All the king's horses and all the king's men are working in *synergy* to reassemble Humpty Dumpty.

7. watershed—[B] turning point. Kira's divorce was a *watershed* in her life—not long after, she changed careers and moved across the country.

8. precipitately—[C] with reckless haste. In a three-legged race, it is never wise to start *precipitately*.

9. entrepreneur—[B] business starter. An *entrepreneur* even as a toddler, Nicki once sold her dollhouse to a schoolmate for $100.

10. stratagem—[C] clever plan. Harold tried various *stratagems* before he finally caught the raccoon that was eating his garbage.

11. aggrandize—[A] enlarge. Carlos used his hefty bonus to *aggrandize* his collection of Rolex watches.

12. vaticinate—[B] predict. It's so difficult to *vaticinate* the weather this time of year, so I always carry a sweater.

13. avant-garde—[B] on the leading edge. Is Elaine's writing style *avant-garde* or just incoherent?

14. incremental—[B] step-by-step. The pharaoh was impatient with the *incremental* progress on his latest pyramid.

15. propagate—[C] spread. Uncle Joe is having a tough time *propagating* his flat-Earth theory.

GO FARTHER OR GO FURTHER?

These near-synonyms cause a lot of confusion, but here's an easy way to know which to use: If you're talking about measurable, physical distance, use *farther*, as in, "How much farther is the station?" But if you're talking about a figurative distance, use *further*, as in, "If you pester me any further, I won't drive you any farther."

POWER WORDS

You might say we're using strong language. Our vocabulary quiz features words about power—having it, getting it, or lacking it. After flexing your mental muscles, turn to the next page for answers.

1. anneal (uh-'neel) *v.*—A: toughen. B: weaken gradually. C: submit to authority.

2. doughty ('dow-tee) *adj.*— A: hesitant. B: willing to yield power. C: stouthearted.

3. enervated ('eh-nur-vay-ted) *adj.*—A: lacking vigor. B: strengthened. C: glorified.

4. dint (dihnt) *n.*—A: heavyweight. B: power. C: electrical unit.

5. proxy ('prahk-see) *n.*— A: strong liking. B: authority to act for another. C: king's royal guard.

6. thew (thoo) *n.*—A: muscular strength. B: castle wall. C: term of surrender.

7. buttress ('buh-tress) *v.*— A: shore up. B: challenge head-to-head. C: dethrone.

8. preponderate (pre-'pahn-duh-rayt) *v.*—A: seize control. B: influence by insidious means. C: have greater importance.

9. duress (du-'rehss) *n.*— A: queen's sister. B: sovereign rule. C: compulsion by threat.

10. puissant ('pwee-sahnt) *adj.*— A: powerful. B: subdued by fear. C: cowardly.

11. arrogate ('ehr-uh-gayt) *v.*— A: supply with weapons. B: seize unjustly. C: crown.

12. effete (eh-'feet) *adj.*— A: marked by weakness. B: brawny. C: able to get things done.

13. attenuate (uh-'ten-yoo-wayt) *v.*—A: make firmer. B: make longer. C: make weaker.

14. coup (coo) *n.*—A: strong signal. B: head honcho. C: power grab.

15. ex officio (eks uh-'fih-shee-oh) *adj.*—A: out of power. B: by virtue of position. C: abstaining from a vote.

The American Dream

"Power Words" Answers

1. anneal—[A] toughen. Fans of the Chicago Cubs were *annealed* by decades of misery.

2. doughty—[C] stouthearted. Prince Ari was a meek little boy, but he grew up to be a *doughty* warrior.

3. enervated—[A] lacking vigor. My bout with the flu left me *enervated* for weeks.

4. dint—[B] power. Chloe doesn't have an ear for languages, but she has become proficient in German by *dint* of hard work.

5. proxy—[B] authority to act for another. Tweedledum couldn't attend the vote, so he gave Tweedledee his *proxy*.

6. thew—[A] muscular strength. That guy Biff is all *thew* and no brains.

7. buttress—[A] shore up. My puny allowance isn't doing much to *buttress* my savings.

8. preponderate—[C] have greater importance. In recent years, online news outlets have begun to *preponderate* over traditional print newspapers.

9. duress—[C] compulsion by threat. Indira will eat broccoli, but only under *duress*.

10. puissant—[A] powerful. Octogenarians can still be plenty *puissant*—think Warren Buffett or Queen Victoria.

11. arrogate—[B] seize unjustly. When my mother comes to visit, she immediately *arrogates* my kitchen.

12. effete—[A] marked by weakness. With every failure, Wile E. Coyote's schemes seem more *effete*.

13. attenuate—[C] make weaker. We wear earplugs to *attenuate* the upstairs neighbors' midnight stomping.

14. coup—[C] power grab. The empress had the two conspirators arrested after their attempted *coup*.

15. ex officio—[B] by virtue of position. All department heads are *ex officio* members of the company softball team.

THE GOLDEN ARCH

Why do we call someone an *archbishop*, an *archduke*, or an *archenemy*? The Greeks gave us *arkhos*, meaning "leader," and we've attached it to things good (*archangel*) and bad (*archfiend*). The ending *–archy* ("rule") appears in the kingly monarchy (*mon-* = "one"), the fatherly patriarchy (*pater-* = "father"), and the chaotic anarchy (*an-* = "without").

STUMPED!

What words perplex us most often? The folks at Merriam-Webster revealed 2012's most frequently searched words on their website, and some of them may surprise you. Answers on the next page.

1. paradigm ('payr-a-diym) *n.*—A: puzzle or problem. B: pattern or archetype. C: fringe.

2. malarkey (muh-'lar-kee) *n.*—A: wild partying. B: foolish talk. C: habitual laziness.

3. ubiquitous (yoo-'bik-wi-tus) *adj.*—A: found everywhere. B: pertaining to a wife. C: spoiling for a fight.

4. hypocrite ('hip-uh-krit) *n.*—A: syringe. B: overstatement. C: phony who acts counter to stated beliefs.

5. louche ('loosh) *adj.*—A: quite comfortable. B: of doubtful morals. C: childlike or naive.

6. didactic (diy-'dak-tik) *adj.*—A: taking bold steps. B: intended to teach. C: shrill as crickets.

7. albeit (awl-'bee-it) *conj.*—A: such as. B: even though. C: because.

8. holistic (hoh-'lis-tik) *adj.*—A: sacred. B: three-dimensional. C: involving entire systems.

9. insidious (in-'sid-ee-uhs) *adj.*—A: treacherous. B: known to a select few. C: coiled like a snake.

10. camaraderie (kahm-'rah-duh-ree) *n.*— A: good fellowship. B: photographic memory. C: odd collection.

11. touché (too-'shay) *inter.*—A: "Bon voyage!" B: "Such is life." C: "Good point."

12. conundrum (kuh-'nun-drum) *n.*—A: monotony. B: riddle. C: instrument in a convent.

13. pragmatic (prag-'ma-tik) *adj.*—A: practical. B: boastful. C: stuck in a rut.

14. esoteric ('es-uh-ter-ik) *adj.*—A: distrustful of foreigners. B: of fossil fuels. C: arcane.

15. schadenfreude ('shah-den-froy-duh) *n.*—A: feeling of déjà vu. B: exact copy. C: taking pleasure in another's misfortune.

The American Dream

"Stumped!" Answers

1. paradigm—[B] pattern or archetype. The wax wings aren't working—I need a new *paradigm* for human flight.

2. malarkey—[B] foolish talk. Tell me why your homework isn't done, and spare me the *malarkey*.

3. ubiquitous—[A] found everywhere. I'm still not sure what the film is about, but the *ubiquitous* posters promoting George Clooney's new movie have made me excited to see it!

4. hypocrite—[C] phony who acts counter to stated beliefs. She lectures us about the importance of promptness and then shows up late, the *hypocrite*!

5. louche—[B] of doubtful morals. If you would prefer a *louche* president, by all means vote for my opponent.

6. didactic—[B] intended to teach. Sarah couldn't discuss being a vegan without going off on *didactic* tangents.

7. albeit—[B] even though. Albeit soaked, Dad seemed to enjoy our water-balloon prank.

8. holistic—[C] involving entire systems. In order to see advances across the board, we need to take a holistic approach to improving our schools.

9. insidious—[A] treacherous. It was rather *insidious* of that wolf to

dress up as my grandmother.

10. camaraderie—[A] good fellowship. Despite a dismal win-loss record, our team has plenty of *camaraderie*.

11. touché—[C] "Good point." After Paul observed that I wouldn't be so broke if I didn't buy Jimmy Choos twice a month, I replied, "*Touché.*"

12. conundrum—[B] riddle. Driving into an Italian town is easy; finding your way out is a *conundrum*.

13. pragmatic—[A] practical. We need something more *pragmatic* than rain dances to water our crops.

14. esoteric—[C] arcane. Our club's secret handshake is so *esoteric* that nobody can remember how to do it.

15. schadenfreude—[C] taking pleasure in another's misfortune. I felt a twinge of *schadenfreude* when the Oscar-winning actor didn't get a coveted part.

CROSSWORD CHAMPS

This month, we feature words from the 2016 American Crossword Puzzle Tournament, an annual contest directed by Will Shortz, crossword editor for the *New York Times*. Competitors encountered these words over eight challenging rounds. If you feel puzzled, peek at the next page for answers.

1. bugbear ('buhg-bair) *n.*—A: petty crime. B: character flaw. C: object of dread.

2. sopor ('soh-puhr) *n.*—A: salty taste. B: deep sleep. C: second-year cadet.

3. parlance ('par-lunts) *n.*—A: manner of speaking. B: secret meeting. C: equality.

4. prate ('prayt) *v.*—A: chatter. B: criticize. C: make a grand show.

5. bireme ('biy-reem) *n.*—A: ancient ship propelled by oars. B: marshy tract. C: case of illogic.

6. tiki ('tee-kee) *n.*—A: kitschy cocktail shaker. B: wooden or stone image of a Polynesian god. C: curry sauce.

7. weir ('wair) *n.*—A: ghost. B: mirror image. C: dam in a stream or river.

8. ovine ('oh-viyn) *adj.*—A: of eggs. B: of sheep. C: of grapes.

9. anathema (uh-'na-thuh-muh) *n.*—A: main topic or theme. B: total opposite. C: someone or something intensely disliked.

10. acolyte ('a-kuh-liyt) *n.*—A: follower. B: spiritual healer. C: circle of stones.

11. vituperate (viy-'too-puh-rayt) *v.*—A: give new life to. B: hiss like a snake. C: use harsh language.

12. lasciviously (luh-'sih-vee-uhs-lee) *adv.*—A: with lust. B: in a careless way. C: snidely.

13. tittle ('tih-tuhl) *n.*—A: dot in writing. B: small songbird. C: mob snitch.

14. auspices ('ahs-pih-sez) *n.*—A: flavorings. B: terms of forgiveness. C: patronage.

15. arboreal (ar-'bor-ee-uhl) *adj.*—A: from the north. B: about winds. C: concerning trees.

The American Dream

"Crossword Champs" Answers

1. bugbear—[C] object of dread. Rain is the biggest *bugbear* for the organizers of our town's annual autumn festival.

2. sopor—[B] deep sleep. Rip Van Winkle wasn't just napp*ing*—he was in a doozy of a *sopor*.

3. parlance—[A] manner of speaking. Juan's keynote speech was "mic drop" good, to use the current *parlance*.

4. prate—[A] chatter. Do you have anything useful to tell me, or are you just *prating* into the air?

5. bireme—[A] ancient ship propelled by oars. Don't the centipede's legs remind you of the oars on a Roman *bireme*?

6. tiki—[B] wooden or stone image of a Polynesian god. I traveled to Maui and returned with a lei, a ukulele, and a wooden *tiki*.

7. weir—[C] dam in a stream or river. The river's *weir* helps to prevent flooding.

8. ovine—[B] of sheep. The *ovine* residents of our farm always bleat loudly when they're sheared.

9. anathema—[C] someone or something intensely disliked. I don't mind snakes, but spiders are *anathema*.

10. acolyte—[A] follower. We couldn't even hear the speaker over the chants of his fervent *acolytes*.

11. vituperate—[C] use harsh language. You will get further by being polite than by *vituperating* at full volume.

12. lasciviously—[A] with lust. Ali dipped her finger into the bowl of frosting and then licked it *lasciviously*.

13. tittle—[A] dot in writing. Ryan meticulously dots each i with a perfect *tittle*.

14. auspices—[C] patronage. Under the *auspices* of her mother, little Courtenay has opened a lemonade stand.

15. arboreal—[C] concerning trees. The birds in my backyard prefer their *arboreal* nests to my adorable birdhouses.

FEELING CROSS?

Fans of crosswords may humorously call themselves *cruciverbalists*. This term for puzzle aficionados is stitched together from the Latin *crux* (for "cross") and *verbum* (for "word"). Of course, a tormented solver might point out that *crux* is also at the root of *excruciating* ("painful") and related to *crucible* ("severe test")—and switch to word searches.

TALK LIKE A GENIUS

Does your lexicon need a lift? Try these terms guaranteed to impress even the most well-versed wordsmiths—from the vocabulary-building book *Talk Like a Genius* by Ed Kozak. Stumped? Check the next page for answers.

1. capitulate (kuh-'pih-chuh-layt) *v.*—A: provide funding. B: stop resisting. C: state formally.

2. unequivocal (uhn-ih-'kwih-vuh-kuhl) *adj.*—A: cool under pressure. B: untamed or out of control. C: leaving no doubt.

3. cavalier (ka-vuh-'lir) *adj.*—A: nonchalant or marked by disdainful dismissal. B: dome shaped. C: undefeated or worthy of praise.

4. leery ('lir-ee) *adj.*—A: untrusting. B: odd. C: off balance.

5. levity ('leh-vuh-tee) *n.*—A: taxation. B: merriment. C: departure.

6. penchant ('pen-chunt) *n.*—A: recital. B: strong liking. C: deep thought.

7. bifurcate ('biy-fer-kayt) *v.*—A: tell lies. B: flash like lightning. C: divide into parts.

8. craven ('kray-vuhn) *adj.*—A: chiseled. B: needy or famished. C: cowardly.

9. coterie ('koh-tuh-ree) *n.*—A: exclusive group. B: takeover. C: birdcage.

10. stalwart ('stahl-wert) *adj.*—A: loyal. B: left-handed. C: disguising one's weakness.

11. travesty ('tra-vuh-stee) *n.*—A: wardrobe. B: long journey on foot. C: absurd imitation.

12. hedonism ('hee-duh-nih-zuhm) *n.*—A: espionage. B: sun worship. C: pursuit of pleasure.

13. obviate ('ahb-vee-ayt) *v.*—A: watch over. B: prevent or render unnecessary. C: leave unfinished.

14. excoriate (ek-'skor-ee-ayt) *v.*—A: hollow out. B: criticize harshly. C: sketch in detail.

15. penurious (peh-'nur-ee-uhs) *adj.*—A: given to fits of rage. B: wordy. C: poor.

"Talk Like a Genius" Answers

1. capitulate—[B] stop resisting. Only when I wrapped the pill in bacon did my dog finally *capitulate*.

2. unequivocal—[C] leaving no doubt. The ump unleashed a resonant, *unequivocal* "Steee-rike!"

3. cavalier—[A] nonchalant or marked by disdainful dismissal. Our driver had a shockingly *cavalier* attitude about the steep mountain road ahead.

4. leery—[A] untrusting. Initially, Eve was a touch *leery* of the apple.

5. levity—[B] merriment. Our family thankfully found moments of *levity* during the memorial.

6. penchant—[B] strong liking. Thomas was warned repeatedly about his *penchant* for daydreaming in meetings.

7. bifurcate—[C] divide into parts. If anything, Donald Trump has certainly managed to *bifurcate* the nation.

8. craven—[C] cowardly. She took a markedly *craven* position against the weak crime bill.

9. coterie—[A] exclusive group. Claire's *coterie* consisted entirely of fellow Mozart enthusiasts and violinists.

10. stalwart—[A] loyal. Throughout the senator's campaign, Kerrie has repeatedly shown *stalwart* support.

11. travesty—[C] absurd imitation. Her lawyer demanded an appeal, calling the jury's decision a *travesty* of justice.

12. hedonism—[C] pursuit of pleasure. In Shakespeare's *Henry IV*, young Prince Hal mistakes *hedonism* for heroism.

13. obviate—[B] prevent or render unnecessary. Gloria's doctor hoped that physical therapy would *obviate* the need for more surgery.

14. excoriate—[B] criticize harshly. Coach Keegan was *excoriated* by the media for the play calling during the game's final minutes.

15. penurious—[C] poor. Paul and Carla entered the casino flush and left it *penurious*.

SMART STORY

If you track down the origins of *intelligence*, you find the Latin *inter* ("between, among") plus *legere* ("choose, read"). To be intelligent, then, is literally "to choose among" or "discern." The versatile *legere* also gives us the words *legend, lecture, election,* and *logo*.

EDUCATION COUNTS

Sharpen your pencil and put on your thinking cap—it's time to head back to school. We've selected a roster of words that will challenge learners of all ages. Will you make the grade or draw a blank? Turn the page for answers.

1. parochial (puh-'roh-kee-uhl) *adj.*—A: rigorous. B: elementary. C: run by a church.

2. conscientious (kon-shee-'en-shuhs) *adj.*—A: extremely careful. B: alert. C: well educated.

3. pore (pohr) *v.*—A: quote at length. B: study intently. C: write by hand.

4. carrel ('kehr-uhl) *n.*—A: library nook. B: songbook. C: punctuation mark.

5. curriculum (kuh-'rih-kyuh-luhm) *n.*—A: lecture hall. B: highest grade. C: set of courses.

6. pedantic (pih-'dan-tik) *adj.*—A: misbehaving. B: making a show of knowledge. C: highly poetic.

7. glean (gleen) *v.*—A: divide equally. B: erase. C: gather.

8. rudiments ('roo-duh-ments) *n.*—A: wrong answers. B: small classes. C: beginner's skills.

9. syntax ('sin-tax) *n.*—A: dictionary. B: sentence structure. C: math equation.

10. semantic (sih-'man-tik) *adj.*—A: related to meaning in language. B: collegiate. C: in essay form.

11. pedagogy ('peh-duh-goh-jee) *n.*—A: art of teaching. B: debate tactic. C: study of children.

12. syllabus ('sih-luh-buhs) *n.*—A: word part. B: class outline. C: textbook.

13. woolgathering ('wool-ga-thuh-ring) *n.*—A: taking notes. B: memorizing. C: daydreaming.

14. cognizant ('cog-nuh-zent) *adj.*—A: engrossed. B: aware. C: automated.

15. empirical (im-'peer-ih-kuhl) *adj.*—A: theoretical. B: quick to learn. C: based on observation.

The American Dream

"Education Counts" Answers

1. parochial—[C] run by a church. Years of wearing *parochial* school uniforms left me hating plaid.

2. conscientious—[A] extremely careful. Carly is so *conscientious*—this sloppy book report isn't like her.

3. pore—[B] study intently. Sam *pored* over his European history notes the night before the midterm.

4. carrel—[A] library nook. In graduate school, I'd practically sleep in a *carrel* before final exams.

5. curriculum—[C] set of courses. The first class in Pierre's cooking *curriculum* is Sauces, Soups, and Stews.

6. pedantic—[B] making a show of knowledge. Professor Riordon knows a lot, but I find his bookish teaching style a bit *pedantic*.

7. glean—[C] gather. From what I *glean* from her essays, Shauna has done a lot of traveling.

8. rudiments—[C] beginner's skills. First-year students at Hogwarts must learn the *rudiments* of wizardry.

9. syntax—[B] sentence structure. This sentence a rather tortured *syntax* has.

10. semantic—[A] related to meaning in language. "What's the *semantic* difference between *clown* and *fool*?" our English teacher asked.

11. pedagogy—[A] art of teaching. "There are no lucrative awards for *pedagogy*," said Mr. Wilcox, "but I find it very rewarding."

12. syllabus—[B] class outline. This *syllabus* has no homework assignments listed—woo-hoo!

13. woolgathering—[C] daydreaming. If you hadn't been *woolgathering* in class, you wouldn't have flunked.

14. cognizant—[B] aware. "I'm *cognizant* of the facts of your case," the vice principal told Mason, "but they don't excuse cheating."

15. empirical—[C] based on observation. Brody's science project presents *empirical* evidence that eating chocolate is good for you.

NONWORKING CLASS

Cramming for tests, slaving over papers—school can be a grind. But the word *school* comes from the Greek *shkole*, meaning "idleness." In ancient Greece, *shkole* referred to how the well-to-do spent their spare time: in philosophical discussion. *Shkole* became the Latin *schola* ("meeting place for teachers and students"), which in turn gave us *school*.

EDUCATION

The whole purpose of education is to turn mirrors into windows.
—**SYDNEY J. HARRIS**

"
Education is what survives when what has been learnt has been forgotten.
—**B. F. SKINNER**

"
[Learning] is the only thing which the mind can never exhaust . . . never fear . . . and never dream of regretting.
—**T. H. WHITE**

"
I think sleeping was my problem in school. If school had started at four in the afternoon, I'd be a college graduate today.
—**GEORGE FOREMAN**

"
Education's purpose is to replace an empty mind with an open one.
—**MALCOLM FORBES**

"
Education is a progressive discovery of our own ignorance.
—**WILL DURANT**

THE PERFECT WORDS FOR
GRADUATION SPEECHES

You can't connect the dots looking forward; you can only connect them looking backward. So you have to trust that the dots will somehow connect. You have to trust in something—your gut, destiny, life, karma.
—STEVE JOBS

"
I was a loser in high school. . . . And I'm here to tell my fellow dweebs and losers that your day will come. High school is not the final word on you. There is hope.
—DOUG MARLETTE

"
How will your experience pave the way for a new voice in America? I hope it will take you out these doors, out into the open air. You will breathe it in your lungs and say, "From now on, this life will be what I stand for. . . . Move over—this is my story now."
—JODIE FOSTER

Getting up in the morning and having work
you love is what makes life different for people.
If you get into a position where you don't love what
you're doing, get off it.
—BOB WOODWARD

"

The really important kind of freedom involves
attention and awareness and discipline,
and being able truly to care about other people
and to sacrifice for them over and over in myriad
petty, unsexy ways every day.
—DAVID FOSTER WALLACE

"

The unfortunate, truly exciting thing about
your life is that there is no core curriculum. . . .
So don't worry about your grade or the results
or success. Success is defined in myriad ways, and
you will find it, and people will no longer
be grading you.
—JON STEWART

> There's an old saying about those who forget history. I don't remember it, but it's good.
>
> —STEPHEN COLBERT

PATRIOTIC & PROUD

History is often written by the winners, but the records of what was said reflect the truth more closely. From politicians, protestors, and patriots, the spirit of our time is collected in the words by which we remember our leaders.

AMERICA

America is a vast conspiracy to make you happy.
—JOHN UPDIKE

America is not just a country. It's an idea.
—BONO

America is not perfect, but it's much better than anywhere else in the world.
—CATHERINE ZETA-JONES

I think the most un-American thing you can say is "You can't say that."
—GARRISON KEILLOR

America is so vast that almost everything said about it is likely to be true, and the opposite is probably equally true.
—JAMES T. FARRELL

The great arrogance of the present is to forget the intelligence of the past.
—KEN BURNS

Poker is to cards and games what jazz is to music. It's this great American thing, born and bred here. We dig it because everybody can play.
—**STEVE LIPSCOMB**

"

What is the essence of our America? Finding and maintaining that perfect, delicate balance between freedom "to" and freedom "from."
—**MARILYN VOS SAVANT**

"

You don't have to be old in America to say of a world you lived in, "That world is gone."
—**PEGGY NOONAN**

"

Whoever wants to know the heart and mind of America had better learn baseball.
—**JACQUES BARZUN**

"

The American dream is not over. America is an adventure.
—**THEODORE WHITE**

"

America did not invent human rights. In a very real sense, it is the other way around. Human rights invented America.
—**JIMMY CARTER**

GOVERNMENT

To lodge all power in one party and keep it there is to insure bad government.
—MARK TWAIN

"

What Washington needs is adult supervision.
—BARACK OBAMA

"

You don't pay taxes—they take taxes.
—CHRIS ROCK

"

It is easier to build strong children than to repair broken men.
—FREDERICK DOUGLASS

One of the fondest expressions around is that we can't be the world's policeman. But guess who gets called when suddenly someone needs a cop.
—GEN. COLIN POWELL

If we don't believe in free expression for those we despise, we don't believe in it at all.
—NOAM CHOMSKY

Governing a large country is like frying a small fish. You spoil it with too much poking.
—LAO-TZU

"
A little government and a little luck are necessary in life, but only a fool trusts either of them.
—P. J. O'ROURKE

"
Everybody wants to eat at the government's table, but nobody wants to do the dishes.
—WERNER FINCK

"
Government can't give us anything without depriving us of something else.
—HENRY HAZLITT

"
When government accepts responsibility for people, then people no longer take responsibility for themselves.
—GEORGE PATAKI

POLITICS

Politics is the only business where doing nothing other than making the other guy look bad is an acceptable outcome.
—MARK WARNER

"
I looked up the word *politics* in the dictionary. It's actually a combination of two words: poli, which means many, and tics, which means bloodsuckers.
—JAY LENO

"
Ideas are great arrows, but there has to be a bow. And politics is the bow of idealism.
—BILL MOYERS

"
Washington, D.C., is to lying what Wisconsin is to cheese.
—DENNIS MILLER

Everybody knows politics is a contact sport
—BARACK OBAMA

Take it from me—elections matter.
—AL GORE

It's in the democratic citizen's nature to be like a leaf that doesn't believe in the tree it's part of.
—DAVID FOSTER WALLACE

"
Disobedience is the true foundation of liberty. The obedient must be slaves.
—HENRY DAVID THOREAU

"
Politics is the art of looking for trouble, finding it everywhere, diagnosing it incorrectly, and applying the wrong remedies.
—GROUCHO MARX

"
I'm older than dirt, I've got more scars than Frankenstein, but I've learned a few things along the way.
—JOHN MCCAIN

"
Where you stand should not depend on where you sit.
—JANE BRYANT QUINN

HISTORY

Each time history repeats itself, the price goes up.
—RONALD WRIGHT

"

Well-behaved women seldom make history.
—LAUREL THATCHER ULRICH

"

The past is a source of knowledge,
and the future is a source of hope.
Love of the past implies faith in the future.
—STEPHEN AMBROSE

"

Live out of your imagination, not your history.
—STEPHEN R. COVEY

QUOTABLE TWEETS

In a thousand years, archaeologists will dig up tanning beds and think we fried people as punishment.
@OLIVIAWILDE

LEADERSHIP

A leader is one who, out of madness or goodness, volunteers to take upon himself the woe of the people. There are few men so foolish, hence the erratic quality of leadership.
—JOHN UPDIKE

"
Being powerful is like being a lady. If you have to tell people you are, you aren't.
—MARGARET THATCHER

"
Power is nothing unless you can turn it into influence.
—CONDOLEEZZA RICE

"
You have to have a vision. It's got to be a vision you articulate clearly and forcefully. You can't blow an uncertain trumpet.
—REV. THEODORE HESBURGH

"
Most people can bear adversity. But if you wish to know what a man really is, give him power.
—ROBERT G. INGERSOLL

THE PERFECT WORDS FOR
PROTEST CAMPAIGNS

There may be times when we are powerless to prevent injustice, but there must never be a time when we fail to protest.
—ELIE WIESEL

"

What is morally wrong cannot be politically right.
—WILLIAM GLADSTONE

"

To sin by silence when they should protest makes cowards of men.
—ABRAHAM LINCOLN

"

A small body of determined spirits fired by an unquenchable faith in their mission can alter the course of history.
—MAHATMA GANDHI

"

You're not supposed to be so blind with patriotism that you can't face reality. Wrong is wrong, no matter who does it or who says it.
—MALCOLM X

IN WORDS WE TRUST

The United States can take credit for scores of contributions to the world's lexicon: Rock 'n' roll, software, teddy bear, and even A-OK are just a few all-American additions. So to celebrate, we've compiled some lesser-known gems with U.S. roots. Answers (plus a little etymology) on next page.

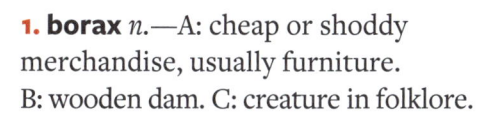

1. borax *n.*—A: cheap or shoddy merchandise, usually furniture. B: wooden dam. C: creature in folklore.

2. highbinder *n.*—A: type of moonshine. B: 19th-century gun. C: corrupt politician or mean person.

3. Holy Joe *n.*—A: meat sandwich. B: clergyman. C: exclamation used in early baseball leagues.

4. spoony *adj.*—A: silly or unduly sentimental. B: drunk. C: slow-witted.

5. alewife *n.*—A: rudimentary log cabin. B: kinship. C: herring common to the Atlantic Coast.

6. blackstrap *n.*—A: type of molasses. B: early horse saddle. C: gambling house.

7. slimsy *adj.*—A: of questionable nature. B: frail. C: slippery.

8. blatherskite *n.*—A: double-edged hunting knife. B: one who speaks nonsense. C: red rock indigenous to North America.

9. sockdolager *n.*—A: decisive blow or answer. B: counselor. C: nickname for a banker.

10. jag *n.*—A: stone step. B: unrestrained activity. C: insult.

11. piker *n.*—A: one who gambles with a small amount of money or does something cheaply. B: one who prefers to walk. C: nickname for a logger.

12. simon-pure *adj.*—A: as fresh as mountain air. B: immoral, from *Uncle Tom's Cabin*. C: of untainted integrity.

13. callithump *n.*—A: boisterous band or parade. B: carnival game. C: rabbit originally found in the Deep South.

14. deadhead *n.*—A: traveler who has not paid for a ticket. B: slang for male witch. C: weed particular to the Florida Everglades.

Patriotic & Proud

"In Words We Trust" Answers

1. borax—[A] cheap or shoddy merchandise, usually furniture (probably from New York's Lower East Side; late 1800s). "What a *borax* of a table!" cried Alison as its legs collapsed.

2. highbinder—[C] corrupt politician or mean person (from the Highbinders, bullies in New York City; early 1800s). While not an evil man, the mayor was at the very least a *highbinder*.

3. Holy Joe—[B] clergyman (slang, especially in the U.S. armed forces; 1800s). The anxious privates all went to visit the *Holy Joe* before shipping out.

4. spoony—[A] silly or unduly sentimental (from *spoon*, "foolish person"; early 1800s). Her *spoony* ex tried to win her back with a truckload of tulips.

5. alewife—[C] herring common to the Atlantic Coast (perhaps an alteration of an American Indian name; 1633). Art prefers *alewife* to typical sea herring.

6. blackstrap—[A] type of molasses (from a mixture of rum and molasses; 1800s). Fran's must-have ingredient for his beans? *Blackstrap* molasses.

7. slimsy—[B] frail (blend of *slim* and *flimsy*; 1845). "I can't knit with *that*," Emilie said. "The cotton is so *slimsy*!"

8. blatherskite—[B] one who speaks nonsense (alteration of Scottish *blether*, "blather," and *skate*, "contemptible person"; U.S. usage from the American Revolution). Can't anyone silence that *blatherskite*?!

9. sockdolager—[A] decisive blow or answer (perhaps from *sock*, "to hit hard"; 1827). The variation *sockdologising* is supposedly one of the last words Lincoln heard before being shot.

10. jag—[B] unrestrained activity (from Jack London's *The Valley of the Moon*; 1913). Joy went on a whining *jag* after losing her phone.

11. piker—[A] one who gambles with a small amount of money or does something cheaply (from frugal residents of Pike County, Missouri; mid-1800s). Always the family's *piker*, Ruthie played only three dollars at the craps table.

12. simon-pure—[C] of untainted integrity (from a character in the English play *A Bold Stroke for a Wife*; U.S. usage, 1840s). Her reputation as a writer? She's *simon-pure*.

13. callithump—[A] boisterous band or parade (from *callithumpian band*, "noisemakers on New Year's Eve"; 1800s). At the much-anticipated *callithump*, the Colts celebrated their gridiron win.

14. deadhead—[A] traveler who has not paid for a ticket (at least as far back as 1840s New York City). "Does that *deadhead* really work for the airline?"

WITHIN REGION

The year 2012 marked the long-anticipated completion of the five-volume *Dictionary of American Regional English*. These tomes feature words and phrases, both old and new, that vary from place to place. Here, some of our favorites (we've added the primary regions for each to help you along). Answers on next page.

1. **pinkletink** *n., Martha's Vineyard*—A: piano. B: light rain shower. C: spring peeper frog.

2. **king's ex** *exclam., Gulf states, west of Mississippi River*—A: get lost! B: good luck! C: time out!

3. **snail** *n., California*—A: cinnamon roll. B: boyfriend. C: sound made with the sides of the hands.

4. **noodle** *v., Arkansas, Missouri, Oklahoma*—A: catch fish barehanded. B: drink from a flask. C: visit neighbors.

5. **silver thaw** *n., Oregon, Washington*—A: brook trout. B: freezing rain. C: 50th wedding anniversary.

6. **on the carpet** *adj., South*—A: under arrest. B: ready to marry. C: exhausted.

7. **remuda** *n., Southwest*—A: herd of horses. B: dry gulch. C: bunk.

8. **punee** *n., Hawaii*—A: loose dress. B: couch or sofa. C: outflow of lava.

9. **pungle** *v., West*—A: bollix. B: pay up. C: make verbal jokes.

10. **givey** *adj., Mid- and South Atlantic*—A: humid or moist. B: too talkative. C: up for anything.

11. **rumpelkammer** *n., Wisconsin*—A: thunderstorm. B: storage closet. C: unruly child.

12. **mug-up** *n., Alaska*—A: mascara kit. B: coffee break. C: robbery.

13. **berm** *n., West Virginia*—A: shoulder of a road. B: tip jar. C: big poker hand.

14. **hook Jack** *v., New England*—A: come up empty. B: add cheese to a dish. C: skip school.

15. **all-overs** *n., South*—A: one-piece suit. B: nervous feelings. C: gossip.

Patriotic & Proud

"Within Region" Answers

1. pinkletink—[C] spring peeper frog. By May, the *pinkletinks* are in their full-throated glory.

2. king's ex—[C] time out! As soon as the dentist reached for his drill, Bucky yelled, "*King's ex!*"

3. snail—[A] cinnamon roll. The edge went off my appetite when I found a hair in my favorite bistro's *snail*.

4. noodle—[A] catch fish bare-handed. For a guy who used to *noodle*, Jeremy sure has clumsy mitts.

5. silver thaw—[B] freezing rain. Hoping to lighten the mood, Audrey did her best Gene Kelly, singing and dancing in the *silver thaw*.

6. on the carpet—[B] ready to marry. Max is *on the carpet*, but Grace is still on the fence.

7. remuda—[A] herd of horses. My brother's two kids hit the house during visits like a galloping *remuda*.

8. punee—[B] couch or sofa. Lounging supine on her *punee*, Clare spends the day watching soaps and eating poi chips.

9. pungle—[B] pay up. If you don't *pungle* soon, they're going to send Biff to visit you.

10. givey—[A] humid or moist. The *givey* August weather left us drawn down and listless come midday.

11. rumpelkammer—[B] storage closet. When we played hide-and-seek, nobody could find little Waldo in the *rumpelkammer*.

12. mug-up—[B] coffee break. Maria gets nothing done, because she yaks through a *mug-up* every ten minutes.

13. berm—[A] shoulder of a road. Thoroughly exhausted by the drive from Portland, Alice pulled to the *berm* for a break.

14. hook Jack—[C] skip school. Whenever there's an algebra test, Moe and I *hook Jack* and head for the river.

15. all-overs—[B] nervous feelings. I get the *all-overs* when my brother lets his pet tarantula loose.

SANDWICH SHOP
Match the city with the sandwich name that is common there.

1. New York City
2. Philadelphia
3. Boston
4. New Orleans
5. Yonkers

A. grinder
B. po'boy
C. hero
D. hoagie
E. wedge

1.C; 2.D; 3.A; 4.B; 5.E

USE YOUR WORDS

AMERICANA

From the land that gave birth to baseball, Budweiser, and bebop, we bring you this homegrown mix of words, phrases, and names. Need help with your Americana? Ask your uncle Sam—or check the next page for answers.

1. pompadour ('pahm-puh-dohr) *n.*—A: parade uniform. B: convertible top. C: men's hairstyle.

2. El Capitan (ehl 'kahp-ee-'tahn) *n.*—A: Alamo general. B: Yosemite rock formation. C: Civil War stronghold.

3. jackalope ('jak-uh-lohp) *n.*—A: rabbit with antlers. B: rodeo bronco. C: crusading journalist.

4. barnstorm ('barn-storm) *v.*—A: travel around performing. B: dance at a hoedown. C: give a ranting speech.

5. ponderosa (pahn-deh-'roh-suh) *n.*—A: gold mine. B: pine tree. C: mountain range.

6. fake book ('fayk book) *n.*—A: recipe folder or container. B: stack of marked playing cards. C: collection of songs.

7. tricorn ('try-korn) *adj.*—A: popped, as in kernels. B: deliberately campy. C: like Paul Revere's hat.

8. bunting ('buhn-ting) *n.*—A: fabric for flags. B: baby boy. C: Roaring Twenties dress.

9. Tin Pan Alley (tihn pan 'a-lee) *n.*—A: hideout for hoboes. B: row of factories. C: pop music center formed in the late 19th century.

10. twain ('twayn) *n.*—A: disguise. B: male suitor. C: two.

11. moxie ('mahk-see) *n.*—A: chorus girl. B: courage. C: double-talk or deceptive message.

12. brushback ('bruhsh-bak) *n.*—A: grooming technique for a horse. B: baseball pitch. C: method of sawing or logging.

13. eighty-six ('ay-tee 'siks) *v.*—A: round up. B: get rid of. C: submerge.

14. copacetic (koh-puh-'seh-tik) *adj.*—A: very satisfactory. B: satirical. C: pepped up.

Patriotic & Proud

"Americana" Answers

1. pompadour—[C] men's hairstyle. The piled-up-in-front do, notably worn by Elvis, was named for France's Madame de Pompadour (1721–1764).

2. El Capitan—[B] Yosemite rock formation. It's Spanish for "the captain"—appropriate, since the landmark impressed early explorers as the dominant rock in the valley.

3. jackalope—[A] rabbit with antlers. In Wild West folklore, it's a cross between a jackrabbit and an antelope.

4. barnstorm—[A] travel around performing. Semipro baseball teams used to tour the country playing exhibition games in their off-season.

5. ponderosa—[B] pine tree. The name of this heavy western North American tree has roots (pun intended) in the word *ponderous*.

6. fake book—[C] collection of songs. Used by jazz and other musicians to quickly learn songs, it has bare-bones melody lines and chord names.

7. tricorn—[C] like Paul Revere's hat. A tricorn hat is bent at three points (*tri* for "three" plus *corn* for "corner").

8. bunting—[A] fabric for flags. Made of worsted wool, it is typically used for Fourth of July banners.

9. Tin Pan Alley—[C] pop music center formed in the late 19th century. It was named for the tinkling pianos in a neighborhood of Manhattan songwriters.

10. twain—[C] two. Where the Mississippi River measured two fathoms in depth, steamship workers would call out, "Mark twain!" (hence the pen name of Samuel Clemens).

11. moxie—[B] courage. The word dates back to a soft drink in the 1800s.

12. brushback—[B] baseball pitch. It forces a batter to step back and breaks his confidence.

13. eighty-six—[B] get rid of. Rhyming with *nix*, it was originally diner slang meaning "to cancel."

14. copacetic—[A] very satisfactory. Its roots are unknown, but tap dancer Bill "Bojangles" Robinson claimed to have invented the word.

PICTURE THIS
Decals, a 19th-century invention, let people transfer pictures from paper to glass and other surfaces. Rumor is that by the early 1900s, fast-talking New Yorkers had jokily mashed the word *decalcomania* (the art of decal transfer) into *cockamamy*, slang for "nonsensical"—though etymologists aren't completely sure how!

TALKING POLITICS

Before you hit the polls, make sure you've mastered the lingo of the campaign trail. Try this quiz to see how politically correct your vocabulary is, then consult the next page for answers.

1. demagogue ('deh-meh-gog) *n.*—A: pollster. B: meeting. C: rabble-rouser.

2. plebiscite ('pleh-beh-siyt) *n.*—A: statement of loyalty. B: volunteer. C: countrywide vote.

3. chauvinist ('sho-veh-nist) *n.*—A: promoter of monarchy. B: political pundit. C: excessive patriot.

4. reactionary (ree-'ak-shuh-nary) *adj.*—A: very liberal. B: very conservative. C: undecided.

5. canvass ('kan-vas) *v.*—A: solicit voters. B: stretch a budget. C: attempt a cover-up.

6. hustings ('huhs-tingz) *n.*—A: nominee's supporters. B: proceedings or locale of a campaign. C: ballot punch-outs.

7. gravitas ('gra-veh-tahs) *n.*—A: perks and freebies. B: local leanings. C: serious bearing.

8. snollygoster ('snahlee-gahster) *n.*—A: unprincipled but shrewd person. B: loud argument. C: close vote.

9. incendiary (in-'sen-dee-er-ee) *adj.*—A: illegal. B: tending to excite or agitate. C: rising in power.

10. suffrage ('suh-frij) *n.*—A: right to vote. B: media exposure. C: civil disobedience.

11. jobbery ('jah-beh-ree) *n.*—A: works program. B: false persona. C: corruption in office.

12. éminence grise (ay-may-nahns 'greez) *n.*—A: confidential agent. B: diplomat. C: elite class.

13. laissez-faire ('le-'say-fair) *adj.*—A: proactive. B: opposing government interference. C: suave.

14. abdicate ('ab-di-kayt) *v.*—A: decline to vote. B: speak out of turn. C: resign from power.

15. junket ('juhn-ket) *n.*—A: government-paid trip. B: smear campaign. C: bad loan.

Patriotic & Proud

"Talking Politics" Answers

1. demagogue—[C] rabble-rouser. The senator's campaign turned ugly once the unofficial *demagogue* became manager.

2. plebiscite—[C] countrywide vote. We're having a *plebiscite* on whether countrywide votes are legitimate.

3. chauvinist—[C] excessive patriot. The governor is a true *chauvinist*: He wears Stars and Stripes boxers to bed. [The term, from purported 19th-century French nationalist Nicolas Chauvin, didn't take on the extremist "male chauvinist" meaning until the 1970s.]

4. reactionary—[B] very conservative. Larry is so *reactionary*, he won't even consider amending the education bill.

5. canvass—[A] solicit voters. Ever the all-American, Sally *canvassed* door-to-door toting a flag and an apple pie.

6. hustings—[B] proceedings or locale of a campaign. He doesn't really care if he wins; he just likes the bus rides to the various *hustings*.

7. gravitas—[C] serious bearing. How can you assume political *gravitas* with a name like Duckwill?

8. snollygoster—[A] unprincipled but shrewd person. There's something of a *snollygoster* in Governor Tooney's public persona.

9. incendiary—[B] tending to excite or agitate. My youngest girl is composing an *incendiary* speech about unionizing.

10. suffrage—[A] right to vote. So I told her, no, she doesn't have *suffrage* on matters of bedtime.

11. jobbery—[C] corruption in office. How is it *jobbery* if my friends just happened to all get on the payroll?

12. éminence grise—[A] confidential agent. It says Joey's Lemonade Stand, but Ella is the business's *éminence grise*.

13. laissez-faire—[B] opposing government interference. Joan seems to have a *laissez-faire* attitude about controlling her classroom.

14. abdicate—[C] resign from power. You can't depose me—I *abdicate*!

15. junket—[A] government-paid trip. I hear the boss went on a Busch Gardens *junket* using our pension fund!

44 USE YOUR WORDS

HIP-HOP *HAMILTON*

The musical *Hamilton* by Lin-Manuel Miranda features a hip-hop libretto packed with rich vocabulary. Here are some words to know before seeing the historical show—if you can get a ticket! But there's no wait for the answers, which are on the next page, complete with lines from the Broadway smash.

1. manumission (man-yoo-'mih-shin) *n.*—A: spy operation. B: the act of freeing from slavery. C: handiwork.

2. complicit (kom-'plih-siht) *adj.*—A: elaborate. B: in total agreement. C: associating with or participating in.

3. equivocate (ih-'kwih-vuh-kayt) *v.*—A: waffle. B: share evenly. C: tremble.

4. enterprising ('ehn-ter-pry-zing) *adj.*—A: go-getting. B: trespassing. C: just beginning.

5. homilies ('hah-muh-leez) *n.*—A: family relations. B: sermons. C: opposites.

6. venerated ('veh-nuh-ray-ted) *adj.*—A: exhausted. B: honored. C: pardoned.

7. restitution (res-tih-'too-shuhn) *n.*—A: truce. B: imprisonment. C: amends.

8. dissidents ('diss-ih-dihnts) *n.*—A: dissenters. B: immigrants. C: tossers of insults.

9. obfuscates ('ahb-fuh-skayts) *v.*—A: substitutes. B: glides gracefully. C: confuses.

10. jettison ('jeh-tih-sen) *v.*—A: turn black. B: rise rapidly. C: throw away.

11. intemperate (ihn-'tem-puh-riht) *adj.*—A: permanent. B: hard to resist. C: unrestrained.

12. vacuous ('va-kew-uhs) *adj.*—A: empty or blank. B: gusting. C: immune.

13. intransigent (ihn-'tran-zih-jent) *adj.*—A: stubborn. B: revolting. C: on the move.

14. inimitable (ihn-'ih-mih-tuh-buhl) *adj.*—A: incomparable or unrivaled. B: undivided. C: countless.

15. disparage (di-'spar-ij) *v.*—A: scatter. B: speak ill of. C: fire, as cannons.

"Hip-Hop *Hamilton*" Answers

1. manumission—[B] the act of freeing from slavery. Alexander Hamilton: "[We are] a bunch of revolutionary *manumission* abolitionists."

2. complicit—[C] associating with or participating in. Thomas Jefferson: "I am *complicit* in watchin' him grabbin' at power and kiss it."

3. equivocate—[A] waffle. Hamilton: "I will not *equivocate* on my opinion."

4. enterprising—[A] go-getting. Jefferson: "These are wise words, *enterprising* men quote 'em."

5. homilies—[B] sermons. Aaron Burr: "These are things that the *homilies* and hymns won't teach ya."

6. venerated—[B] honored. George Washington: "I'm … the *venerated* Virginian veteran."

7. restitution—[C] amends. Burr: "He woulda been dead or destitute without a cent or *restitution*."

8. dissidents—[A] dissenters. Jefferson: "If Washington isn't gon' listen to disciplined *dissidents* …"

9. obfuscates—[C] confuses. James Madison: "Ask him a question: It glances off, he *obfuscates*, he dances."

10. jettison—[C] throw away. Hamilton: "There isn't a plan he doesn't *jettison*."

11. intemperate—[C] unrestrained. Burr: "*Intemperate* indeed, good man."

12. vacuous—[A] empty or blank. Jefferson: "Gimme some dirt on this *vacuous* mass so we can at last unmask him."

13. intransigent—[A] stubborn. Hamilton: "These Virginians are … being *intransigent*."

14. inimitable—[A] incomparable or unrivaled. Burr: "I am *inimitable*. I am an original."

15. disparage—[B] speak ill of. Philip Hamilton: "He *disparaged* my family's legacy in front of a crowd."

SHAPE SHIFTING

In the play, Alexander Hamilton is described as *protean*. This adjective comes to us from Proteus, a Greek sea god who could transform his shape at will—in Homer's *Odyssey*, Proteus transforms into a lion, a tree, and even running water. In human terms, it refers to someone who has great versatility or someone whose personality seems ever-changing. If you've had two or three wildly different careers, you might be called protean.

NATIVE AMERICAN ROOTS

Some Native American words adopted into English are as common as a backyard chipmunk (that's from the Ojibwa tribe), but there are plenty that are as unusual as a manatee in a mackinaw. For answers and etymology, turn to the next page.

1. mackinaw ('ma-kuh-naw) *n.*—A: mountain creek. B: makeshift bed. C: wool coat.

2. dory ('dohr-ee) *n.*—A: dry gulch. B: flat-bottomed boat. C: small red potato.

3. hogan ('hoh-gahn) *n.*—A: town meeting. B: log home. C: ceremonial pipe.

4. punkie ('puhn-kee) *n.*—A: wooden sled. B: biting bug. C: runt of a litter.

5. dowitcher ('dow-ih-chur) *n.*—A: wading bird. B: widow. C: gifted healer.

6. Podunk ('poh-dunk) *n.*—A: small town. B: swimming hole. C: fried cake.

7. manatee ('ma-nuh-tee) *n.*—A: carved face. B: sea cow. C: hard-fought contest.

8. pogonip ('pah-guh-nihp) *n.*—A: ball game. B: organic snack. C: cold fog.

9. potlatch ('paht-lach) *n.*—A: straw hat. B: red pigment. C: celebratory feast.

10. kachina (kuh-'chee-nuh) *n.*—A: rain shower. B: wooden doll. C: drum.

11. savanna (suh-'va-nuh) *n.*—A: voyage on foot. B: expression of adoration. C: grassland.

12. terrapin ('tehr-uh-pin) *n.*—A: spring flower. B: swampland. C: turtle.

13. hackmatack ('hak-muh-tak) *n.*—A: larch tree. B: machete. C: ambush.

14. sachem ('say-chum) *n.*—A: hex or curse. B: puff of smoke. C: leader.

15. chinook (shih-'nook) *n.*—A: convicted thief. B: warm wind. C: campfire.

Patriotic & Proud

"Native American Roots" Answers

1. mackinaw—[C] wool coat. Joseph always wears his *mackinaw*, even on warm, sunny days. (Algonquian)

2. dory—[B] flat-bottomed boat. Susan's favorite way to relax is fishing from her *dory* on the bay. (Miskito)

3. hogan—[B] log home. The doorway of a traditional *hogan* faces east, toward the sunrise. (Navajo)

4. punkie—[B] biting bug. Whether you call them midges, no-see-ums, or *punkies*, they're all out for blood! (Delaware)

5. dowitcher—[A] wading bird. According to my field guide, that bird is a long-billed *dowitcher*. (Iroquois)

6. Podunk—[A] small town. Who could have imagined that this kid from *Podunk* would make it big? (Algonquian)

7. manatee—[B] sea cow. *Manatees* use their flippers to "walk" along the seabed while grazing on plants. (Cariban)

8. pogonip—[C] cold fog. Thanks to this morning's *pogonip*, I have ice crystals in my eyebrows. (Shoshone)

9. potlatch—[C] celebratory feast. Geno's mac and cheese is a favorite at his family's annual *potlatch*. (Nootka)

10. kachina—[B] wooden doll. The museum has an impressive collection of hand-carved *kachinas*. (Hopi)

11. savanna—[C] grassland. On his tour of African *savannas*, Eli spotted elephants, zebras, and rhinos. (Taino)

12. terrapin—[C] turtle. On summer days, *terrapins* sun themselves on flat rocks in the marsh. (Algonquian)

13. hackmatack—[A] larch tree. Will you have a picnic under the *hackmatack* with me? (Algonquian)

14. sachem—[C] leader. The CEO may sit in the corner office, but in this company the marketing director is the real *sachem*. (Narragansett)

15. chinook—[B] warm wind. The *chinook* blew in from the southwest, melting the last of the winter snow. (Chehalis)

SAY THAT AGAIN?

We can thank the Nipmuc people of Massachusetts for the longest place name in America. With 45 letters and 14 syllables, Lake Chargoggagoggmanchauggagoggchaubunagungamaugg certainly presents a challenge to sign painters. Fortunately, it's also known by a shorter (and more pronounceable) name: Webster Lake.

GIVING THANKS

Add some zest to your vocabulary with this feast of nutritious words and phrases, perfect for Thanksgiving—or any time you're hungry. If you can't stand the heat in our kitchen, cool off with the answers on the next page.

1. gustatory ('guh-stuh-tohr-ee) *adj.*—A: full-bellied. B: relating to taste. C: rich and flavorful.

2. au gratin (oh 'grah-tin) *adj.*—A: cooked to medium rare. B: free of charge. C: covered with cheese and browned.

3. succulent ('suh-kyu-lent) *adj.*—A: sun-dried. B: juicy. C: sipped with a straw.

4. mesclun ('mess-klen) *n.*—A: mix of greens. B: shellfish. C: Cajun dipping sauce.

5. piquant ('pee-kent) *adj.*—A: in season. B: in small amounts. C: spicy.

6. chiffonade (shih-fuh-'nayd) *n.*—A: whipped margarine. B: shredded herbs or veggies. C: lemon pudding.

7. toothsome ('tooth-sum) *adj.*—A: chewy. B: delicious. C: hungry.

8. sous vide (soo 'veed) *adv.*—A: without salt. B: on the side. C: cooked in a pouch.

9. culinary ('kuh-lih-nehr-ee) *adj.*—A: of the kitchen. B: buttery. C: cage-free.

10. umami (ooh-'mah-mee) *n.*—A: oven rack. B: chopsticks. C: savory taste.

11. tempeh ('tem-pay) *n.*—A: part-time chef. B: soy cake. C: fondue pot.

12. fricassee ('frih-kuh-see) *v.*—A: cut and stew in gravy. B: deep-fry. C: sauté with mushrooms.

13. oenophile ('ee-nuh-fiyl) *n.*—A: wine lover. B: food critic. C: egg fancier.

14. poach (pohch) *v.*—A: cook in simmering liquid. B: fry in a small amount of fat. C: heat slowly in a covered pot.

15. fondant ('fahn-duhnt) *n.*—A: food lover. B: cake icing. C: large bib.

"Giving Thanks" Answers

1. gustatory—[B] relating to taste. Here, try my new *gustatory* experiment—beet ice cream!

2. au gratin—[C] covered with cheese and browned. Is there anything better than onion soup *au gratin* on a cold, rainy day?

3. succulent—[B] juicy. For dessert, the chef served pound cake topped with *succulent* pears.

4. mesclun—[A] mix of greens. "You call this a salad? It's just a plate of wilted *mesclun*."

5. piquant—[C] spicy. The *piquant* smells from the Mexican restaurant wafted out onto the street.

6. chiffonade—[B] shredded herbs or veggies. If you add a *chiffonade* of fresh basil, this frozen pizza isn't half bad!

7. toothsome—[B] delicious. Hattie makes the most *toothsome* cherry pie I've ever tasted.

8. sous vide—[C] cooked in a pouch. Though preparing steak *sous vide* takes time, it will cook your meat evenly and retain the moisture.

9. culinary—[A] of the kitchen. Julia Child was a true *culinary* icon.

10. umami—[C] savory taste. *Umami* is one of the five basic tastes, along with sweet, sour, salty, and bitter.

11. tempeh—[B] soy cake. Ezra, a devoted vegan, serves *tempeh* burgers and tofu dogs at his cookouts.

12. fricassee—[A] cut and stew in gravy. Tired of turkey sandwiches and turkey soup, Hector decided to *fricassee* the leftovers from his Thanksgiving bird.

13. oenophile—[A] wine lover. A serious *oenophile*, Adrienne was horrified when her date added ice cubes to his pinot noir.

14. poach—[A] cook in simmering liquid. For breakfast, Sasha loves to *poach* an egg and pair it with avocado toast topped with tomato.

15. fondant—[B] cake icing. Kelly flunked her cake-making class when she slathered on too much *fondant*.

WHAT KIND OF FOOD PERSON ARE YOU?

If you appreciate fine dining, you might call yourself a *gourmet*, an *epicure*, or a *bon vivant*. If you have a healthy but unrefined appetite, you're a *gourmand* or a *trencherman*. And if you've done your homework on the history and rituals of haute cuisine, you're a *gastronome* (*gastronomy* is the art or science of good eating).

IDEAS & IDEALS

It's one thing to feel that you are on the right path, but it's another to think that yours is the only path.
—PAULO COELHO

"

Injustice anywhere is a threat to justice everywhere.
—REV. MARTIN LUTHER KING JR.

"

A bookstore is one of the only pieces of evidence we have that people are still thinking.
—JERRY SEINFELD

"

Curious learning not only makes unpleasant things less unpleasant but also makes pleasant things more pleasant.
—BERTRAND RUSSELL

"

When a generation talks just to itself, it becomes more filled with folly than it might have otherwise.
—STEWART BRAND

"

I think everybody has a right to happiness and freedom and security and health care and education and guitar lessons.
—BONNIE RAITT

THE PERFECT WORDS FOR
OPEN COURT

A great many people in this country are worried about law-and-order. And a great many people are worried about justice. But one thing is certain: you cannot have either until you have both.
—RAMSEY CLARK

Justice is the insurance we have on our lives, and obedience is the premium we pay for it.
—WILLIAM PENN

Injustice is relatively easy to bear; what stings is justice.
—H. L. MENCKEN

The worst form of injustice is pretended justice.
—PLATO

That old law about "an eye for an eye" leaves everybody blind.
—REV. MARTIN LUTHER KING JR.

In matters of truth and justice, there is no difference between large and small problems, for issues concerning the treatment of people are all the same.
—**ALBERT EINSTEIN**

"

It's every man's business to see justice done.
—**SIR ARTHUR CONAN DOYLE**

"

I would uphold the law if for no other reason but to protect myself.
—**THOMAS MORE**

"

It is better to risk saving a guilty man than to condemn an innocent one.
—**VOLTAIRE**

"

Injustice alone can shake down the pillars of the skies, and restore the reign of Chaos and Night.
—**HORACE MANN**

"

Defending the truth is not something one does out of a sense of duty or to allay guilt complexes, but is a reward in itself.
—**SIMONE DE BEAUVOIR**

> I am simple, complex, generous, selfish, unattractive, beautiful, lazy, and driven.
> —BARBRA STREISAND

AGING GRACEFULLY

The older we get, the more we learn about the world—or so we hope. It may not be fun to watch our faces and bodies change over the years, but the life lessons we've learned are reflected back at us each time we look in the mirror.

LOVE THE ONE YOU'RE WITH

Be happy in your body. . . . It's the only one you've got, so you might as well like it.
—**KEIRA KNIGHTLEY**

"

I really don't think I need buns of steel. I'd be happy with buns of cinnamon.
—**ELLEN DEGENERES**

"

I'm not overweight. I'm just nine inches too short.
—**SHELLEY WINTERS**

"

If you want to look young and thin, hang around old fat people.
—**JIM EASON**

"

I'd rather be a few pounds heavier and enjoy life than be worried all the time.
—**DREW BARRYMORE**

"

Even the worst haircut eventually grows out.
—**LISA KOGAN**

Happiness is the best facelift.
—**DIANA KRALL**

> Beauty, to me, is about being comfortable in your own skin. That, or a kick-ass red lipstick.
—**GWYNETH PALTROW**

> I would rather be called funny than pretty.
—**NIA VARDALOS**

> The most beautiful makeup for a woman is passion. But cosmetics are easier to buy.
—**YVES ST. LAURENT**

> It seems with every match I win, I get better-looking to other people.
—**ANDY RODDICK**

> It's great to be a blonde. With low expectations it's very easy to surprise people.
—**PAMELA ANDERSON**

🐦 QUOTABLE TWEETS

It's all about lovin' not only who we see in the mirror, but what we feel about ourselves when we look in the mirror.
@TYRABANKS

Aging Gracefully

WORKING IT OUT

I don't exercise. If God had wanted me to bend over, he would have put diamonds on the floor.
—**JOAN RIVERS**

> The word *aerobics* came about when the gym instructors got together and said, "If we're going to charge $10 an hour, we can't call it jumping up and down."
—**RITA RUDNER**

> I'm so unfamiliar with the gym I call it James.
—**CHI MCBRIDE**

> It's all right letting yourself go, as long as you can get yourself back.
—**MICK JAGGER**

> I decided I can't pay a person to rewind time, so I may as well get over it.
—**SERENA WILLIAMS**

🐦 QUOTABLE TWEETS

People always ask me: "WHY?! OH GOD WHY?!!?" Mostly at the beach.
@CONANOBRIEN

TO YOUR HEALTH

The first wealth is health.
—**RALPH WALDO EMERSON**

"

The best beauty secret is sunblock.
—**CHRISTIE BRINKLEY**

"

Eat right, exercise regularly, die anyway.
—**UNKNOWN**

"

God gave us the gift of life; it is up to us to give ourselves the gift of living well.
—**VOLTAIRE**

"

I believe that how you feel is very important to how you look—that healthy equals beautiful.
—**VICTORIA PRINCIPAL**

AGING WELL

You can get old pretty young if you don't take care of yourself.

—YOGI BERRA

❝

The ball doesn't know how old I am.

—MARTINA NAVRATILOVA

❝

I don't want to get to the end of my life and find that I have lived just the length of it. I want to have lived the width of it as well.

—DIANE ACKERMAN

❝

Forget aging. If you're six feet above ground, it's a good day.

—FAITH HILL

🐦 QUOTABLE TWEETS

Happy Birthday, Thomas Hayward. Unfortunately he's dead, he would have been 177 today. Only a year younger than me…

@JOHNCLEESE

The only thing that has ever made me feel old is those few times where I allow myself to be predictable.
—**CARLOS SANTANA**

"

The heart ages last.
—**SYLVESTER STALLONE**

"

Maturity is a high price to pay for growing up.
—**TOM STOPPARD**

"

I don't feel old. I don't feel anything till noon. That's when it's time for my nap.
—**BOB HOPE**

"

One day I woke up and I was the oldest person in every room.
—**BILL CLINTON**

"

Life asks us to make measurable progress in reasonable time. That's why they make those fourth-grade chairs so small—so you won't fit in them at age 25.
—**JIM ROHN**

"

The older I get, the better I used to be.
—**JOHN MCENROE**

Aging Gracefully

THE PERFECT WORDS FOR
GET-WELL CARDS

I wonder why you can always read a doctor's bill and you can never read his prescription.
—FINLEY PETER DUNNE

"
If you're going through hell, keep going.
—WINSTON CHURCHILL

"
Sleep, riches, and health to be truly enjoyed must be interrupted.
—JOHANN PAUL FRIEDRICH RICHTER

"
When you come to the end of your rope, tie a knot and hang on.
—FRANKLIN D. ROOSEVELT

"
To array a man's will against his sickness is the supreme art of medicine.
—HENRY WARD BEECHER

"
Sickness comes on horseback but departs on foot.
—DUTCH PROVERB

FAMOUS WORDS

The words in this quiz come from the book *Favorite Words of Famous People* by Lewis Burke Frumkes. Turn the page for answers—and to see which notable names picked these terms for top billing.

1. **plangent** ('plan-jent) *adj.*— A: flexible. B: very loud. C: carefully detailed.

2. **ruckus** ('ruh-kuhs) *n.*— A: backpack. B: melee. C: dry gully.

3. **vermilion** (ver-'mil-yun) *n.*—A: ten-figure number. B: moth larva. C: bright red.

4. **chthonic** ('thah-nik) *adj.*— A: of the underworld. B: frozen solid. C: having sharp claws.

5. **gormless** ('gorm-les) *adj.*—A: nonflowering. B: lacking firm shape. C: stupid.

6. **interstitial** (ihn-ter-'stih-shuhl) *adj.*—A: beyond our solar system. B: in the spaces between. C: joined by stitches.

7. **unilateral** (yoo-nih-'la-tuh-ruhl) *adj.*—A: one-sided. B: in alliance with. C: flat.

8. **palimpsest** ('pa-lehmp-sehst) *n.*—A: spotted pony. B: leg brace. C: written-over document.

9. **beguiling** (bih-'guy-ling) *adj.*—A: twisted together. B: complementary. C: cleverly deceptive.

10. **lambent** ('lam-buhnt) *adj.*— A: easily dissolved. B: submissive. C: luminous.

11. **incarnadine** (ihn-'kar-nuh-dine) *adj.*—A: flesh-colored. B: reborn. C: not digestible.

12. **phosphorescent** (fos-fuh-'reh-sent) *adj.*—A: of ocean depths. B: glittering. C: soapy.

13. **ramshackle** ('ram-sha-kuhl) *adj.*—A: barnlike. B: rickety-looking. C: falsely imprisoned.

14. **pixilated** (pick-suh-'lay-ted) *adj.*—A: grainy or blurry. B: elfin. C: mentally unbalanced.

15. **qua** ('kwah) *prep.*—A: in the capacity of. B: starting from. C: in the immediate neighborhood of.

Aging Gracefully

"Famous Words" Answers

1. **plangent**—[B] very loud. My nephew blasts *plangent*, sad music in his room. (director Wes Craven)

2. **ruckus**—[B] melee. There was quite a *ruckus* when the fire alarm went off. (Penn Jillette of Penn & Teller)

3. **vermilion**—[C] bright red. The theater had eye-catching *vermilion* walls. (writer A. S. Byatt)

4. **chthonic**—[A] of the underworld. I love the story of Orpheus's *chthonic* journey. (Margaret Atwood)

5. **gormless**—[C] stupid. The writer dismissed his critics as *gormless* twits. (author Barbara Taylor Bradford)

6. **interstitial**—[B] in the spaces between. The film's action sequences were thrilling; I found the *interstitial* scenes rather dull. (Al Gore)

7. **unilateral**—[A] one-sided. The volleyball squad had a *unilateral* advantage in height. (editor Helen Gurley Brown)

8. **palimpsest**—[C] written-over document. My address book is a *palimpsest*—I keep erasing names and adding new ones. (Joyce Carol Oates)

9. **beguiling**—[C] cleverly deceptive. Those *beguiling* ads persuaded me to buy a phone I didn't really need. (playwright Wendy Wasserstein)

10. **lambent**—[C] luminous. Sofia loved hiking by the *lambent* moonlight. (activist Andrea Dworkin)

11. **incarnadine**—[A] flesh-colored. Mia chose a pretty *incarnadine* dress for the wedding. (Arthur C. Clarke)

12. **phosphorescent**—[B] glittering. The *phosphorescent* firefly flew right into the jar. (John Updike)

13. **ramshackle**—[B] rickety-looking. Jack carefully stepped onto the *ramshackle* bridge. (Ray Bradbury)

14. **pixilated**—[C] mentally unbalanced. Dad's *pixilated* behavior has us worried. (Mark Hamill)

15. **qua**—[A] in the capacity of. Forget the painter's political views—can we enjoy her art *qua* art? (Dave Barry)

OTHER FAVORITES

Crime writer Edna Buchanan liked *berserk* ("crazed") and *amok* ("in a murderously frenzied state") best. Actor and dancer Gene Kelly chose *plethora* ("excess"). Comedian Bob Hope went with *laughter*, while journalist Dan Rather selected *courage*. And TV host Larry King singled out *why*, saying, "It's the best word in the universe. Think about it."

USE YOUR WORDS

SHARP DRESSER

This time, we challenge your fashion sense—that is, your knowledge of words about clothing and style. Fit to be tied? Turn the page for answers.

1. **décolletage** (day-kah-le-'tazh) *n.*—A: low-cut neckline. B: school uniform. C: clothing sale.

2. **sartorial** (sar-'tor-ee-ul) *adj.*—A: relating to a tailor or tailored clothes. B: relating to shoes. C: made out of wool.

3. **ruched** ('roosht) *adj.*—A: tied in a bow. B: pleated or bunched. C: dyed blue.

4. **argyle** ('ar-giyl) *adj.*—A: in pinstripes. B: in diamond patterns. C: polka-dotted.

5. **twee** ('twee) *adj.*—A: spotted with stains. B: having a veil over the face. C: excessively dainty or cute.

6. **salopettes** ('sal-eh-pets) *n.*—A: wooden shoes. B: skier's overalls. C: cuff links.

7. **caparison** (ke-'per-uh-sun) *n.*—A: selection of hats. B: ornamental covering for a horse. C: jester's costume.

8. **bouffant** (boo-'fahnt or 'boo-fahnt) *adj.*—A: flowery. B: puffed-out. C: skin-tight.

9. **ikat** ('ee-kaht) *n.*—A: head scarf. B: shoelace tip. C: tie-dyed fabric.

10. **bespoke** (bih-'spohk) *adj.*—A: custom-made. B: color-coordinated. C: with circular designs.

11. **clew** ('klew) *n.*—A: ball of yarn. B: run in a stocking. C: alligator skin.

12. **regalia** (ri-'gayl-yeh) *n.*—A: everyday wear. B: magnificent attire. C: lingerie.

13. **panache** (puh-'nash or -'nahsh) *n.*—A: handkerchief. B: untucked shirttail. C: flamboyance in style.

14. **prink** ('prink) *v.*—A: perforate. B: dress carefully. C: go down one size.

15. **sporran** ('spor-en) *n.*—A: lobster bib. B: pouch worn with a kilt. C: ruffed collar or sleeve.

Aging Gracefully

"Sharp Dresser" Answers

1. décolletage—[A] low-cut neckline. A stray rolling pea disappeared down Lady Buxton's *décolletage*.

2. sartorial—[A] relating to a tailor or tailored clothes. If you had any *sartorial* respect, you wouldn't dunk my Burberry jacket sleeve in gravy.

3. ruched—[B] pleated or bunched. Taking a trend too far, Lucy had *ruched* tablecloths, curtains, and slipcovers.

4. argyle—[B] in diamond patterns. Roy found that his *argyle* socks worked well as meatball catapults.

5. twee—[C] excessively dainty or cute. That pink dress might suit you, but isn't it a bit *twee* for the barbecue?

6. salopettes—[B] skier's overalls. Carl's *salopettes* may have stood out on the slope, but they did nothing to enhance his downhill performance.

7. caparison—[B] ornamental covering for a horse. The "medieval" battle looked authentic to us, right down to the *caparisons* for the horses.

8. bouffant—[B] puffed-out. The gown's *bouffant* skirt was the perfect complement to the bride's hairdo.

9. ikat—[C] tie-dyed fabric. In head-to-toe *ikat*, Rufus looked rather psychedelic.

10. bespoke—[A] custom-made. Lyle enjoyed showing off his *bespoke* ten-gallon hat at dinner last night.

11. clew—[A] ball of yarn. Follow this unraveled *clew* far enough, and you'll find Casper, my tabby kitten.

12. regalia—[B] magnificent attire. Eva's *regalia* sure made a statement at last night's state dinner.

13. panache—[C] flamboyance in style. Yes, Charlie leads an exciting, outrageous life, but he doesn't quite have the *panache* of a Hollywood playboy.

14. prink—[B] dress carefully. Lauren *prinks* for hours before each date.

15. sporran—[B] pouch worn with a kilt. Rushing out the door for the parade, my brother shouted, "Has anyone seen my *sporran*?"

USE YOUR WORDS

NEWSWORTHY

Each week, the folks at merriam-webster.com highlight a word that's in the news. Here's a sampling from their Trend Watch section from May 2015. Check the next page for answers.

1. **amnesty** ('am-neh-stee) *n.*—
A: treason. B: pardon. C: safe haven.

2. **harridan** ('har-eh-den) *n.*—
A: brief, wild storm. B: mercenary soldier. C: haggard, old woman.

3. **repudiate** (rih-'pyu-dee-ayt) *v.*—A: overthrow. B: refuse to accept or support. C: divulge.

4. **indict** (en-'diyt) *v.*—A: point out. B: charge with a crime. C: vote.

5. **gentrification** (jen-treh-feh-'kay-shehn) *n.*—A: gender switch. B: uncultured upbringing. C: displacement of the poor by the affluent.

6. **sovereignty** ('sahv-er-en-tee) *n.*—A: full knowledge. B: supreme power. C: communal state.

7. **conflate** (kon-'flayt) *v.*—A: barter or deal. B: ignore. C: confuse or combine into a whole.

8. **solipsistic** (soh-lep-'sis-tik) *adj.*—A: highly egocentric. B: slick. C: applied to the lips.

9. **intransigence** (in-'tran-sih-jents) *n.*—A: stubbornness. B: hard travel. C: secret information.

10. **subterfuge** ('sub-ter-fyewj) *n.*—A: deceptive stratagem. B: underwater dwelling. C: cheap replica.

11. **inherent** (in-'hir-ent) *adj.*—A: inborn. B: granted by a will. C: leased for low cost.

12. **eponymous** (ih-'pah-neh-mes) *adj.*—A: unsigned. B: opposite in meaning. C: named for a person.

13. **intrepid** (in-'treh-pid) *adj.*—A: stumbling. B: unpleasantly hot. C: fearless.

14. **sectarian** (sek-'ter-ee-an) *adj.*—A: related to a horse. B: of religious factions. C: having six parts.

15. **culpable** ('kuhl-peh-buhl) *adj.*—A: blameworthy. B: likely to happen. C: not competent.

Aging Gracefully

"Newsworthy" Answers

1. amnesty—[B] pardon. President Obama's deportation *amnesty* is a key controversy across the nation.

2. harridan—[C] haggard, old woman. During trial, former Virginia governor Bob McDonnell portrayed his wife as a *harridan*, said the *New York Times*.

3. repudiate—[B] refuse to accept or support. After the midterm elections, Senator Paul said, "Tonight is a *repudiation* of Barack Obama's policies."

4. indict—[B] charge with a crime. Darren Wilson was not *indicted* for the killing of Michael Brown.

5. gentrification—[C] displacement of the poor by the affluent. Spike Lee has denounced the *gentrification* in neighborhoods such as Fort Greene.

6. sovereignty—[B] supreme power. Ukraine will not settle its conflicts with Russia until it regains full *sovereignty* over Crimea.

7. conflate—[C] confuse or combine into a whole. Newsman Brian Williams doesn't know what caused him to "*conflate* one aircraft with another."

8. solipsistic—[A] highly egocentric. Some view Facebook as a simply *solipsistic* forum.

9. intransigence—[A] stubbornness. The government shutdown was a display of *intransigence*, said the *Los Angeles Times*.

10. subterfuge—[A] deceptive stratagem. Democratic leader Nancy Pelosi said the Republicans' intent to sue the president was a "*subterfuge*."

11. inherent—[A] inborn. When the Declaration of Independence refers to "unalienable" rights, it is describing the *inherent* privileges people are entitled to.

12. eponymous—[C] named for a person. Who was the original Oscar behind the *eponymous* statuette?

13. intrepid—[C] fearless. After "stealing" a block while playing, Prince George was called "very *intrepid*."

14. sectarian—[B] of religious factions. The UN has warned of "further *sectarian* violence" in Iraq.

15. culpable—[A] blameworthy. Oscar Pistorius was found guilty of *culpable* homicide in South Africa.

WHY WE CAST ABOUT

The word *cast* has its roots in Middle English via the Old Norse *kasta*, meaning "to throw." This is close to the modern definition of "to put forth." So it makes sense that now a newscaster can broadcast the forecast.

BODY LANGUAGE

When the ancient Greeks inscribed the phrase "Know thyself" at the temple of Apollo, we're pretty sure they meant it in the philosophical sense. But how well do you know thyself in a physical sense? This month's quiz tests your knowledge of words related to the body. Can't put your finger on a definition? See the next page for answers.

1. mental *adj.*—of or relating to… A: the navel. B: the chin. C: the hands or feet.

2. visage *n.*—A: face. B: lens of the eye. C: type of birthmark.

3. hirsute *adj.*—A: bent over with hands on knees. B: barrel-chested. C: hairy.

4. pectoral *adj.*—A: of the side. B: of the back. C: of the chest.

5. corpulent *adj.*—A: of or relating to the skull. B: bulky or stout. C: frail, as a bone.

6. alopecia *n.*—A: skin reddening. B: baldness. C: mythological beauty.

7. nuque *n.*—A: back of the neck. B: arch of the foot. C: tip of the tongue.

8. hemic *adj.*—A: of the liver. B: of the blood. C: of the stomach.

9. gangling *adj.*—A: infected. B: bunched, as nerves. C: awkwardly tall and thin.

10. cerumen *n.*—A: type of leg brace. B: essential protein. C: earwax.

11. pollex *n.*—A: kneecap or the tissue surrounding it. B: thumb. C: bridge between the nostrils.

12. ventral *adj.*—A: around the stomach. B: leaving the body, as exhaled air. C: fully developed, as a muscle.

13. axilla *n.*—A: network of nerves along the spine. B: long bone of the leg. C: armpit.

14. ossicles *n.*—A: small bones in the ear. B: nerves attached to the eye. C: eyelashes.

15. fontanel *n.*—A: bone in the finger. B: lower-back muscle. C: soft spot in a young skull.

Aging Gracefully

"Body Language" Answers

1. mental—[B] of or relating to the chin. The boxing vet gave the cocky kid a little *mental* reminder halfway through the first round.

2. visage—[A] face. Harlan stared hard at the *visage* in the painting, curious about its smile.

3. hirsute—[C] hairy. "That's a great costume," Alan admitted. "But you're missing the *hirsute* hobbit feet."

4. pectoral—[C] of the chest. The weight lifter flexed his *pectoral* muscles in a truly Hulkian spectacle.

5. corpulent—[B] bulky or stout. Tara wouldn't call her brother overweight, just a little *corpulent*.

6. alopecia—[B] baldness. Art has been shaving his head since he was 21, hoping to hide his *alopecia*.

7. nuque—[A] back of the neck. Grazing Mary's *nuque*, Hugo thought, was a subtle sign of affection. She disagreed.

8. hemic—[B] of the blood. Would it be fair to say the *Twilight* characters have a slight *hemic* obsession?

9. gangling—[C] awkwardly tall and thin. The new teacher was a *gangling* figure from Sleepy Hollow, best known for another spindly pedagogue, Ichabod Crane.

10. cerumen—[C] earwax. "I certainly doubt *cerumen* is keeping you from hearing me," the instructor barked, glaring at her student's headphones.

11. pollex—[B] thumb. "That's a thimble," Gracie explained to her granddaughter during their sewing lesson. "It's the best way to protect your *pollex*."

12. ventral—[A] around the stomach. His *ventral* fat, the *Biggest Loser* contestant hoped, would be the first to go.

13. axilla—[C] armpit. The second grader's favorite gag involved his cupped hand and his *axilla*.

14. ossicles—[A] small bones in the ear. "For extra credit, what are the smallest bones in the human body?" Mr. Griffin asked. "The *ossicles*!" Tad shouted out.

15. fontanel—[C] soft spot in a young skull. "Mind his *fontanel*," the new mom said, handing her son to his nervous father.

USE YOUR WORDS

MEASURING UP

We're counting on you to figure out these useful words about numbers, amounts, and measurements. Having trouble putting two and two together? Turn the page for answers.

1. fourscore ('fohr-skohr) *adj.*—
A: sixteen. B: forty. C: eighty.

2. tabulate ('ta-byuh-layt) *v.*—
A: rank by weight and height.
B: count or arrange systematically.
C: indent a column.

3. copious ('coh-pee-uhss) *adj.*—
A: plentiful. B: scanty. C: carefully reproduced.

4. gross (grohss) *n.*—A: twelve dozen. B: 51 percent. C: two bushels.

5. aggregate ('a-grih-get) *adj.*—
A: increasing exponentially.
B: amounting to a whole. C: left over as a fraction.

6. googol ('goo-gaul) *n.*—
A: negative number. B: value of pi.
C: 1 followed by 100 zeros.

7. paucity ('paw-sih-tee) *n.*—
A: overabundance. B: shortage.
C: average.

8. myriad ('meer-ee-uhd) *adj.*—
A: very heavy. B: immeasurably small. C: countless.

9. troika ('troy-kuh) *n.*—
A: numbered wheel. B: group of three. C: ancient calculator.

10. calibrate ('ka-luh-brayt) *v.*—
A: adjust according to a standard.
B: divide into equal parts.
C: gain heat.

11. manifold ('man-uh-fold) *adj.*—A: diverse. B: dwindling.
C: doubled.

12. quota ('kwoh-tuh) *n.*—
A: estimated profit. B: bottom line.
C: preset percentage.

13. brace (brayss) *n.*—A: pair.
B: trio. C: quartet.

14. cipher ('sy-fer) *n.*—
A: zero. B: exponent. C: equal proportion.

15. cubed (kyoobd) *adj.*—
A: tripled. B: cut into thirds.
C: multiplied by itself twice.

Aging Gracefully

"Measuring Up" Answers

1. fourscore—[C] eighty. That's the strangest thing I've heard in all my *fourscore* years.

2. tabulate—[B] count or arrange systematically. The committee has *tabulated* the votes—and determined that it's a tie!

3. copious—[A] plentiful. Harriet's notes from history class are *copious* but completely illegible.

4. gross—[A] twelve dozen. How many *gross* of cupcakes did you order for the Halloween party?

5. aggregate—[B] amounting to a whole. Analysts are expecting the *aggregate* demand for electric cars to skyrocket.

6. googol—[C] 1 followed by 100 zeros. Emile's chances of dating Jacqueline are about one in a *googol*.

7. paucity—[B] shortage. Given the *paucity* of evidence against the murder suspect, the detective reluctantly let her go.

8. myriad—[C] countless. Brooke plans to consume *myriad* pumpkin-spice-flavored products this fall.

9. troika—[B] group of three. In my opinion, Larry, Curly, and Moe are a *troika* of numbskulls.

10. calibrate—[A] adjust according to a standard. The post office *calibrates* its scale each morning before opening for business.

11. manifold—[A] diverse. There are *manifold* reasons why Cory's time machine experiment failed.

12. quota—[C] preset percentage. Are you saying one lousy cookie is my *quota* from this jar?

13. brace—[A] pair. We just adopted a *brace* of puppies, so it's kind of crazy around our house.

14. cipher—[A] zero. If you felt like a *cipher* in middle school, join the club!

15. cubed—[C] multiplied by itself twice. Three *cubed* is 27, the last time I checked.

THE NAME IS DEEP

When the young writer Samuel Clemens worked as a Mississippi riverboat pilot, he surely saw crewmen *sounding* the river—measuring its depth—with the call "Mark twain!" This meant they had measured two *fathoms*; a single fathom is six feet, and *twain* means "two." Clemens first used the byline Mark Twain in 1863, as a Nevada newspaper reporter.

USE YOUR WORDS

WORDS OF YESTERYEAR

Language, colorful and complex, is always evolving. Some words are rooted in their time; others are merely useful for a time. This group is probably well known to grandparents if not to today's whippersnappers. How many do you know? Answers on next page.

1. cordial—A: garden party. B: fruit-flavored liqueur. C: flower for buttonhole.

2. gumption—A: foolhardiness. B: resourcefulness. C: stickiness.

3. ragamuffin—A: child in dirty clothes. B: pie made with fruit and stale crumbs. C: abandoned house pet.

4. jalopy—A: beat-up car. B: vacant building. C: elderly gentleman.

5. ewer—A: wide-mouthed water jug. B: hand-crank pump. C: paddock for sheep.

6. lollygag—A: play a trick on someone. B: wolf down food. C: dawdle.

7. bustle—A: padding at the rear of a woman's skirt. B: undergarment used to constrict the waist. C: strapless bodice.

8. rapscallion—A: bitter vegetable. B: mischievous person. C: musical style.

9. gumshoe—A: detective. B: burglar. C: athlete.

10. gitches—A: arguments. B: underwear. C: silly people.

11. apothecary—A: fortune teller. B: pharmacist. C: evangelical minister.

12. balderdash—A: slang. B: exaggeration. C: nonsense.

13. dickey—A: chest pocket on overalls. B: false shirtfront. C: high-necked cape.

14. providence—A: happy coincidence. B: physical comfort. C: divine care.

15. naughty-naught—A: badly behaved child. B: girl's tangled hair. C: the year 1900.

16. pedal pushers—A: bicycle gears. B: calf-length trousers. C: two-tone shoes.

17. humdinger—A: laughable. B: modern. C: someone or something extraordinary.

Aging Gracefully

"Words of Yesteryear" Answers

1. cordial—[B] fruit-flavored liqueur. Only favored guests were offered Aunt Millie's homemade raspberry *cordial*.

2. gumption—[B] resourcefulness. The Wright brothers sure had *gumption* to make and fly their planes.

3. ragamuffin—[A] child in dirty clothes. After picking up Arnie from the petting zoo, Grandma proclaimed, "He looks like the *ragamuffin* Oliver Twist!"

4. jalopy—[A] beat-up car. A constant eyesore, our neighbor's *jalopy* is ready for the junkyard.

5. ewer—[A] widemouthed water jug. A basin and *ewer* predate the modern bathroom sink.

6. lollygag—[C] dawdle. Don't *lollygag* on the way to school or you'll be late.

7. bustle—[A] padding at the rear of a woman's skirt. The *bustle* added some unneeded curves to her profile.

8. rapscallion—[B] mischievous person. That *rapscallion* tricked everyone into doing all his chores for him.

9. gumshoe—[A] detective. Who is your favorite *gumshoe*, Philip Marlowe or Sam Spade?

10. gitches—[B] underwear. It was so warm outside that little Sammy stripped down to his *gitches*.

11. apothecary—[B] pharmacist. Check with the *apothecary* about side effects before taking that drug.

12. balderdash—[C] nonsense. In response to vehement claims that the earth is flat, Galileo would always yell, "What *balderdash!*"

13. dickey—[B] false shirtfront. My great-uncle wore a *dickey*, saving my great-aunt from heaps of shirt washing.

14. providence—[C] divine care. Trusting in *providence*, Lillie booked a transatlantic voyage during hurricane season.

15. naughty-naught—[C] the year 1900. *Naughty-naught* cleverly hints at a daring new generation.

16. pedal pushers—[B] calf-length trousers. The costume designer had her hands full making *pedal pushers* for the play's revival.

17. humdinger—[C] something or someone extraordinary. That was a real *humdinger* of a storm last night.

VERBAL MISUSE AND ABUSE

Combat conversation miscues with our quiz—which tackles some too-frequent examples of verbal misuse (and abuse!). How sure are you about these troublemaking morphemes? Answers on next page.

1. noisome ('noy-sum) *adj.*— A: loud. B: stinky. C: crowded.

2. enervated ('eh-ner-vayt-ed) *adj.*—A: lacking energy. B: refreshed. C: feeling anxiety.

3. proscribe (proh-'skriyb) *v.*— A: encourage. B: dispense a medicine. C: forbid.

4. nonplussed (non-'pluhst) *adj.*—A: baffled. B: cool under pressure. C: subtracted.

5. principle ('prin-seh-pul) *n.*— A: interest-earning money. B: basic rule. C: school head.

6. flout ('flowt) *v.*—A: display proudly. B: scorn. C: defeat decisively.

7. discrete (dis-'kreet) *adj.*— A: separate and distinct. B: showing good manners. C: whole and undamaged.

8. ingenuous (in-'jen-yew-us) *adj.*—A: showing innocence or simplicity. B: extremely clever. C: one-of-a-kind.

9. cachet (ka-'shay) *n.*— A: secret stockpile. B: perfumed bag. C: prestige.

10. allusion (uh-'lew-zhun) *n.*— A: misleading image or perception. B: crazy idea. C: indirect reference.

11. reticent ('reh-tuh-sent) *adj.*—A: inclined to keep silent. B: reluctant. C: backward.

12. bemused (bih-'myuzd) *adj.*— A: entertained. B: puzzled. C: inspired.

13. diffuse (di-'fyuz) *v.*—A: make less dangerous. B: come together. C: spread or pour out freely.

14. eminent ('eh-muh-nent) *adj.*—A: prominent. B: about to happen. C: inherent.

15. apprise (uh-'priyz) *v.*— A: estimate a value. B: promote. C: inform of or give notice.

Aging Gracefully **75**

"Verbal Misuse and Abuse" Answers

1. noisome—[B] stinky. Because of its deceptive root, *noisome* is often confused with *noisy*.

2. enervated—[A] lacking energy. From the sound of it, you'd think *enervated* means "full of energy"—nope, it's the exact opposite.

3. proscribe—[C] forbid. Careful: *Prescribe* means "to dispense a drug."

4. nonplussed—[A] baffled. The *non* is the deceiver here, leading many to equate *nonplussed* with *calm*.

5. principle—[B] basic rule. A classic gaffe. Sibling *principal* is the head of a school (think "pal") or a capital sum.

6. flout—[B] scorn. Though some sources are doing away with the distinction, *flout* doesn't mean "to flaunt," i.e., "to show off."

7. discrete—[A] separate and distinct. This is a spell-check snafu. Its homonym, *discreet*, means "prudent."

8. ingenuous—[A] showing innocence or simplicity. Not—we repeat—not *ingenious*, "showing an aptitude."

9. cachet—[C] prestige. What a difference a letter makes: Lop off the *t*, and you've got "a secret stockpile" or "a short-lived computer memory."

10. allusion—[C] indirect reference. Another infamous faux pas. *Illusion* is the one referring to a sleight of hand.

11. reticent—[A] inclined to keep silent. It's in the ballpark with *reluctant*, or "unwilling," so be reticent if you're unsure of the difference.

12. bemused—[B] puzzled. As with *noisome*, you may *want* this to mean "entertained." But as the Rolling Stones said, "You can't always get ..."

13. diffuse—[C] spread or pour out freely. You defuse a bomb or a heated situation, but a photographer might diffuse light.

14. eminent—[A] prominent. It's typically mistaken for *imminent*, or "about to happen."

15. apprise—[C] inform of or give notice. The president is apprised of a crisis; antiques are appraised (given an estimated value).

IS IT IRONIC?

Strictly speaking, irony involves a reversal. A traffic cop who has 13 unpaid traffic tickets is ironic because that is not expected. Rain on a wedding day may be dampening, and a tall man named Tallman might be coincidental—but it's properly ironic only if the rain falls on a sun festival or if Mr. Tallman is short.

FEELING YOUNG

The most sophisticated people I know—
inside they are all children.
—JIM HENSON

"
Adults are always asking children what
they want to be when they grow up because
they're looking for ideas.
—PAULA POUNDSTONE

"
The key to successful aging is to pay
as little attention to it as possible.
—JUDITH REGAN

"
If only I'd known that one day my differentness
would be an asset, then my early life
would have been much easier.
—BETTE MIDLER

"
Youth would be an ideal state if it came
a little later in life.
—HERBERT ASQUITH

"
Everybody, no matter how old you are,
is around 24, 25 in their heart.
—BRUCE WILLIS

THE PERFECT WORDS FOR
BIRTHDAY CARDS

One of the best parts of growing older? You can flirt all you like since you've become harmless.
—**LIZ SMITH**

"
The more you praise and celebrate your life, the more there is in life to celebrate.
—**OPRAH**

"
You are only young once, but you can stay immature indefinitely.
—**OGDEN NASH**

"
Age is an issue of mind over matter. If you don't mind, it doesn't matter.
—**MARK TWAIN**

"
Middle age is the awkward period when Father Time starts catching up with Mother Nature.
—**HAROLD COFFIN**

There is still no cure for the common birthday.
—JOHN GLENN

"
The secret of staying young is to live honestly, eat slowly, and lie about your age.
—LUCILLE BALL

"
Birthdays are good for you. Statistics show that the people who have the most live the longest.
—LARRY LORENZONI

"
Those who love deeply never grow old; they may die of old age, but they die young.
—DOROTHY CANFIELD FISHER

"
You know you're getting old when the candles cost more than the cake.
—BOB HOPE

> This is a sign, having a broken heart. It means we have tried for something.
>
> —ELIZABETH GILBERT

LOVE & MARRIAGE

We can't live without love, but often living with it isn't that easy either. Gaining insight from different perspectives helps us understand our own relationships and be thankful for the one we've got.

MEN ON MARRIAGE

Being a good husband is like being a stand-up comic. You need 10 years before you can even call yourself a beginner.
—**JERRY SEINFELD**

As a man in a relationship, you have a simple choice: You can be right or you can be happy.
—**RALPHIE MAY**

They say marriages are made in heaven. But so is thunder and lightning.
—**CLINT EASTWOOD**

We accept the love we think we deserve.
—**STEPHEN CHBOSKY**

🐦 QUOTABLE TWEETS

No one in America should ever be afraid to walk down the street holding hands with the person they love.
@BARACKOBAMA

If you marry for money, you will earn every penny.
—DR. PHIL MCGRAW

My parents just had their 50th anniversary and they're happier than ever. They have each other's back— I think that's what it's about.
—BEN STILLER

"

Behind every great man is a woman rolling her eyes.
—JIM CARREY

"

I love being married. I was single for a long time, and I just got so sick of finishing my own sentences.
—BRIAN KILEY

"

My wife tells me that if I ever decide to leave, she's coming with me.
—JON BON JOVI

"

Never marry anyone you could not sit next to during a three-day bus trip.
—ROGER EBERT

Love & Marriage

WOMEN ON MARRIAGE

Sexiness wears thin after a while, and beauty fades, but to be married to a man who makes you laugh every day, ah, now that's a real treat.
—**JOANNE WOODWARD**

"

Grief is the price we pay for love.
—**QUEEN ELIZABETH II**

"

Marriage is very difficult. It's like a 5,000-piece jigsaw puzzle, all sky.
—**CATHY LADMAN**

"

The opposite of love isn't hate—it's indifference. And if you hate me, that means you still care.
—**MARCIA CROSS**

QUOTABLE TWEETS

Don't make mountains out of molehills. If your partner says that everything is OK, believe it.
@ASKDRRUTH

It is only when you see people looking ridiculous that you realize just how much you love them.
—AGATHA CHRISTIE

"

The three words every woman really longs to hear: I'll clean up.
—MOLLY SHANNON

"

Love is blind, but marriage is a real eye-opener.
—PAULA DEEN

"

One of the few articles of clothing that a man won't try to remove from a woman is an apron.
—MARILYN VOS SAVANT

"

Why does a woman work ten years to change a man's habits and then complain that he's not the man she married?
—BARBRA STREISAND

"

For marriage to be a success, every woman and every man should have her and his own bathroom. The end.
—CATHERINE ZETA-JONES

A LITTLE HEART

Want to improve your relationships?
See love as a verb rather than as a feeling.
—STEPHEN R. COVEY

"

I know love at first sight can work.
It happened to my parents.
—GEORGE CLOONEY

"

You know how they say we only use 10 percent of our brains? I think we only use 10 percent of our hearts.
—OWEN WILSON

"

In a nutshell, loving someone is about
giving, not receiving.
—NICHOLAS SPARKS

QUOTABLE TWEETS

What matter is it where you find a real love
that makes this life a little easier?
@ALECBALDWIN

To wear your heart on your sleeve isn't a very good plan. You should wear it inside, where it functions best.
—MARGARET THATCHER

That's what real love amounts to—letting a person be what he really is.
—JIM MORRISON

"
I still believe that love is all you need. I don't know a better message than that.
—PAUL MCCARTNEY

"
If grass can grow through cement, love can find you at every time in your life.
—CHER

"
Love is like quicksilver in the hand. Leave the fingers open, and it stays. Clutch it, and it darts away.
—DOROTHY PARKER

Love & Marriage

THE PERFECT WORDS FOR
WEDDING SPEECHES

The formula for a successful relationship is simple: Treat all disasters as if they were trivialities, but never treat a triviality as if it were a disaster.
—QUENTIN CRISP

"

Marriage should, I think, always be a little hard and new and strange. It should be breaking your shell and going into another world, and a bigger one.
—ANNE MORROW LINDBERGH

"

Getting married is an incredible act of hopefulness.
—ASHLEY JUDD

"

Story writers say that love is concerned only with young people, and the excitement and glamour of romance end at the altar. How blind they are. The best romance is inside marriage; the finest love stories come after the wedding, not before.
—IRVING STONE

"

Love is a game that two can play and both win.
—EVA GABOR

VALENTINE WORDS

Before sending a card this Valentine's Day, be sure you know the language of love. Here are some words perfect for would-be Romeos and Juliets. Don't know them by heart? See the next page for answers.

1. **ardent** ('ar-dent) *adj.*—
A: engaged. B: lyrical. C: passionate.

2. **paramour** ('pa-ruh-mor) *n.*—
A: chaperone. B: lover. C: token of affection.

3. **buss** ('buhs) *v.*—A: kiss. B: elope. C: carve initials in a tree.

4. **swain** ('swayn) *n.*—A: intense crush. B: male suitor. C: gondola for two.

5. **connubial** (kuh-'new-bee-uhl) *adj.*—A: coy. B: of marriage. C: about the heart.

6. **troth** ('trawth) *n.*—A: wooden or rustic altar. B: fidelity. C: Celtic wedding ring.

7. **coquettish** (koh-'ket-ish) *adj.*—
A: flirtatious. B: alluring. C: shy.

8. **macushla** (muh-'koosh-luh) *n.*—A: darling. B: fainting spell. C: best man.

9. **platonic** (pluh-'tah-nik) *adj.*—
A: of a honeymoon. B: smitten. C: without physical desire.

10. **liaison** (lee-'ay-zahn) *n.*—
A: secret affair. B: exchange of vows. C: pet nickname.

11. **beaux** ('bohz) *n.*—
A: traditional string used to join hands in marriage. B: winks of an eye. C: boyfriends.

12. **requite** (rih-'kwiyt) *v.*—
A: ask for someone's hand.
B: give back, as affection. C: fondly remember.

13. **epistolary** (ih-'pis-tuh-la-ree) *adj.*—A: serenading. B: set in an arbor. C: relating to letters.

14. **philter** ('fil-ter) *n.*—A: love potion. B: caress. C: family keepsake or hand-me-down.

15. **cupidity** (kyu-'pih-duh-tee) *n.*—A: valentine shape. B: lust or desire for wealth. C: condition of instant romance, as love at first sight.

Love & Marriage **89**

"Valentine Words" Answers

1. ardent—[C] passionate. Though he's a native New Yorker, Peter is an *ardent* Red Sox fan.

2. paramour—[B] lover. Claire was overwhelmed by the devotion and affection of her new *paramour*.

3. buss—[A] kiss. During the bus ride, Lauren and Alex sneaked off to *buss* in the backseat.

4. swain—[B] male suitor. The princess gave a weary sigh as she awaited the entreaties of her *swains*.

5. connubial—[B] of marriage. Aside from their celebrity status, Paul Newman and Joanne Woodward were famous for their *connubial* bliss.

6. troth—[B] fidelity. "It was in this gazebo, 20 years ago, dear, that we pledged our *troth*," said Arthur.

7. coquettish—[A] flirtatious. Alison caught Dean's eye with a *coquettish* smile and nod.

8. macushla—[A] darling. In *Million Dollar Baby*, boxing trainer Clint Eastwood gave his dear protégé Hilary Swank the nickname *macushla*.

9. platonic—[C] without physical desire. I hate to disappoint the paparazzi, but my current relationships are all *platonic*.

10. liaison—[A] secret affair. The young couple stole away at midnight each evening for their *liaison*.

11. beaux—[C] boyfriends. I doubt that Sharon considers young Timothy one of her best *beaux*.

12. requite—[B] give back, as affection. Her lyrics tend toward *requited* love rather than heartbreak.

13. epistolary—[C] relating to letters. The romance between Elizabeth Barrett Browning and Robert Browning is marked by an *epistolary* trail.

14. philter—[A] love potion. Hoping for attention from my crush, I went to Madam Ava for her purported *philter*.

15. cupidity—[B] lust or desire for wealth. The testimony gave clear evidence of the *cupidity* of the accused investors.

> ### GONE A-COURTIN' ...
> You may know that *horticulture* pertains to gardening. It comes from the Latin *hortus* ("garden"). Add the prefix *co-* ("with") to that root, and you get both *court* (a yard) and *cohort* (a companion). In royal settings of old, and still today, a flowery yard is an ideal spot for courting a sweetheart. (A quaint old synonym of *courting* is *pitching woo*. But etymologists aren't sure where *woo* came from.)

TWO OF A KIND

Whether you're from Walla Walla, Washington, or Wagga Wagga, Australia, we double-dare you to master this month's quiz—all about words with repeating sets of letters. (Don't go gaga, though.) See the next page for answers.

1. baba ('bah-bah) *n.*—A: rum-soaked cake. B: maternal relative. C: mild bruise or scrape.

2. muumuu ('moo-moo) *n.*—A: radical militant. B: lagoon in an atoll. C: long, loose dress.

3. pupu ('poo-poo) *n.*—A: tree with yellow fruit. B: sea breeze. C: Asian appetizer.

4. chichi ('shee-shee) *adj.*—A: frigid, icy. B: loose, lanky. C: showy, frilly.

5. Isis ('eye-sis) *n.*—A: fiery river of Hades. B: Egyptian nature goddess. C: rainbow personified.

6. furfur ('fer-fer) *n.*—A: about 1.25 miles. B: dandruff. C: bow-shaped pasta.

7. tsetse ('set-see or 'teet-) *n.*—A: type of fly. B: Greek hierarchy. C: opposing force of energy or gravity.

8. chop-chop (chop-'chop) *adv.*—A: sarcastically. B: intently. C: promptly.

9. nene ('nay-nay) *n.*—A: endangered state bird of Hawaii. B: forbidden behavior. C: cheap trinket.

10. tam-tam ('tam-tam) *n.*—A: pouty look. B: gong. C: skiing maneuver.

11. chin-chin ('chin-chin) *n.*—A: broom. B: type of dog. C: salutation or toast.

12. juju ('joo-joo) *n.*—A: West African music style. B: trophy. C: candy.

13. couscous ('coos-coos) *n.*—A: semolina dish. B: Moroccan beach strip. C: Congolese dance.

14. meme ('meem) *n.*—A: perfect imitation. B: recycling symbol. C: idea or trait that spreads within a culture.

15. bulbul ('bull-bull) *n.*—A: songbird. B: knobbed head on a cane. C: croak of a male frog.

Love & Marriage

"Two of a Kind" Answers

1. baba—[A] rum-soaked cake. Nothing completes a holiday feast like Becky's homemade *baba*.

2. muumuu—[C] long, loose dress. Natalie was jealous of the authentic *muumuu* her sister brought back from her honeymoon.

3. pupu—[C] Asian appetizer. Art's favorite part of the meal? The *pupu* platter of fried shrimp and egg rolls.

4. chichi—[C] showy, frilly. As we'd predicted, Lucy got just what she wanted: an over-the-top, *chichi* engagement ring.

5. Isis—[B] Egyptian nature goddess. Certainly, Bob Dylan was inspired by the mystical *Isis* when he penned his famous song.

6. furfur—[B] dandruff. "I have a great remedy for that *furfur* on your dog's coat," Tiffany offered.

7. tsetse—[A] type of fly. Sleeping sickness, a disease marked by lethargy and confusion, is transmitted by the *tsetse* fly.

8. chop-chop—[C] promptly. Yes, the soup arrived *chop-chop*, but I seriously doubt it's homemade.

9. nene—[A] endangered state bird of Hawaii. A bird lover, Marty was delighted to see the *nene* up close during his trip.

10. tam-tam—[B] gong. Lauren was fascinated by the *tam-tam* player in the orchestra.

11. chin-chin—[C] salutation or toast. Neville looked forward to saying *"chin-chin"* to his classmates at the reunion.

12. juju—[A] West African music style. Featuring a breathtaking beat, Alec's *juju* composition relies on heavy percussion.

13. couscous—[A] semolina dish. Our family's *couscous* recipe is five generations old.

14. meme—[C] idea or trait that spreads within a culture. The abuse of the word *like* is an unfortunate *meme* dating back to the '80s.

15. bulbul—[A] songbird. The *bulbul* makes frequent appearances in Persian poetry, Emily learned during her graduate studies.

OOH LA, LA

Thousands of English words, from *archery* to *zest*, have their origins in French. Think you're a word connoisseur? Take a tour through this petite list of terms, then sashay to the next page for answers.

1. raconteur (ra-kahn-'ter) *n.*—
A: skillful storyteller. B: blackmailer. C: court jester.

2. faience (fay-'ans) *n.*—A: false pretenses. B: fidelity. C: glazed pottery.

3. couturier (koo-'tuhr-ee-er) *n.*—
A: head chef. B: fashion designer. C: museum guide.

4. laissez-faire (leh-say-'fair) *adj.*—A: festive. B: noninterfering. C: done by women.

5. cabal (kuh-'bahl) *n.*—
A: plotting group. B: young horse. C: crystal wineglass.

6. fait accompli (fayt ah-cahm-'plee) *n.*—A: done deal. B: lucky charm. C: partner in crime.

7. au courant (oh kuh-'rahn) *adj.*—A: on the contrary. B: with cherries on top. C: up-to-date.

8. interlard (ihn-ter-'lahrd) *v.*—
A: encroach on. B: vary by intermixing. C: fluctuate in weight.

9. soupçon (soop-'sohn) *n.*—
A: wooden ladle. B: swindle. C: small amount.

10. milieu (meel-'yeu) *n.*—
A: environment. B: thousand. C: armed force.

11. aubade (oh-'bahd) *n.*—
A: gold pendant. B: babysitter. C: morning song.

12. pince-nez (pahns-'nay) *n.*—
A: clipped-on eyeglasses. B: rude interruption. C: narrow hallway.

13. sangfroid (sahn-'fwah) *n.*—
A: intense heat wave. B: composure under strain. C: mind reading.

14. fracas ('fray-kuhs) *n.*—
A: wool scarf. B: noisy quarrel. C: utter failure.

15. roué (roo-'ay) *n.*—A: thick meat sauce. B: rakish man. C: illegal gambling game.

Love & Marriage

"Ooh La, La" Answers

1. raconteur—[A] skillful storyteller. No one would call me a *raconteur*—I tend to ramble and say "um" a lot.

2. faience—[C] glazed pottery. Catherine hoped to sell the rare *faience* she'd found at the tag sale for a huge profit.

3. couturier—[B] fashion designer. C*outuriers* such as Christian Dior and Jean-Paul Gaultier have shaped fashion history.

4. laissez-faire—[B] noninterfering. In our family, Mom's the enforcer, while Dad takes more of a *laissez-faire* attitude.

5. cabal—[A] plotting group. There's a *cabal* among the dictator's aides, who are all vying for control of the country.

6. fait accompli—[A] done deal. Well, we've painted the bedroom dark purple—it's a *fait accompli*.

7. au courant—[C] up-to-date. To stay *au courant*, Rafael snaps up all the newest apps.

8. interlard—[B] vary by intermixing. I didn't understand your film—why did you *interlard* the narrative with those bizarre dream sequences?

9. soupçon—[C] small amount. Dylan detected a *soupçon* of sarcasm in his teenage son's remark.

10. milieu—[A] environment. "The briar patch," said Brer Rabbit, "is my natural *milieu*."

11. aubade—[C] morning song. Ah, the tuneful *aubade* of my alarm!

12. pince-nez—[A] clipped-on eyeglasses. I've never understood how you keep your *pince-nez* on your nose while you dance.

13. sangfroid—[B] composure under strain. We had to admire Magda's *sangfroid* as she stood up to her obnoxious boss.

14. fracas—[B] noisy quarrel. I wouldn't call it a *fracas*. It's just a difference of opinion.

15. roué—[B] rakish man. Steer clear of that guy Casanova—he's a shameless *roué*.

WATCH YOUR TONGUE

The Académie Française, which has set the country's linguistic standards for centuries, has a special distaste for English tech terms. It nixed *e-mail* and *software* in favor of *courriel* and *logiciel*. And in 2013, francophones were urged to slash *hashtag*. The French version: *mot-dièse* (*mot* for "word," *dièse* for a musical sharp symbol).

USE YOUR WORDS

IN SHORT

In recognition of February, the shortest month (even during a leap year), we celebrate all things diminutive. Zip through this quiz in short order, then baby step to the next page for answers.

1. **transient** ('tran-shee-nt or -zee-ent) *adj.*—A: short-range. B: short-handed. C: short-lived.

2. **vignette** (vin-'yet) *n.*—A: small glass. B: short literary sketch or scene. C: thin line.

3. **bagatelle** (ba-geh-'tel) *n.*—A: child's rucksack. B: cell nucleus. C: something of little value.

4. **scintilla** (sin-'ti-luh) *n.*—A: short vowel. B: minute amount. C: minor crime.

5. **myopic** (miy-'oh-pik) *adj.*—A: too tiny for the naked eye. B: shortsighted. C: early.

6. **irascible** (i-'ra-se-bul) *adj.*—A: small-minded. B: narrow-waisted. C: marked by a short temper.

7. **expeditiously** (ek-speh-'di-shes-lee) *adv.*—A: promptly and efficiently. B: incompletely. C: tersely or rudely.

8. **tabard** ('ta-bird) *n.*—A: short-sleeved coat. B: booklet of verses. C: dwarf evergreen.

9. **arietta** (ar-ee-'eh-tuh) *n.*—A: tot's playpen. B: miniature figurine. C: short melody.

10. **niggling** ('nih-gehling) *adj.*—A: petty. B: stunted. C: short-winded.

11. **aphorism** ('a-feh-ri-zuhm) *n.*—A: concise saying. B: shorthand writing. C: cut-off sentence.

12. **staccato** (ste-'kah-toh) *adj.*—A: of cemented fragments. B: formed into droplets. C: disconnected.

13. **nib** ('nib) *n.*—A: crumb on a plate. B: point of a pen. C: matter of seconds.

14. **exiguous** (ig-'zi-gye-wes) *adj.*—A: inadequate, scanty. B: momentary. C: reduced by one tenth.

15. **truncate** ('trun-kayt) *v.*—A: compress by squeezing. B: speed up. C: shorten by lopping off.

Love & Marriage

"In Short" Answers

1. transient—[C] short-lived. The first-quarter lead proved *transient*, as the Ravens racked up 42 points in the second.

2. vignette—[B] short literary sketch or scene. Dickens created characters from prose *vignettes* like little photographs.

3. bagatelle—[C] something of little value. My stories aren't prized works, just personal *bagatelles*.

4. scintilla—[B] minute amount. There's not one scintilla of evidence against my client.

5. myopic—[B] shortsighted. Kim's *myopic* view of the project surely led to its collapse.

6. irascible—[C] marked by a short temper. If Jack were any more *irascible*, he'd have smoke coming out his ears.

7. expeditiously—[A] promptly and efficiently. As a pick-me-up, a triple espresso works *expeditiously*.

8. tabard—[A] short-sleeved coat. My entire Hamlet costume consists of a wooden sword and this *tabard*.

9. arietta—[C] short melody. The goldfinch trilled an *arietta*, reminding us that spring would come soon.

10. niggling—[A] petty. Mom, you're driving me bonkers with your *niggling* complaints!

11. aphorism—[A] concise saying. My father has an *aphorism* for any situation.

12. staccato—[C] disconnected. Lucy's hilarious laugh comes in sharp, *staccato* dog barks.

13. nib—[B] point of a pen. A faulty *nib*, Beth complained, ruined her first pass at her final drawing project.

14. exiguous—[A] inadequate, scanty. Ever a big eater, Art found even the jumbo burger a bit *exiguous*.

15. truncate—[C] shorten by lopping off. According to mythology, the gruesome Procrustes would *truncate* his guests if they were too long for the bed.

OPPOSITES ATTRACT

Within the month of March, we greet the proverbial lion and lamb of weather. This quiz brings you other extremes and polar opposites. So go all out (but don't overexert yourself!), then turn the page for the answers.

1. **nethermost** ('neth-er-mohst) *adj.*—A: coldest. B: thinnest. C: lowest.

2. **extravagant** (ik-'stra-vi-gent) *adj.*—A: all gone. B: irate. C: over the top.

3. **acme** ('ak-mee) *n.*—A: verge. B: highest point. C: overflow.

4. **culminate** ('kul-mih-nayt) *v.*—A: fly into space. B: hit the bottom. C: reach a climax.

5. **acute** (uh-'kyoot) *adj.*—A: intense, urgent. B: tiny, insignificant. C: pretty, appealing.

6. **precipice** ('preh-sih-pis) *n.*—A: very steep side of a cliff. B: earliest moment. C: towering spire.

7. **superlative** (soo-'per-leh-tiv) *adj.*—A: outstanding. B: excessive. C: final.

8. **antithesis** (an-'ti-theh-sis) *n.*—A: exact opposite. B: end of time. C: extremely negative reaction.

9. **surfeit** ('sur-fet) *n.*—A: utter wreck. B: more than needed. C: intense heat.

10. **exorbitant** (ig-'zor-bih-tent) *adj.*—A: on a shore's edge. B: at a mountain's summit. C: far exceeding what is fair or reasonable.

11. **overweening** (oh-ver-'wee-ning) *adj.*—A: arrogant. B: too fond of food. C: severely strict.

12. **optimal** ('ahp-tih-mul) *adj.*—A: best. B: surplus. C: out of sight.

13. **radical** ('ra-di-kul) *n.*—A: supreme leader. B: extremist. C: middle-of-the-roader.

14. **penultimate** (peh-'nul-teh-mit) *adj.*—A: next to last. B: most recent. C: cream of the crop.

15. **maximal** ('mak-sih-mul) *adj.*—A: greatest possible. B: conflicting. C: most important.

16. **zealotry** ('ze-luh-tree) *n.*—A: extreme greed. B: overdone fervor. C: excess of noise.

"Opposites Attract" Answers

1. nethermost—[C] lowest. No one dares explore the *nethermost* dungeons of this castle.

2. extravagant—[C] over the top. How can Monty afford to throw such *extravagant* parties?

3. acme—[B] highest point. Going to the top of the Empire State Building was literally the *acme* of our trip.

4. culminate—[C] reach a climax. Nearly every scene with the Stooges in a cafeteria *culminates* in a pie fight.

5. acute—[A] intense, urgent. Joey has an *acute* hankering for chocolate.

6. precipice—[A] very steep side of a cliff. As Alex peered over the *precipice*, he developed a sudden case of acrophobia.

7. superlative—[A] outstanding. Despite Willie's *superlative* effort to catch the ball, it landed in the bleachers.

8. antithesis—[A] exact opposite. Slovenly Oscar is the *antithesis* of a neatnik.

9. surfeit—[B] more than needed. We have a *surfeit* of nachos but absolutely no salsa!

10. exorbitant—[C] far exceeding what is fair or reasonable. I nearly fainted from sticker shock when I saw the *exorbitant* price.

11. overweening—[A] arrogant. I enjoy the art class, but not Professor Prigg's *overweening* attitude.

12. optimal—[A] best. Now is not the *optimal* time to pester the boss about a raise. [Note: The synonym *optimum* is best used as a noun.]

13. radical—[B] extremist. We knew Carey loved her pup, but we didn't realize what a *radical* she was until she tattooed its face on her arm.

14. penultimate—[A] next to last. My *penultimate* finish in the marathon was my best showing ever.

15. maximal—[A] greatest possible. "OK" is *maximal* praise from that old curmudgeon. [Like *optimum*, the synonym *maximum* is best used as a noun.]

16. zealotry—[B] overdone fervor. *Zealotry* gets TV attention, but it rarely brings compromise.

EARTHLY EXTREMES

At its farthest point from the sun, Earth reaches its apogee; when nearest the sun, Earth is at its perigee. In these examples, *gee* means "Earth." Meanwhile, in Greek, *apo* means "far from," and *peri* means "near to."

MIXING AND MINGLING

The rules of social engagement are always changing. But whether you interact mouse-to-mouse or face-to-face (now, *there's* a novel idea), it helps to speak the language of social harmony. Here's a primer on words concerned with schmoozing, mixing, and mingling. Answers on next page.

1. **diffident** *adj.*—A: argumentative. B: unmatched. C: shy.

2. **comity** *n.*—A: hilarious misunderstanding. B: social harmony. C: lack of respect.

3. **interlocutor** *n.*—A: formal escort. B: meddler. C: person in a conversation.

4. **gregarious** *adj.*—A: a little tipsy. B: fond of company. C: markedly rude.

5. **accost** *v.*— A: aggressively approach. B: offer to pay. C: decline to join.

6. **propriety** *n.*—A: home of a host. B: good social form. C: tendency to gossip.

7. **fulsome** *adj.*— A: broad-minded. B: physically attractive. C: excessively flattering.

8. **confabulate** *v.*—A: chat. B: get things backward. C: greet with a hug.

9. **brusque** *adj.*—A: clownish. B: discourteously blunt. C: full of questions.

10. **decorum** *n.*—A: high praise. B: dignified behavior or speech. C: showy jewelry or makeup.

11. **unctuous** *adj.*—A: avoiding eye contact. B: on pins and needles. C: smug.

12. **urbane** *adj.*—A: suave and polished. B: known by everyone. C: pertinent to the subject.

13. **malapert** *adj.*—A: socially awkward. B: bold and saucy. C: disappointed.

14. **audacity** *n.*— A: long-windedness. B: good listening skills. C: gall.

15. **genteel** *adj.*— A: polite. B: macho. C: timid.

Love & Marriage

"Mixing and Mingling" Answers

1. diffident—[C] shy. I would hardly call Veronica *diffident*—she's the center of attention at every party she attends.

2. comity—[B] social harmony. Ducking for cover as the food fight intensified, Millie realized all *comity* at her table was lost.

3. interlocutor—[C] person in a conversation. Ever the gentleman, Professor Windham was sure to give other *interlocutors* time to speak.

4. gregarious—[B] fond of company. Dad is so *gregarious*, it's all we can do to keep him from hugging total strangers.

5. accost—[A] aggressively approach. Ariana can't even walk across the room without someone *accosting* her for an autograph.

6. propriety—[B] good social form. "Someone should tell your daughter that *propriety* dictates that she eat her spaghetti with a fork," the hostess said, groaning.

7. fulsome—[C] excessively flattering. When meeting Bev's mom, Eddie praised her with such *fulsome* remarks that she rolled her eyes.

8. confabulate—[A] chat. Luca wants to *confabulate* a bit about the new office's blueprints.

9. brusque—[B] discourteously blunt. Alice did her best to hold her tongue after listening to the coach's *brusque* advice.

10. decorum—[B] dignified behavior or speech. In a surprising show of *decorum*, the tipsy best man gave an endearing toast.

11. unctuous—[C] smug. Ramona, don't believe a thing that *unctuous*, money-grubbing sneak tells you.

12. urbane—[A] suave and polished. Cary's *urbane* persona was obvious as soon as he stepped into the room.

13. malapert—[B] bold and saucy. After the audition, Jenny gave the director a wink in a most *malapert* manner.

14. audacity—[C] gall. Did you hear the gossip that Eli had the *audacity* to repeat?

15. genteel—[A] polite. Clare had to remind the twins to be *genteel* around their grandparents.

COCKTAIL CONVERSATION

Do you ever toss off an impressive-sounding word at a cocktail party only to wonder: Did I get that right? The terms in this month's quiz, inspired by the book *You're Saying It Wrong* by Ross and Kathryn Petras, will make you sound like the smartest person in the room—*if* your pronunciation is correct. See the next page for answers.

1. **detritus** (dih-'try-tuss) *n.*—A: subtracted amount. B: debris. C: falsified claim.

2. **prerogative** (prih-'rah-guh-tiv) *n.*—A: educated guess. B: first choice. C: special right.

3. **segue** ('sehg-way) *v.*—A: transition. B: completely surround. C: begin a court case.

4. **hegemony** (hih-'jeh-muh-nee) *n.*—A: domination. B: smooth blend. C: large family.

5. **dais** ('day-iss) *n.*—A: group leader. B: garden fountain. C: raised platform.

6. **kefir** (keh-'feer) *n.*—A: verbal skirmish. B: fermented milk. C: painting technique.

7. **peremptory** (puh-'remp-tuh-ree) *adj.*—A: allowing no disagreement. B: coming first. C: walking quickly.

8. **quay** (kee) *n.*—A: wharf. B: small island. C: dram of brandy.

9. **machination** (ma-kuh-'nay-shun) *n.*—A: study of robotics. B: talkativeness. C: scheme.

10. **slough** (sloo) *n.*—A: soft breeze. B: heavy club. C: swamp.

11. **spurious** ('spyuhr-ee-us) *adj.*—A: hasty. B: fake. C: livid.

12. **nuptial** ('nuhp-shuhl) *adj.*—A: just starting. B: relating to marriage. C: present during all seasons.

13. **coxswain** ('kahk-suhn) *n.*—A: innkeeper. B: secret lover. C: sailor in charge.

14. **geoduck** ('goo-ee-duhk) *n.*—A: earth tremor. B: wooden footstool. C: large Pacific clam.

15. **plethora** ('pleh-thuh-ruh) *n.*—A: person not of noble rank. B: abundance. C: spiritual journey.

Love & Marriage

"Cocktail Conversation" Answers

1. detritus—[B] debris. People on our block are still picking up *detritus* from Billy's birthday bash.

2. prerogative—[C] special right. If Dad wants to regift his dinosaur tie, that's his *prerogative*.

3. segue—[A] transition. But enough about you; let's *segue* to the topic of snakes.

4. hegemony—[A] domination. Brian has complete *hegemony* over this Monopoly board.

5. dais—[C] raised platform. The crowd threw tomatoes at the *dais* as the mayor began her press conference.

6. kefir—[B] fermented milk. Beth always eats the same breakfast: *kefir* mixed with nuts and fruit.

7. peremptory—[A] allowing no disagreement. "I am not going to bed!" the toddler yelled in a *peremptory* tone.

8. quay—[A] wharf. Passengers waiting on the *quay* prepared to board the ferry.

9. machination—[C] scheme. Despite all his *machinations*, Wile E. Coyote can't catch Road Runner.

10. slough—[C] swamp. The *slough* is home to a variety of species, including salmon, ducks, and otters.

11. spurious—[B] fake. So that UFO sighting in Central Park turned out to be *spurious*?

12. nuptial—[B] relating to marriage. I've attached a string of tin cans to the *nuptial* sedan.

13. coxswain—[C] sailor in charge. It's traditional for a winning crew to toss its *coxswain* overboard.

14. geoduck—[C] large Pacific clam. A *geoduck* can weigh over ten pounds—and live for more than 150 years!

15. plethora—[B] abundance. Joe claims a *plethora* of proof that Bigfoot exists.

DULL AS WHICH WATER?

People often say a boring thing is as *dull as dishwater*. But before the phrase was misspoken, it was actually as *dull as ditchwater*. Most dictionaries now accept either, but here are a few phrases that are just plain wrong: *butt naked* (for *buck naked*), *hare's breath* (for *hair's breadth*), and *road to hoe* (for *row to hoe*).

DATING

You've got to date a lot of Volkswagens before you get to your Porsche.
—**DEBBY ATKINSON**

> Being in therapy is great.
> I spend an hour just talking about myself.
> It's kinda like being the guy on a date.
—**CAROLINE RHEA**

> Falling in love and having a relationship are two different things.
—**KEANU REEVES**

> I don't have a girlfriend. But I do know a woman who'd be mad at me for saying that.
—**MITCH HEDBERG**

🐦 QUOTABLE TWEETS

Women fall in love on the date, and men fall in love after the date.
@PATTISTRANGER

Love & Marriage

THE PERFECT WORDS FOR
ANNIVERSARY TOASTS

Let there be space in your togetherness
and let the winds of the heavens dance between you.
—KAHLIL GIBRAN

"

A wedding anniversary is the celebration of love,
trust, partnership, tolerance, and tenacity.
The order varies for any given year.
—PAUL SWEENEY

"

A long marriage is two people trying to dance
a duet and two solos at the same time.
—ANNE TAYLOR FLEMING

"

A good marriage is like an incredible retirement
fund. You put everything you have into it
during your productive life, and over the years
it turns from silver to gold to platinum.
—WILLARD SCOTT

Love is what you've
been through with somebody.
—JAMES THURBER

A successful marriage requires falling in love many times, always with the same person.
—**MIGNON MCLAUGHLIN**

Love endures only when the lovers love many things together and not merely each other.
—**WALTER LIPPMANN**

"
Getting married is easy. Staying married is more difficult. Staying happily married for a lifetime should rank among the fine arts.
—**ROBERTA FLACK**

"
One advantage of marriage is that when you fall out of love with him or he falls out of love with you, it keeps you together until you fall in again.
—**JUDITH VIORST**

"
You don't marry one person; you marry three: the person you think they are, the person they are, and the person they are going to become as the result of being married to you.
—**RICHARD NEEDHAM**

I have the worst memory ever, so no matter who comes up to me, they're just like, "I can't believe you don't remember me!" I'm like, "Oh Dad, I'm sorry!"

—ELLEN DEGENERES

FAMILY & FRIENDS

It has been said that family is everything: all there is, all your love, all your life. Families, and the friends that become as close as family, shape our worldview and inspire us to greatness.

HEARTH & HOME

The ordinary acts we practice every day
at home are of more importance to the soul
than their simplicity might suggest.
—THOMAS MOORE

"
I still close my eyes and go home. . . .
I can always draw from that.
—DOLLY PARTON

"
One's home is like a delicious piece of pie
you order in a restaurant on a country road one
cozy evening—the best piece of pie you have ever
eaten in your life—and can never find again.
—LEMONY SNICKET

"
Home is the place where, when you have
to go there, they have to take you in.
—ROBERT FROST

"
Home lies in the things you carry with you everywhere
and not the ones that tie you down.
—PICO IYER

FAMILY FIRST

Acting is just a way of making a living; the family is life.
—DENZEL WASHINGTON

"
No matter what you've done for yourself or for humanity, if you can't look back on having given love and attention to your own family, what have you really accomplished?
—LEE IACOCCA

"
I'm not going to have a better day, a more magical moment, than the first time I heard my daughter giggle.
—SEAN PENN

"
What is a family, after all, except memories?— haphazard and precious as the contents of a catchall drawer in the kitchen.
—JOYCE CAROL OATES

"
A family is a unit composed not only of children but of men, women, an occasional animal, and the common cold.
—OGDEN NASH

Family & Friends

I would give everything if I could only keep my family.
—JOHNNY DEPP

"
You don't choose your family. They are God's gift to you, as you are to them.
—DESMOND TUTU

"
Happiness is having a large, caring, close-knit family in another city.
—GEORGE BURNS

"
Call it a clan, call it a network, call it a tribe, call it a family. Whatever you call it, whoever you are, you need one.
—JANE HOWARD

"
A happy family is but an earlier heaven.
—SIR JOHN BOWRING

QUOTABLE TWEETS

Your #family is depending on you. No better reason to bring all your game all the time.
@GRANTCARDONE

CHILDREN

Having children is like living in a frat house—nobody sleeps, everything's broken, and there's a lot of throwing up.
—RAY ROMANO

"
I would be most content if my children grew up to be the kind of people who think decorating consists mostly of building enough bookshelves.
—ANNA QUINDLEN

"
Work is the least important thing and family is the most important.
—JERRY SEINFELD

"
Ask your child what he wants for dinner only if he's buying.
—FRAN LEBOWITZ

"
All of us have to recognize that we owe our children more than we have been giving them.
—HILLARY CLINTON

🐦 QUOTABLE TWEETS

@ItsMyTyme09 biggest mistake in helping underserved kids is NOT RAISING the BAR high enough. Children will believe if you believe in them.

@OPRAH

The best way to keep children at home
is to make the home atmosphere pleasant—
and let the air out of the tires.

—DOROTHY PARKER

❝

Having five children in six years is the best
training in the world for Speaker of the House.

—NANCY PELOSI

❝

Just be good and kind to your children.
Not only are they the future of the world, they're
the ones who can sign you into the home.

—DENNIS MILLER

Kids are life's only guaranteed bona fide upside surprise.

—JACK NICHOLSON

PARENTS

You can hit my father over the head with a chair and he won't wake up, but my mother, all you have to do to my mother is cough somewhere in Siberia and she'll hear you.
—J. D. SALINGER

"

A new survey found that 12 percent of parents punish their kids by banning social-networking sites. The other 88 percent punish their kids by joining social-networking sites.
—JIMMY FALLON

"

Imagine if you succeeded in making the world perfect for your children what a shock the rest of life would be for them.
—JOYCE MAYNARD

"

A rich person should leave his kids enough to do something, but not enough to do nothing.
—WARREN BUFFETT

"

My parents treated me like I had a brain—which, in turn, caused me to have one.
—DIANE LANE

THE PERFECT WORDS FOR
NEW-BABY CARDS

I think, at a child's birth, if a mother could ask
a fairy godmother to endow it with
the most useful gift, that gift should be curiosity.
—ELEANOR ROOSEVELT

"

If you can give your child only one gift,
let it be enthusiasm.
—BRUCE BARTON

"

Making the decision to have a child is momentous.
It is to decide forever to have your heart go
walking around outside your body.
—ELIZABETH STONE

"

Having a baby is like falling in love again,
both with your husband and your child.
—TINA BROWN

"

Babies are bits of stardust, blown from
the hand of God. Lucky the woman who knows
the pangs of birth, for she has held a star.
—LARRY BARRATTO

GOOD GENES

You can't pick your family, but you can at least talk about them. Here are a few familial, if sometimes unfamiliar, words to bring to the next reunion. For quiz answers, turn the page.

1. **filial** ('fill-ee-ul) *adj.*—A: related by marriage. B: of sons and daughters. C: of brothers.

2. **kith** ('kith) *n.*—A: friends. B: in-laws. C: homestead.

3. **agnate** ('ag-nate) *adj.*—A: related on the father's side. B: descended from royalty. C: of a child with unmarried parents.

4. **sororal** (suh-'roar-ul) *adj.*—A: grandmotherly. B: motherly. C: sisterly.

5. **cognomen** (cog-'no-mun) *n.*—A: clan emblem. B: name. C: last of the male line.

6. **progeny** ('proj-uh-nee) *n.*—A: ancestors. B: descendants. C: extended family.

7. **cousin once removed** *n.*—A: your cousin's cousin. B: your cousin's child. C: your cousin's ex-spouse.

8. **nepotism** ('nep-uh-tiz-um) *n.*—A: marriage of first cousins. B: ninth generation. C: favoritism toward a relative.

9. **congenital** (kun-'jen-uh-tul) *adj.*—A: acquired in utero. B: generation-skipping. C: of a multiple birth.

10. **ménage** (may-'nazh) *n.*—A: marriage vow. B: household. C: golden years.

11. **misopedia** (miss-oh-'pee-dee-uh or my-so-) *n.*—A: hatred of children. B: middle age. C: family history.

12. **pedigree** ('ped-uh-gree) *n.*—A: lineage. B: inheritance. C: birth announcement.

13. **avuncular** (uh-'vunk-yuh-lur) *adj.*—A: without cousins. B: adopted. C: like an uncle.

14. **polyandry** ('pah-lee-an-dree) *n.*—A: having two or more husbands. B: having two or more children. C: having male and female traits.

15. **bairn** ('bayrn) *n.*—A: gap in genealogical record. B: poor relation. C: child.

Family & Friends

"Good Genes" Answers

1. filial—[B] of sons and daughters. Francis still lives with his mother, partly out of *filial* devotion, partly out of an aversion to doing laundry.

2. kith—[A] friends. With all her *kith* and kin assembled, the bride got cold feet and fled the church.

3. agnate—[A] related on the father's side. My last name has no vowels because immigration officials misheard my *agnate* grandfather.

4. sororal—[C] sisterly. After a day of looking for Polly Pocket's shoes and refereeing *sororal* squabbles, the girls' mother collapsed onto the couch.

5. cognomen—[B] name. Eugene added the *cognomen* "the Great" to his business cards and letterhead.

6. progeny—[B] descendants. With seven siblings and all their spouses and *progeny*, we have a lot of birthdays to remember.

7. cousin once removed—[B] your cousin's child. The university allows only two commencement guests for each graduate: What am I going to tell all my great-aunts and *cousins once removed*?

8. nepotism—[C] favoritism toward a relative. When the umpire—who happened to be the base runner's dad—yelled, "Safe!" the other team cried *nepotism*.

9. congenital—[A] acquired in utero. Nathaniel told the gym teacher that he has a *congenital* heart defect just so he won't have to play dodgeball.

10. ménage—[B] household. It's not a mansion, but it's just right for our little *ménage*.

11. misopedia—[A] hatred of children. W.C. Fields, who turned *misopedia* into comedic masterpieces, once said, "I love children. Yes, if properly cooked."

12. pedigree—[A] lineage. The freshman senator has a distinguished political *pedigree*, since both her father and grandfather held public office.

13. avuncular—[C] like an uncle. The pilot's *avuncular* voice was reassuring to the nervous flier.

14. polyandry—[A] having two or more husbands. *Polyandry* is rare in human societies, mostly because women object to picking up that many socks off the floor.

15. bairn—[C] child. Duncan has been playing the bagpipes since he was a wee *bairn*.

USE YOUR WORDS

STANDING TALL

The confidence you project hugely affects how others perceive you. Test yourself on these words about proof, opinion, and even doubt. Unsure of your answers? Turn the page to be certain you are right.

1. **waffle** ('wah-ful) *v.*—A: flip-flop in opinion. B: press a point firmly. C: invent a wild story.

2. **conjecture** (con-'jek-cher) *n.*—A: group agreement. B: guess. C: optimistic outlook.

3. **equivocal** (ih-'kwi-veh-kel) *adj.*—A: open to interpretations. B: firmly settled. C: in the form of a question.

4. **corroborate** (kuh-'rah-beh-rayt) *v.*—A: support with evidence. B: steal another's ideas. C: pretend to be sure.

5. **allegation** (a-lih-'gay-shun) *n.*—A: proof. B: suspicion. C: claim.

6. **precarious** (pri-'kar-ee-us) *adj.*—A: false. B: depending on uncertain circumstances. C: having foreknowledge.

7. **expound** (ik-'spownd) *v.*—A: take back. B: carefully state. C: contradict.

8. **intuition** (in-too-'ih-shun) *n.*—A: instinctive knowledge. B: formal teaching. C: logical paradox.

9. **indubitably** (in-'doo-beh-teh-blee) *adv.*—A: certainly. B: doubtfully. C: deceitfully.

10. **bona fide** ('boh-neh fiyd) *adj.*—A: with high hopes. B: genuine. C: in contention.

11. **nebulous** ('neh-byeh-les) *adj.*—A: vague. B: all-knowing. C: making a breakthrough.

12. **surmise** (sir-'miyz) *v.*—A: sum up. B: suppose on limited evidence. C: apply logic.

13. **spurious** ('spyur-ee-us) *adj.*—A: sharply worded. B: false or deceitful. C: impossible to refute.

14. **tentative** ('ten-teh-tiv) *adj.*—A: forceful. B: all-inclusive. C: hesitant.

15. **apocryphal** (uh-'pah-kreh-ful) *adj.*—A: mathematical or scientific. B: not fully developed, as an idea. C: of doubtful authenticity.

Family & Friends

"Standing Tall" Answers

1. waffle—[A] flip-flop in opinion. Quit *waffling*: Goobers or Raisinets?!

2. conjecture—[B] guess. Whether this ladder can reach that roof's gutter is anyone's *conjecture*.

3. equivocal—[A] open to interpretations. The umpire gestured, but his meaning was *equivocal*.

4. corroborate—[A] support with evidence. "I can *corroborate* Amy's excuse," her mom said. "Here's what's left of her homework after Rufus got to it."

5. allegation—[C] claim. Please don't believe the wild *allegations* that Adrienne is making about me.

6. precarious—[B] depending on uncertain circumstances. Everyone's job is *precarious* in this poor economy.

7. expound—[B] carefully state. On the first day of school, Alex's teacher *expounded* on the basics of physics to a befuddled classroom.

8. intuition—[A] instinctive knowledge. A good private eye trusts her *intuition* on a case.

9. indubitably—[A] certainly. "These footprints, Watson," said Sherlock Holmes, "*indubitably* belong to the butler!"

10. bona fide—[B] genuine. Yet again, our AA baseball team is starting the season without a *bona fide* shortstop.

11. nebulous—[A] vague. The point of practicing seemed *nebulous* to Jill until the recital started.

12. surmise—[B] suppose on limited evidence. From your white mustache, I *surmise* that you've been drinking my milk.

13. spurious—[B] false or deceitful. Tom Sawyer played hooky using a *spurious* note from the doctor.

14. tentative—[C] hesitant. An infant's first steps are always *tentative* and awkward.

15. apocryphal—[C] of doubtful authenticity. Jake gave an *apocryphal* story about having to tough it out at summer camp.

> **DO YOU IMPLY OR INFER?**
> When you're the speaker and you suggest something indirectly, you *imply* it. When you're the listener and you draw a conclusion from what someone else says, you *infer* it. Example: If you say, "Everyone needs a good diet," a friend might *infer* that you mean her. She might say, "What are you *implying*?"

DECORATING TIPS

With spring in full swing and summer sneaking up, it's time to shake off the decor doldrums and set your inner home stylist free. Before you start testing paint chips and fabric swatches, test yourself with this month's quiz, full of words you might encounter while sprucing up. Answers on next page.

1. **cabriole** *n.*—A: china cabinet. B: curved furniture leg. C: tea cart.

2. **trug** *n.*—A: shallow basket. B: triangular jug. C: padded footrest.

3. **bolster** *n.*—A: comforter cover. B: bed skirt. C: long pillow.

4. **pilaster** *n.*—A: column jutting from a wall. B: ornate molding on ceiling. C: recessed cubbyhole.

5. **torchère** *n.*—A: propane fireplace. B: stand for a candlestick. C: wall-mounted light.

6. **grommet** *n.*—A: sliding drawer. B: eyelet to protect an opening. C: anchor chain for hanging lamps.

7. **pounce** *v.*—A: transfer a stencil design. B: add light. C: combine fabrics.

8. **patina** *n.*—A: weathered look of copper or bronze. B: two-toned floors. C: high-gloss surface.

9. **finial** *n.*—A: ornament at the tip of a lamp or a curtain rod. B: pull string. C: metal drawer handle.

10. **organdy** *n.*—A: polka-dot pattern. B: insulating lining. C: transparent muslin.

11. **newel** *n.*—A: sunny nook. B: central post of a circular staircase. C: arched doorway between adjoining rooms.

12. **bergère** *n.*—A: upholstered chair with exposed wood. B: one-armed couch. C: semicircular occasional table.

13. **ceruse** *n.*—A: eye-catching color. B: table runner. C: pigment composed of white lead.

14. **Bauhaus** *adj.*—of or relating to … A: rococo style. B: a German school of functional design. C: an eco-friendly house.

15. **incise** *v.*—A: prune. B: slice. C: engrave.

Family & Friends

"Decorating Tips" Answers

1. cabriole—[B] curved furniture leg. "That *cabriole* shape mimics Rufus's hind leg!" the collector's son boasted.

2. trug—[A] shallow basket. Barbara's handmade *trugs* are ideal for carrying flowers.

3. bolster—[C] long pillow. A pair of comfy bolsters soften the ends of a daybed.

4. pilaster—[A] column jutting from a wall. Two enormous *pilasters* flanked the entrance, dwarfing the hand-carved door.

5. torchère—[B] stand for a candlestick. "Would you mind bringing the *torchère* over here?" Dean's grandmother intoned from the dark corner.

6. grommet—[B] eyelet to protect an opening. The *grommets* jangled as I yanked open the drapes and tried to duck out.

7. pounce—[A] transfer a stencil design. Diane tried to duplicate her drawing by *pouncing* it, but the effect was lost.

8. patina—[A] weathered look of copper or bronze. "How long before the roof dulls to that fantastic *patina*?" Janice asked.

9. finial—[A] ornament at the tip of a lamp or a curtain rod. Tacky *finials* cluttered the stark window treatments.

10. organdy—[C] transparent muslin. To soften your bedroom, try *organdy* curtains—they'll filter the light.

11. newel—[B] central post of a circular staircase. The handrail is sound, but the *newel* needs replacing.

12. bergère—[A] upholstered chair with exposed wood. Invented in the 1700s, the *bergère* was designed for lounging.

13. ceruse—[C] pigment composed of white lead. Applying a *ceruse* finish may help conceal the table's flaws.

14. Bauhaus—[B] of or relating to a German school of functional design. The *Bauhaus* influence was clear in her early drawings.

15. incise—[C] engrave. A carpenter may *incise* his name into his furniture.

USE YOUR WORDS

THE MEANING OF NAMES

The meanings of some given names (Rose, Faith, Dawn) are as plain as the nose on your face. And then there are names such as Cameron, which actually comes from the Gaelic for "crooked nose." We've compiled some of the more interesting names and their derivations here. Can you use your word smarts to guess the meanings? Turn the page for answers and etymology.

1. **Sophia**—A: summer rainstorm. B: great wisdom. C: tremendous wealth.

2. **Felix**—A: faithful. B: happy. C: catlike.

3. **Dolores**—A: lady of sorrows. B: maiden of mirth. C: weaver of tales.

4. **Natalie**—A: birthday. B: first snowstorm of the year. C: princess.

5. **Quincy**—A: fruit tree. B: the fifth in a series. C: belonging to an ancient family.

6. **Melanie**—A: circular path. B: melodious. C: dark.

7. **Clement**—A: warrior-like. B: studious. C: mild.

8. **Philip**—A: as hard as a rock. B: lover of horses. C: son of Time.

9. **Sylvia**—A: obsessed with beautiful things. B: inhabiting the woods. C: having clean lines.

10. **Benedict**—A: ruled by earthly passions. B: emancipated. C: blessed.

11. **Phyllis**—A: butterfly. B: waterfall. C: foliage.

12. **Ursula**—A: little bear. B: constellation. C: giant octopus.

13. **Vincent**—A: winemaker. B: conqueror. C: wandering minstrel.

14. **Vera**—A: evening. B: true. C: raven.

15. **Chandler**—A: maker of candles. B: shooter of bows. C: rider of wild hogs.

Family & Friends

"The Meaning of Names" Answers

1. Sophia—[B] great wisdom. *Sophia* is majoring in philosophy. (Greek *sophos* = wise)

2. Felix—[B] happy. Being in love has given *Felix* a new felicity in life. (Latin *felix* = happy)

3. Dolores—[A] lady of sorrows. Why does *Dolores* always sing such dolorous dirges? (Latin *dolor* = pain)

4. Natalie—[A] birthday. Each December, *Natalie* plays an angel in her church's nativity play. (Latin *natalis* = of birth)

5. Quincy—[B] the fifth in a series. *Quincy* was the only boy among the quintuplets. (Latin *quintus* = fifth)

6. Melanie—[C] dark. Of late, *Melanie* has been in a melancholy funk. (Greek *melaina* = black, dark)

7. Clement—[C] mild. *Clement's* ballgame was postponed because of inclement weather. (Latin *clementem* = mild, gentle)

8. Philip—[B] lover of horses. On Sundays you'll find *Philip* down at the hippodrome. (Greek *philos* = friend; Greek *hippos* = horse)

9. Sylvia—[B] inhabiting the woods. *Sylvia* uprooted herself and moved to Pennsylvania. (Latin *silva* = forest)

10. Benedict—[C] blessed. Pope *Benedict* issued a benevolent edict to his followers. (Latin *bene* = well; *dictio* = speaking)

11. Phyllis—[C] foliage. If you need a lesson on chlorophyll, just talk to *Phyllis*. (Greek *phyllon* = leaf)

12. Ursula—[A] little bear. *Ursula* is telling the story of Goldilocks and her three ursine hosts. (Latin *ursa* = she-bear)

13. Vincent—[B] conqueror. *Vincent* won by a convincing margin. (Latin *vincere* = to overcome)

14. Vera—[B] true. The jury doubted the veracity of *Vera's* claim. (Latin *verus* = true)

15. Chandler—[A] maker of candles. *Chandler* keeps a candelabra on his grand piano. (Latin *candela* = candle)

ARCANE NAME GAME

Cameron isn't the only name derived from an odd physical trait: Calvin means "bald" (from the Latin *calvus*). Other monikers with curious meanings: Portia ("pig," from the Latin *porcus*) and Emily ("rival," from the Latin *aemulus*). But our favorite curious source belongs to Alfred, who was apparently "given advice by elves" (Old English *ælf* = elf, *ræd* = counsel).

SPORTING

Test your gaming vocabulary with this playful quiz. There's no harm, no foul, and no penalty for flipping to the next page for the answers.

1. aficionado (uh-fish-ee-uh-'nah-doh) *n.*—A: referee. B: expert. C: buff.

2. wheelhouse ('weel-howse) *n.*—A: batter's ideal swinging range. B: overhand pitch. C: cycling stadium.

3. laugher ('laff-er) *n.*—A: close game. B: lopsided win. C: joker in a deck.

4. gambit ('gam-bit) *n.*—A: opening maneuver. B: single inning. C: intense rival.

5. arbitrate ('ahr-bi-trayt) *v.*—A: protest a call. B: serve as umpire. C: settle for a tie.

6. chaff ('chaf) *v.*—A: tease. B: discard. C: advance a pawn.

7. thimblerig ('thim-buhl-rig) *n.*—A: party platter. B: con game. C: handspring.

8. see ('see) *v.*—A: match, as a poker bet. B: leapfrog over. C: strike and open a piñata.

9. ludic ('loo-dik) *adj.*—A: following the rules. B: playful. C: easy to learn.

10. baize ('bayz) *n.*—A: pool-table fabric. B: long-range pass. C: sculling boat.

11. maffick ('maf-ik) *v.*—A: celebrate joyfully. B: enter a raffle. C: play solitaire.

12. cat's game ('kats 'gaym) *n.*—A: tie in tic-tac-toe. B: Parcheesi. C: yo-yo trick.

13. token ('toh-kin) *n.*—A: loss of a turn. B: signal to a partner. C: game piece.

14. ruff ('ruhf) *v.*—A: sail on a new tack. B: play a trump card. C: drive a ball off the fairway.

15. hat trick ('hat 'trik) *n.*—A: fancy outfield catch. B: three hockey goals by one player. C: "grand slam" of tennis.

Family & Friends

"Sporting" Answers

1. aficionado—[C] buff. A nascent fishing *aficionado*, Jonathan insists on using spinning lures instead of worms as bait.

2. wheelhouse—[A] batter's ideal swinging range. To his chagrin, the pitcher threw into the slugger's *wheelhouse* and cost his team a run.

3. laugher—[B] lopsided win. Even though the game was a *laugher*, the victors graciously greeted the losing team.

4. gambit—[A] opening maneuver. That sneaky *gambit* might earn you a four-move checkmate, but it will cost you willing opponents.

5. arbitrate—[B] serve as umpire. When an argument broke out over the team's last cupcake, a coach stepped in to *arbitrate*.

6. chaff—[A] tease. Chloe *chaffs* Alex each time she beats him at badminton.

7. thimblerig—[B] con game. Tom thought he could outsmart the *thimblerig*, but he lost his temper and $**5**.

8. see—[A] match, as a poker bet. I'll *see* your pie bet with some ice cream.

9. ludic—[B] playful. Fans of the Harlem Globetrotters enjoy their *ludic* antics on the basketball court.

10. baize—[A] pool-table fabric. Eddie is such a billiards fanatic that his man cave is carpeted in *baize*.

11. maffick—[A] celebrate joyfully. The team *mafficked* its victory by rushing the field.

12. cat's game—[A] tie in tic-tac-toe. It took a hasty, careless move to break the longstanding series of *cat's games*.

13. token—[C] game piece. My family plays Parcheesi with buttons because the official *tokens* were lost long ago.

14. ruff—[B] play a trump card. I smiled at her taunts, knowing I would *ruff* on the next hand.

15. hat trick—[B] three hockey goals by one player. After Gretzky's *hat trick*, the ice was littered with fans' caps.

USE YOUR WORDS

SUMMER FAMILY FUN

Before you splash in a pool, bask on a beach, or putter in your garden, master this list of summertime words. You won't find a lemonade stand on the next page, but you will find answers.

1. **torrid** ('tohr-ihd) *adj.*—
A: blooming. B: scorching.
C: perspiring.

2. **deluge** ('dehl-yooj) *n.*—
A: heavy downpour. B: squirt gun.
C: greenhouse.

3. **verdant** ('vurh-dint) *adj.*—
A: sandy. B: green. C: buggy.

4. **tack** (tak) *v.*—A: hook a fish.
B: upend a raft. C: change direction when sailing.

5. **pyrotechnics** (py-ruh-'tek-niks) *n.*—A: sunspots. B: fireworks.
C: heat waves.

6. **chigger** ('chih-ger) *n.*—
A: fastball. B: biting mite.
C: beer garden.

7. **estivate** ('eh-stuh-vayt) *v.*—
A: lounge outdoors. B: nurture until grown. C: spend the summer.

8. **pattypan** ('pa-tee-pan) *n.*—
A: playground. B: heat rash.
C: summer squash.

9. **alfresco** (al-'freh-skoh) *adv.*—A: with cheese sauce.
B: outdoors. C: in a fresh state.

10. **hibachi** (hih-'bah-chee) *n.*—
A: raincoat. B: charcoal griller.
C: Asian eggplant.

11. **pergola** ('per-guh-luh) *n.*—
A: umbrella. B: trellis. C: paid vacation.

12. **glamping** ('glam-ping) *n.*—
A: cave exploring. B: glamorous camping. C: sunbathing.

13. **plage** (plahzh) *n.*—
A: lawn tennis. B: lightning strike.
C: beach at a resort.

14. **espadrilles** ('eh-spuh-drillz) *n.*—A: rope-soled shoes. B: hedge pruners. C: pair of matching beach chairs.

15. **horticulture** ('hohr-tih-kul-cher) *n.*—A: seaside community.
B: pond wildlife. C: science of growing plants.

Family & Friends

"Summer Family Fun" Answers

1. torrid—[B] scorching. This has been the most *torrid* August I can remember!

2. deluge—[A] heavy downpour. Tatiana threw on her black slicker and headed out into the *deluge*.

3. verdant—[B] green. Vermont is famous for its *verdant* mountain ranges.

4. tack—[C] change direction when sailing. The catamaran had to *tack* quickly to avoid the floating debris.

5. pyrotechnics—[B] fireworks. Every Fourth of July, my neighbors set off *pyrotechnics* in their yard until three a.m.

6. chigger—[B] biting mite. Miranda doused herself in bug spray before her hike to ward off *chiggers*.

7. estivate—[C] spend the summer. After hockey season ends, the Myers family *estivates* by the ocean.

8. pattypan—[C] summer squash. Has that pesky rabbit been nibbling my *pattypan* again?

9. alfresco—[B] outdoors. "Whose idea was it to dine *alfresco*?" Ira grumbled, flicking an ant off his sandwich.

10. hibachi—[B] charcoal griller. Come on over—I'm going to throw some burgers on the *hibachi* tonight.

11. pergola—[B] trellis. Legend has it that couples who kiss under this *pergola* will live happily ever after.

12. glamping—[B] glamorous camping. Hayden goes *glamping* with every amenity, then tells everyone he "roughed it."

13. plage—[C] beach at a resort. I never hit the *plage* until I'm completely slathered in sunscreen.

14. espadrilles—[A] rope-soled shoes. Melissa used to live in flip-flops every summer, but now she prefers *espadrilles*.

15. horticulture—[C] science of growing plants. The coveted *Horticulture* Award is a statuette of a green thumb.

THE IDIOMS OF SUMMER

When it comes to coining notable phrases, baseball is *in a league of its own*. If you think that claim is *off base*, we'll list the evidence *right off the bat*. Consider *in the ballpark*, *throw a curveball*, *pinch-hit*, and every shopper's favorite: *rain check*. Still think we haven't *covered our bases*? Then *step up to the plate* and name another sport that has hit more syntactical home runs.

GAME NIGHT

Puzzles and games, mind-benders and puns—they're all unleashed in this quiz. For answers and a clerihew (cleriwhat???), turn the page.

1. pangram *n.*—A: jumble of a word's letters. B: phrase using all 26 letters of the alphabet. C: person's surname used as a common noun.

2. spoonerism *n.*—A: saying "wabbit" for "rabbit." B: saying "right lane" for "light rain." C: saying "I scream" for "ice cream."

3. palindrome *n.*—A: writing that omits the letter e. B: earliest Latin acrostic puzzle. C: text that reads the same in reverse.

4. portmanteau word *n.*—A: French word playfully Anglicized. B: sailors' slang. C: word blend of two other words.

5. homophones *n.*—A: words with the same vowels. B: words with the same etymological root. C: words with the same pronunciation.

6. retronym *n.*—A: form of mirror writing. B: modified name for an old item. C: guessing game invented by bored astronauts.

7. double entendre *n.*—A: word with two of each letter. B: word identical in two different languages. C: term with an extra, often racy meaning.

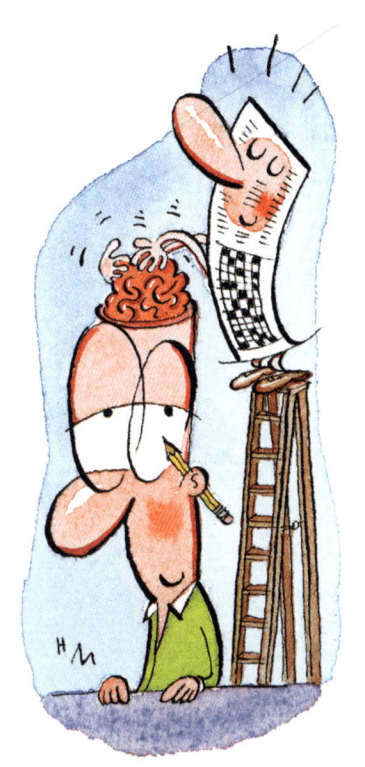

8. malapropism *n.*—A: comic misuse of language. B: misspelled word. C: polite word used to replace a rude one.

9. neologism *n.*—A: made-up or coined word. B: word that has changed its meaning over time. C: long word with a short word tucked inside.

10. cruciverbalist *n.*—A: lover of crossword puzzles. B: speaker of many different languages. C: punster.

11. paronomasia *n.*—A: tongue twister. B: pantomime skit. C: pun.

Family & Friends **127**

"Game Night" Answers

1. pangram—[B] phrase using all 26 letters of the alphabet. Watch *Jeopardy!*, Alex Trebek's fun TV quiz game.

2. spoonerism—[B] saying "right lane" for "light rain." I'm obsessed with lopping sweaters—er, swapping letters.

3. palindrome—[C] text that reads the same in reverse. Straw? No, too stupid a fad—I put soot on warts.

4. portmanteau word—[C] word blend of two other words. I had to chortle (chuckle + snort) while having brunch (breakfast + lunch) in the smog (smoke + fog).

5. homophones—[C] words with the same pronunciation. You've heard of my herd? The flocks eat phlox, but the ewes use yews.

6. retronym—[B] modified name for an old item. Sid wears an analog watch and plays acoustic guitar.

7. double entendre—[C] term with an extra, often racy meaning. In a nudist camp, men and women freely air their differences.

8. malapropism—[A] comic misuse of language (named after Richard Sheridan's character Mrs. Malaprop in *The Rivals*). What are you incinerating, that I'll fade into Bolivian?

9. neologism—[A] made-up or coined word. She just had a big brainstorm—she calls it a psyclone.

10. cruciverbalist—[A] lover of crossword puzzles. I shun *cruciverbalists*. They're either cross or down.

11. paronomasia—[C] pun. Regarding beetles, I always choose the lesser of two weevils.

HOT WORD

A *Clerihew* is a four-line poem that pokes fun at the famous. Invented by British writer Edmund Clerihew Bentley (1875–1956), these mini-verses have three rules: They rhyme aabb, they're about a celebrity named in the first line, and as for the meter? There are no rules! Here's an example:

Actor Harrison Ford / Was feeling extraordinarily bored. / So he grabbed his hat and picked up his bones / And starred in yet another *Indiana Jones*.

FRIENDS

A true friend is one who overlooks your failures and tolerates your successes.
—**DOUG LARSON**

A real friend is one who walks in when the rest of the world walks out.
—**WALTER WINCHELL**

To remember friendship is to recall those conversations that it seemed a sin to break off: the ones that made the sacrifice of the following day a trivial one.
—**CHRISTOPHER HITCHENS**

You can always tell a real friend: when you make a fool of yourself, he doesn't feel you've done a permanent job.
—**LAURENCE PETER**

You don't have to have anything in common with people you've known since you were five. With old friends, you've got your whole life in common.
—**LYLE LOVETT**

THE PERFECT WORDS FOR
FRIENDSHIP

The bird a nest, the spider a web, man friendship.
—**WILLIAM BLAKE**

Strangers are friends that you have yet to meet.
—**ROBERTA LIEBERMAN**

Be slow in choosing a friend, slower in changing.
—**BENJAMIN FRANKLIN**

The most called-upon prerequisite of a friend is an accessible ear.
—**MAYA ANGELOU**

Some of the most rewarding and beautiful moments of a friendship happen in the unforeseen open spaces between planned activities. It is important that you allow these spaces to exist.
—**CHRISTINE LEEFELDT AND ERNEST CALLENBACH**

A friend is someone who can see through you and still enjoys the show.
—***FARMERS' ALMANAC***

Friends are those rare people who ask how we are and then wait to hear the answer.
—ED CUNNINGHAM

"

We love those who know the worst of us and don't turn their faces away.
—WALKER PERCY

"

No man can be called friendless when he has God and the companionship of good books.
—ELIZABETH BARRETT BROWNING

"

I value the friend who for me finds time on his calendar, but I cherish the friend who for me does not consult his calendar.
—ROBERT BRAULT

"

Don't make friends who are comfortable to be with. Make friends who will force you to lever yourself up.
—THOMAS J. WATSON SR.

> We cherish our friends not for the ability to amuse us, but for our ability to amuse them.
> —THOMAS J. WATSON SR.

Family & Friends

There's only now.
—BILL MURRAY

LIFE IS GOOD

Hard work pays off in the moments
that are filled with beauty—
the ones that allow us to sit back,
take a deep breath, and elate in that
which we truly enjoy.

KICKING BACK

There's never enough time to do all the nothing you want.
—BILL WATTERSON

"

For fast-acting relief, try slowing down.
—LILY TOMLIN

"

Sometimes the most important thing in a whole day is the rest we take between two deep breaths.
—ETTY HILLESUM

"

Doing nothing is very hard to do—you never know when you're finished.
—LESLIE NIELSEN

"

Bed is like the womb, only drier and with better TV reception.
—LINDA RICHMAN

QUOTABLE TWEETS

Life is supposed to be fun!
When you're having fun,
you feel great and you receive great things!
@BYRNERHONDA

How many inner resources one needs to tolerate
a life of leisure without fatigue.
—**NATALIE CLIFFORD BARNEY**

"

Time you enjoy wasting was not wasted.
—**JOHN LENNON**

A GOOD MEAL

There is no love sincerer than the love of food.
—**GEORGE BERNARD SHAW**

"

The only time to eat diet food is while
you're waiting for the steak to cook.
—**JULIA CHILD**

"

The trouble with eating Italian food is that
five or six days later, you're hungry again.
—**GEORGE MILLER**

"

Large, naked, raw carrots are acceptable
as food only to those who live
in hutches eagerly awaiting Easter.
—**FRAN LEBOWITZ**

A good slice of pizza can be as good
as a $200 meal in a restaurant.
—BENICIO DEL TORO

"

Life is too short to drink the house wine.
—HELEN THOMAS

"

Just try to be angry with someone
who fed you something delicious.
—CARMEN COOK

"

Stress cannot exist in the presence of a pie.
—DAVID MAMET

TRAVEL & VACATIONS

Not all those who wander are lost.
—J. R. R. TOLKIEN

"

Travel is fatal to prejudice, bigotry,
and narrow-mindedness.
—MARK TWAIN

"

I'm still ready to go to the moon, if they'll take me.
—WALTER CRONKITE

🐦 QUOTABLE TWEETS

You knows what's amazing about life. Enjoying what you see.
@DENNISRODMAN

Airplane travel is nature's way of making you look like your passport photo.
—AL GORE

❝

Most of American life is driving somewhere and then driving back wondering why the hell you went.
—JOHN UPDIKE

❝

If you don't know where you're going, any road will take you there.
—LEWIS CARROLL

❝

Travel is glamorous only in retrospect.
—PAUL THEROUX

❝

Camping: nature's way of promoting the motel industry.
—DAVE BARRY

Life Is Good

HOLIDAY TIME

No matter how carefully you stored the lights last year, they will be snarled again this Christmas.
—ROBERT KIRBY

"
Christmas: It's the only religious holiday that's also a federal holiday. That way, Christians can go to their services, and everyone else can sit at home and reflect on the true meaning of the separation of church and state.
—SAMANTHA BEE

"
Christmas is a time when everybody wants his past forgotten and his present remembered.
—PHYLLIS DILLER

"
Oh, joy, Christmas Eve. By this time tomorrow, millions of Americans, knee-deep in tinsel and wrapping paper, will utter those heartfelt words: "Is this all I got?"
—KELSEY GRAMMER

I get really grinchy right up until Christmas morning.
—DAN AYKROYD

Oh, volunteer work! That's what I like about the holiday season. That's the true spirit of Christmas. People being helped by people other than me.
—JERRY SEINFELD

We're having something a little different this year for Thanksgiving. Instead of a turkey, we're having a swan. You get more stuffing.
—GEORGE CARLIN

Thanksgiving is the one occasion each year when gluttony becomes a patriotic duty.
—MICHAEL DRESSER

Airport screeners are now scanning holiday fruitcakes. Not even the scanners can tell what those little red things are.
—DAVID LETTERMAN

THE PERFECT WORDS FOR
HOLIDAY CARDS

May peace be your gift at Christmas
and your blessing through the year.
—UNKNOWN

>

The darkness of the whole world cannot
swallow the glowing of a candle.
—ROBERT ALTINGER

>

At Christmas play and make good cheer,
for Christmas comes but once a year.
—THOMAS TUSSER

>

Christmas gift suggestions: to your enemy,
forgiveness. To an opponent, tolerance. To a friend,
your heart. To a customer, service. To all, charity.
To every child, a good example. To yourself, respect.
—OREN ARNOLD

>

Christmas is not a time or a season but a state of
mind. To cherish peace and good will, to be plenteous
in mercy, is to have the real spirit of Christmas.
—CALVIN COOLIDGE

CAROLING, CAROLING

Carolers at the doorstep, ice scrapers working overtime, the cat swatting ornaments off the tree—the season is rife with signature sounds. In keeping with the spirit, we offer up this "aural" exam. Answers on next page.

1. carillon ('ker-eh-'lahn) *n.*—A: Christmas choir. B: trombone blast. C: set of bells.

2. dulcet ('dul-set) *adj.*—A: monotonous. B: staccato. C: pleasing to the ear.

3. skirl ('skeruhl) *v.*—A: play a bagpipe. B: change musical keys. C: make a whoosh.

4. stertor ('ster-ter) *n.*—A: snoring. B: howling. C: whimpering.

5. bombinate ('bahm-beh-nayt) *v.*—A: pop like a balloon. B: bang on a gong. C: buzz.

6. euphony ('yew-feh-nee) *n.*—A: perfect pitch. B: pleasing or sweet sound. C: solo singing.

7. cacophony (ka-'kawf-oh-nee) *n.*—A: complete silence. B: audio interruption. C: harsh sound.

8. sternutation ('ster-nyu-'tay-shun) *n.*—A: scolding tone. B: sneeze. C: sound of a backfire.

9. paradiddle ('pa-reh-'di-del) *n.*—A: lilting duet. B: wrong note on a horn. C: rapid drumbeat.

10. canorous (kuh-'nor-us) *adj.*—A: honking like geese. B: echoing. C: melodious.

11. purl ('perl) *n.*—A: rippling sound. B: hum of contentment. C: heavy accent.

12. sough ('sow) *v.*—A: moan or sigh. B: squeak annoyingly. C: chug like an engine.

13. cachinnate ('ka-keh-nayt) *v.*—A: laugh loudly. B: eavesdrop. C: sizzle.

14. clarion ('klehr-ee-uhn) *adj.*—A: fast, as a song. B: repeated, as a verse. C: brilliantly clear.

15. strident ('striy-dnt) *adj.*—A: full of static. B: discordant. C: hard to discern.

Life Is Good

"Caroling, Caroling" Answers

1. carillon—[C] set of bells. By far the highlight of the Christmas concert was the debut of the hall's restored *carillon*.

2. dulcet—[C] pleasing to the ear. Bev's tones are so *dulcet*, Jerry sat mesmerized for the entire afternoon.

3. skirl—[A] play a bagpipe. We awoke the next morning to Jimmy *skirling* away on his new gift.

4. stertor—[A] snoring. When Uncle Hal naps, the *stertor* could blow shingles off the roof.

5. bombinate—[C] buzz. The lackluster rehearsal *bombinated* in his head for the rest of the week.

6. euphony—[B] pleasing or sweet sound. There is no *euphony* like the words "Kids, time for bed!"

7. cacophony—[C] harsh sound. Nor is there any *cacophony* like the 4 a.m. pronouncement "Dad, Santa came! Santa came!"

8. sternutation—[B] sneeze. With one impressive *sternutation*, Maggie sent the startled pup ducking for cover.

9. paradiddle—[C] rapid drumbeat. "I truly appreciate Zack's devotion and practice habits, but that *paradiddle* is going to be the end of me," cried his mom.

10. canorous—[C] melodious. To Dale, the tearing of wrapping paper is the most *canorous* sound imaginable.

11. purl—[A] rippling sound. Hampered by writer's block, Alison finally found inspiration in the simple *purl* of the mountain brook.

12. sough—[A] moan or sigh. *Soughing* as loud as she could, Kate dropped off yet another plate of hors d'oeuvres for her husband's "guests."

13. cachinnate—[A] laugh loudly. I say, didn't you think Beth was overly *cachinnating* about her good fortune?

14. clarion—[C] brilliantly clear. I was enraptured by the opera thanks to the soprano's *clarion* voice.

15. strident—[B] discordant. To say Alex's new punk band is a touch *strident* is a mild understatement.

WORDS TO TRAVEL BY

Before you start cramming your suitcase for that dream getaway, make sure you've got the travel lingo down. Take a tour of these terms, then jet to the next page for answers.

1. docent ('doh-sent) *n.*—A: tour guide. B: side trip. C: frequent flier.

2. sojourn ('soh-jern) *v.*—A: travel nonstop. B: take a guided tour. C: stay temporarily.

3. cosmopolitan (kahz-meh-'pah-leh-tin) *adj.*—A: between stops. B: worldly wise. C: of space travel.

4. prix fixe ('pree feeks or fiks) *n.*—A: confirmed reservation. B: meal with a set price. C: race car.

5. couchette (koo-'shet) *n.*—A: round-trip ticket. B: French pastry. C: train's sleeping compartment.

6. funicular (fyu-'nih-kye-ler) *n.*—A: pleasure cruise. B: cable railway. C: stretch limousine.

7. jitney ('jit-nee) *n.*—A: day trip. B: duty-free shop. C: small bus.

8. valise (vuh-'lees) *n.*—A: car parker. B: small suitcase. C: country cottage.

9. sabbatical (seh-'ba-ti-kul) *n.*—A: break from work. B: lodging overseas. C: seating upgrade.

10. ramada (ruh-'mah-duh) *n.*—A: shelter with open sides. B: dude ranch. C: in-house maid service.

11. incidental (in-seh-'den-tul) *adj.*—A: waiting in a long line. B: minor. C: causing a scandal.

12. transient ('tran-shee- or zee-ent) *adj.*—A: going by rail. B: passing through. C: on foot.

13. manifest ('ma-neh-fest) *n.*—A: red-eye flight. B: reservation. C: passenger list.

14. rack rate ('rak rayt) *n.*—A: overhead-luggage charge. B: takeoff speed. C: full price for lodging.

15. peripatetic (per-uh-puh-'teh-tik) *adj.*—A: speaking many languages. B: traveling from place to place. C: crossing a border illegally.

Life Is Good

"Words to Travel By" Answers

1. docent—[A] tour guide. I followed a *docent* through the museum, pretending to be with a school group.

2. sojourn—[C] stay temporarily. "Will you *sojourn* with us long?" asked the receptionist as I reclined on a bench.

3. cosmopolitan—[B] worldly wise. Apparently, Sara wasn't *cosmopolitan* enough for the maître d' to seat her at any of the best tables.

4. prix fixe—[B] meal with a set price. Alison knew it was a *prix fixe*, but naturally she tried to haggle with the waiter anyway.

5. couchette—[C] train's sleeping compartment. My *couchette* mates snored peacefully in their bunks.

6. funicular—[B] cable railway. The *funicular* disappeared into the mist halfway up the mountain.

7. jitney—[C] small bus. We chartered a *jitney* for our trip to the cape.

8. valise—[B] small suitcase. Eric grew suspicious after finding someone else's credentials in his *valise*.

9. sabbatical—[A] break from work. "I'm here on a six-month *sabbatical*," I tried to explain to the customs agent.

10. ramada—[A] shelter with open sides. My ideal vacation: sipping some colorful cocktail seaside under a *ramada*.

11. incidental—[B] minor. "*Incidental* items can add weight quickly, so pack wisely," my wife advised.

12. transient—[B] passing through. Thankfully, the brute was a *transient* customer, not a permanent guest.

13. manifest—[C] passenger list. I came from such a big family, we had to keep an official *manifest* for every trip.

14. rack rate—[C] full price for lodging. Savvy travelers never settle for a hotel's *rack rate*.

15. peripatetic—[B] traveling from place to place. After two *peripatetic* years in Asia, Jason settled down.

DOWNTIME, REDEFINED

These days, vacations come in myriad forms. A *staycation* is when you don't go anywhere and just enjoy free time at or near home. A *paycation* is when you moonlight as you travel. A *daycation* is a 24-hour getaway. We've also heard of a *praycation* (a religious trip) and even a *bakeation* (a foodie's holiday dedicated to sampling pastries).

EAT YOUR WORDS

Gastronomy—the art of eating—is a rich source of vocabulary in all languages (Italians have far more words for pasta than Eskimos have for snow). See how many culinary words you know, even if you can't boil water. For answers, turn the page.

1. **eupeptic** (yoo-'pep-tick) *adj.*—A: perfectly ripe. B: having a peppery flavor. C: promoting good digestion.

2. **dim sum** ('dim 'soom or 'sum) *n.*—A: dark meat of a duck. B: made with a blended soy sauce. C: small portions of a variety of foods.

3. **sommelier** (sum-ull-'yay) *n.*—A: wine steward. B: head chef. C: light salad dressing.

4. **dredge** ('drej) *v.*—A: lightly coat, as with flour. B: grind into meal. C: bind the wings and legs of a fowl.

5. **Florentine** ('floor-un-teen or -tine) *adj.*—A: prepared with a cream sauce. B: prepared with spinach. C: prepared with mozzarella.

6. **julienne** (joo-lee-'en or zhoo-) *v.*—A: season with herbs. B: steam. C: cut into thin strips.

7. **roux** ('roo) *n.*—A: spicy stew containing okra. B: bead-shaped grain. C: thickener for sauces.

8. **coddle** ('cod-dull) *v.*— A: unmold candy. B: beat with a whisk. C: cook gently in hot water.

9. **bain-marie** (ban-muh-'ree) *n.*—A: cheese slicer. B: double boiler's lower pot. C: small pastry tip for icing petits fours.

10. **nori** ('noh-ree or 'nor-ee) *n.*—A: dipping bowls. B: seaweed wrapper for sushi. C: drink made from fermented rice.

11. **macerate** ('mass-uh-rate) *v.*—A: sizzle. B: soften by steeping. C: break into crumbs.

12. **tandoori** (tahn-'dure-ee) *adj.*—A: flavored with curries. B: sweetened with tamarind. C: roasted in a charcoal oven.

13. **trencherman** ('tren-chur-mun) *n.*—A: hearty eater. B: salad chef. C: waiter's assistant.

14. **clabber** ('clab-ur) *n.*—A: gristle. B: curdled milk. C: corn whiskey.

15. **sapid** ('sap-ud) *adj.*—A: flavorful. B: syrupy. C: stale.

Life Is Good

"Eat Your Words" Answers

1. eupeptic—[C] promoting good digestion. Dad claims that watching the Super Bowl after a big meal is *eupeptic*.

2. dim sum—[C] small portions of a variety of foods. It's not worth it to take Paige out for *dim sum*—one dumpling and she's full.

3. sommelier—[A] wine steward. When Harry ordered a wine spritzer, the *sommelier* turned pale.

4. dredge—[A] lightly coat, as with flour. Rodney *dredged* everything in the kitchen but the chicken.

5. Florentine—[B] prepared with spinach. We don't use the word "spinach" in front of our five-year-old; instead we call it a *Florentine* dish.

6. julienne—[C] cut into thin strips. The puppy methodically *julienned* every pillow in the house.

7. roux—[C] thickener for sauces. If the gravy won't pour, you've used too much *roux*.

8. coddle—[C] cook gently in hot water. His joke's punch line was "Cannibals don't *coddle* their children."

9. bain-marie—[B] double boiler's lower pot. I won't make any recipe that calls for a *bain-marie*—my most exotic kitchen utensil is a pizza cutter.

10. nori—[B] seaweed wrapper for sushi. In his full-body wet suit, Uncle Ned emerged from the water looking like a jumbo shrimp wrapped in *nori*.

11. macerate—[B] soften by steeping. For dessert, our hostess served Anjou pears *macerated* in 25-year-old Armagnac, but we would have preferred Twinkies.

12. tandoori—[C] roasted in a charcoal oven. The restaurant's unrestrained menu included both steak fajitas and *tandoori* chicken.

13. trencherman—[A] hearty eater. Our teenage son, with his *trencherman's* appetite, will eat us out of house and home.

14. clabber—[B] curdled milk. Searching the fridge shelves for a little milk for my coffee, I found only a carton full of *clabber*.

15. sapid—[A] flavorful. This soup is about as sapid as dishwater.

WALTZING THROUGH LIFE

This month we premiere an eclectic medley of musical terms—some classical, some modern, and some slangy. If you're missing a few beats, waltz over to the next page for answers.

1. clam (klam) *n.*—A: silent measure. B: wrong note. C: set of maracas.

2. legato (lih-'gah-toh) *adv.*—A: smoothly. B: quickly. C: loudly.

3. woodshed ('wood-shehd) *v.*—A: serenade. B: drum loudly. C: practice an instrument.

4. busk (busk) *v.*—A: sing baritone. B: work as an accompanist. C: play for donations.

5. ska (skah) *n.*—A: hip-hop club. B: microphone stand. C: Jamaican music.

6. nonet (noh-'net) *n.*—A: ditty for kids. B: composition for nine voices. C: unrehearsed performance.

7. pipes (piyps) *n.*—A: singing voice. B: tuba mouthpieces. C: emcees.

8. da capo (dah 'kah-poh) *adv.*—A: from the top. B: up-tempo. C: raised a half step.

9. beatboxer ('beet-bok-ser) *n.*—A: band competition. B: vocal percussionist. C: instrument case.

10. barrelhouse ('bear-el-hous) *n.*—A: bass trombone. B: rhythmic style of jazz. C: drumroll.

11. tonic ('tah-nik) *n.*—A: first tone of a scale. B: counterpoint. C: harmony.

12. noodle ('noo-duhl) *v.*—A: change key. B: croon. C: improvise casually.

13. hook (hook) *n.*—A: stolen lyric. B: saxophone line. C: catchy musical phrase.

14. skiffle ('skih-ful) *n.*—A: swing step. B: music played on rudimentary instruments. C: fast tempo.

15. earworm ('eer-wurm) *n.*—A: bassoon. B: tune that repeats in one's head. C: power chord.

Life Is Good **147**

"Waltzing Through Life" Answers

1. clam—[B] wrong note. Emmett's violin solo was going wonderfully—until he hit a *clam*.

2. legato—[A] smoothly. Lullabies should always be sung *legato*.

3. woodshed—[C] practice an instrument. If Lydia wants to make it to Carnegie Hall, she needs to *woodshed* a lot more often.

4. busk—[C] play for donations. I'm between gigs right now, unless you count *busking* in the park.

5. ska—[C] Jamaican music. Blake's *ska* band is holding open auditions for horn players this weekend.

6. nonet—[B] composition for nine voices. Our baseball team is also a singing group; we perform only *nonets*!

7. pipes—[A] singing voice. Brandon killed "Livin' on a Prayer" at karaoke last night—who knew he had such great *pipes*?

8. da capo—[A] from the top. Even though the score said *da capo*, the bandleader enjoyed bellowing to his musicians, "Take it from the top!"

9. beatboxer—[B] vocal percussionist. Marina is such an amazing *beatboxer* that you'd swear there was a drummer in the room.

10. barrelhouse—[B] rhythmic style of jazz. Cynthia played an old *barrelhouse* tune on the piano.

11. tonic—[A] first tone of a scale. "This concerto is in C major, so the *tonic* is C," the professor explained.

12. noodle—[C] improvise casually. I was just *noodling* around on my guitar when I wrote this riff.

13. hook—[C] catchy musical phrase. The Beatles had an undeniable knack for melodic *hooks*.

14. skiffle—[B] music played on rudimentary instruments. Our family *skiffle* band features Mom on kazoo, Dad on washboard, and Uncle John on slide whistle.

15. earworm—[B] tune that repeats in one's head. That TV jingle has become my latest *earworm*, and it's driving me crazy!

SING, SING, SING

Many vocal terms have their roots in the Latin verb *cantare* ("to sing"). *Cantatas* are pieces for singers, and *bel canto* (literally "beautiful singing" in Italian) is operatic singing. A *chanson* is a cabaret song, and its female singer is a *chanteuse*. Chants and incantations are often sung. And a long poem, whether recited or sung, may be divided into *cantos*.

THE PLAY'S THE THING

Americans spell it *theater*. The British spell it *theatre*. And the most annoying of us pronounce it "thee-ay-tuh." Find out how dramatic you are by seeing if you can identify all 15 of these theatrical expressions. Ladies and gentlemen, please take your seat. The quiz is about to begin… Answers on the next page.

1. odeum (oh-'dee-uhm) *n.*—A: song of praise. B: air of menace. C: classic theater or concert hall.

2. revue (ree-'vyu) *n.*—A: show consisting of loosely connected skits. B: critics' seating. C: final rehearsal.

3. downstage *adv.*—A: toward the audience. B: away from the audience. C: at an exit.

4. ad libitum (add 'lih-beh-tum) *adv.*—A: intently. B: spontaneously. C: slowly.

5. proscenium (pro-'see-nee-uhm) *n.*—A: introduction. B: list of characters. C: arched wall separating a stage from the auditorium.

6. histrionic (his-tree-'ah-nik) *adj.*—A: enacting past events. B: overly dramatic. C: villainous.

7. dramaturge ('dra-ma-terj) *n.*— A: plot. B: literary adviser and specialist. C: acting bug.

8. strike *v.*—A: hit one's mark onstage. B: disassemble a set. C: speak louder than a fellow actor.

9. scrim *n.*—A: swordfight. B: wig. C: gauze curtain.

10. Grand Guignol (grahn geen-'yol) *n.*—A: horror show. B: player piano. C: high comedy.

11. busk *v.*—A: entertain in public for donations. B: take tickets. C: forget lines.

12. stalls *n.*—A: prop closets. B: late-arriving viewers. C: front orchestra seating.

13. allegorical (a-le-'gor-i-kel) *adj.*—A: written in verse. B: with timely significance. C: having symbolic meaning.

14. flies *n.*—A: departures from the script. B: rapid dialog. C: overhead storage space.

15. pas de deux (pah 'de 'dur) *n.*—A: dance for two people. B: second act. C: encore.

Life Is Good **149**

"The Play's the Thing" Answers

1. odeum—[C] classic theater or concert hall. The opera troupe made its debut in the 1910 *odeum* downtown.

2. revue—[A] show consisting of loosely connected skits. I think the last *revue* I saw was *Side by Side by Sondheim*.

3. downstage—[A] toward the audience. Meryl forgot her lines and ambled *downstage* to ask the audience for suggestions.

4. ad libitum—[B] spontaneously. Discovering a man asleep in the front row, she delivered the rest of the scene *ad libitum*.

5. proscenium—[C] arched wall separating a stage from the auditorium. Rachel spotted the villain peeking out from atop the *proscenium*.

6. histrionic—[B] overly dramatic. "Your readings are needlessly *histrionic*!" the director bellowed at the diva.

7. dramaturge—[B] literary adviser and specialist. "When the lights blow, don't blame me. I'm just the *dramaturge*."

8. strike—[B] disassemble a set. The cast didn't at all mind helping to *strike* the set for *The Fantasticks*.

9. scrim—[C] gauze curtain. Reaching for her love from the balcony, Juliet got tangled in the *scrim*.

10. Grand Guignol—[A] horror show. The garish makeup, surreal staging, and *Grand Guignol* aesthetic was all wrong for *Oklahoma!*

11. busk—[A] entertain in public for donations. "Well, even Sutton Foster had to start somewhere," Kate's dad said when he heard his daughter was going to *busk* in subway stations.

12. stalls—[C] front orchestra seating. During the *Spider-Man* previews, viewers in the *stalls* were advised to take out falling-actor insurance.

13. allegorical—[C] having symbolic meaning. When the character named Eve said, "What do you know?" and bit an apple—was that *allegorical*?

14. flies—[C] overhead storage space. Audrey delighted in the snow onstage; her dad hoped she wouldn't spot the "flakes" falling from the *flies*.

15. pas de deux—[A] dance for two people. The revue featured a complicated *pas de deux* for Carla and Eli.

150   USE YOUR WORDS

MUSEUM MOTS

Planning a visit to the Louvre, the Met, London's National Gallery, or another grand museum this summer? First take our quiz to make sure you have an artful vocabulary. Turn the page for answers.

1. graphic ('gra-fik) *adj.*—A: clearly pictured. B: sculpted of marble. C: roughly composed.

2. canon ('ka-nen) *n.*—A: string of images. B: standard for evaluation. C: negative review.

3. symmetry ('si-meh-tree) *n.*—A: framing and matting. B: balanced proportions. C: imitation.

4. cartography (kahr-'tah-gre-fee) *n.*—A: mapmaking. B: painted wagons. C: traveling exhibits.

5. panoramic (pan-oh-'ram-ik) *adj.*—A: of film artistry. B: shown in miniature. C: sweeping.

6. opaque (oh-'payk) *adj.*—A: deceptive. B: not transparent. C: molded in plaster.

7. juxtapose ('juks-tuh-pohz) *v.*—A: sit for a portrait. B: render precisely. C: place side by side.

8. kinetic (kih-'neh-tik) *adj.*—A: copied identically. B: showing movement. C: picturing countryside.

9. kitschy ('ki-chee) *adj.*—A: in a collage. B: tacky. C: macraméd.

10. baroque (buh-'rohk) *adj.*—A: highly ornamented. B: plain in style. C: traditional.

11. manifesto (ma-neh-'fes-toh) *n.*—A: statement of principles. B: gallery opening. C: watercolor technique.

12. avant-garde (ah-vahnt-'gard) *adj.*—A: retro. B: scandalous. C: cutting-edge.

13. aesthetics (es-'theh-tiks) *n.*—A: acid engravings. B: pleasing appearance. C: works in the outdoor air.

14. anthropomorphic (an-throh-puh-'mohr-fik) *adj.*—A: of cave art. B: made from clay. C: humanlike.

15. analogous (uh-'na-leh-ges) *adj.*—A: shapeless. B: made of wood. C: having a likeness.

Life Is Good

"Museum Mots" Answers

1. graphic—[A] clearly pictured. The depiction of the embrace was a little too *graphic* for me.

2. canon—[B] standard for evaluation. Monet's works are certainly the *canon* by which to measure other Impressionist paintings.

3. symmetry—[B] balanced proportions. Ever the jokester, Dean asked, "When Picasso looked in the mirror, was his face all out of *symmetry* too?"

4. cartography—[A] mapmaking. No need to test my *cartography* skills when I've got a GPS in the car.

5. panoramic—[C] sweeping. Eric and Christine were overwhelmed by the photo's *panoramic* proportions.

6. opaque—[B] not transparent. Notice the *opaque* colors he chose for the backdrop.

7. juxtapose—[C] place side by side. Now that you've *juxtaposed* the photos, I agree—they're not at all alike.

8. kinetic—[B] showing movement. I thought someone was behind me, but it was a particularly *kinetic* statue.

9. kitschy—[B] tacky. Leo thinks anything that isn't Rembrandt is just *kitschy*.

10. baroque—[A] highly ornamented. Alex's *baroque*-inspired sketches were criticized for being too busy.

11. manifesto—[A] statement of principles. Art *manifestos* often come across as pretentious and superior.

12. avant-garde—[C] cutting-edge. Holly dropped out of school to join an *avant-garde* painting troupe.

13. aesthetics—[B] pleasing appearance. Ironically, Joziah's darker portraits most accurately captured the *aesthetics* of the city.

14. anthropomorphic—[C] humanlike. The artist combined everyday street items into an *anthropomorphic* figure.

15. analogous—[C] having a likeness. Right now, my brain is *analogous* to that flat, empty canvas.

SHORT AND SWEET

When people save tickets, clippings, or menus—items intended to last only briefly but often placed in scrapbooks—they are collecting *ephemera* (from the Greek *ephemeros*, "lasting a day"). Such items may not have been made by artists, but over time they acquire value for their place in history. And a cultural trend that passes away quickly is considered *ephemeral*.

SEAWORDY

In honor of Herman Melville and his masterpiece *Moby Dick*, we offer seafaring words. See answers on the next page.

1. natatorial (nay-tuh-'tor-ee-ul or nat-uh-) *adj.*—A: of swimming. B: of boating. C: of sunbathing.

2. shingle *n.*—A: gravelly beach. B: exposed sandbar. C: group of dolphins.

3. maillot (my-'oh or mah-'yo) *n.*—A: lace-up sandal. B: scuba mask. C: one-piece swimsuit.

4. jibe ('jybe) *v.*—A: dig for clams. B: turn a boat's stern. C: tread water.

5. dugong ('doo-gong) *n.*—A: sea cow. B: sea serpent. C: sea horse.

6. founder *v.*—A: sail. B: splash. C: sink.

7. thalassic (thuh-'lass-ick) *adj.*—A: of lighthouses. B: of sand. C: of seas and oceans.

8. ho-dad ('ho-dad) *n.*—A: lighted buoy. B: wannabe surfer. C: boardwalk food stand.

9. littoral ('lit-uh-rul) *adj.*—A: polluted. B: pertaining to mollusks. C: along a seashore.

10. sargasso (sar-'gas-oh) *n.*—A: tropical breeze. B: floating seaweed. C: warming current.

11. alee (uh-'lee) *adv.*—A: toward sea. B: ashore. C: away from the wind.

12. pike *n.*—A: perfect surfing wave. B: jackknife dive. C: waterskiing trick.

13. pelagic (puh-'laj-ick) *adj.*—A: of the open sea. B: threatening to storm. C: infected, as a sting.

14. mal de mer (mal duh 'mare) *n.*—A: seasickness. B: undertow. C: monster.

15. undulate ('un-juh-late or 'un-dyuh-) *v.*—A: raise a mainsail. B: move like waves. C: skinny-dip.

16. conchologist (konk-'ka-luh-jist) *n.*—A: shell expert. B: shark expert. C: erosion expert.

17. Davy Jones *n.*—A: lifeguards' CPR dummy. B: discoverer of Hawaiian Islands. C: the sea personified.

Life Is Good

"Seawordy" Answers

1. natatorial—[A] of swimming. My *natatorial* specialty is the dog paddle.

2. shingle—[A] gravelly beach. "Ow! I should have worn my flip-flops," cried Walter, wincing as he crossed the *shingle*.

3. maillot—[C] one-piece swimsuit. The only good thing about that neon-green *maillot* is that you won't be hard to spot on a crowded beach.

4. jibe—[B] turn a boat's stern. As the storm intensified, we *jibed*, and the swinging boom knocked Stanley overboard.

5. dugong—[A] sea cow. He has the mild mien of a *dugong* but the grin of a shark.

6. founder—[C] sink. Helplessly, Joey watched as his remote-controlled boat capsized and *foundered*.

7. thalassic—[C] of seas and oceans. Though landlocked, the town, with its Nantucket-style houses and laid-back atmosphere, has a distinct *thalassic* feel.

8. ho-dad—('60s surfing slang) [B] wannabe surfer. He may have a righteous board, but that *ho-dad* couldn't surf in a bathtub.

9. littoral—[C] along a seashore. Walking slowly up and down the beach, the marine biologist collected samples of *littoral* flora.

10. sargasso—[B] floating seaweed. Columbus and his crew were nervous that their ships would become tangled in the sprawling *sargasso* of the North Atlantic.

11. alee—[C] away from the wind. "Hard *alee*!" shouted Grandpa, a former navy man, as he steered the Chevy around a corner.

12. pike—[B] jackknife dive. Uncle Hank's attempt at a forward double somersault *pike* ended up as a slap-tastic belly flop.

13. pelagic—[A] of the open sea. Petrels are *pelagic* birds that return to land only to breed.

14. mal de mer—[A] seasickness. Lloyd, green with *mal de mer*, looked up at Lucy gratefully as she mercifully handed him a packet of Dramamine.

15. undulate—[B] move like waves. Back onshore, Lloyd couldn't stomach even the sight of the beach grass *undulating* in the wind.

16. conchologist—[A] shell expert. An amateur *conchologist*, Edith was never happier than the day she found a rare paper nautilus shell.

17. Davy Jones—[C] the sea personified. Any old salt will tell you that *Davy Jones* is a fickle friend.

MUSIC

Country music has always been the best shrink that 15 bucks can buy.
—DIERKS BENTLEY

"
Where words fail, music speaks.
—HANS CHRISTIAN ANDERSON

"
Every musical phrase has a purpose. It's like talking. If you talk with a particular purpose, people listen to you, but if you just recite, it's not as meaningful.
—ITZHAK PERLMAN

"
Great music is as much about the space between the notes as it is about the notes themselves.
—STING

"
I think my music is like anchovies—some people like it, some people get nauseous.
—BARRY MANILOW

"
Talking about music is like talking about sex. Can you describe it? Are you supposed to?
—BRUCE SPRINGSTEEN

QUOTABLE MOVIES

Love means never having to say you're sorry.
—**LOVE STORY**

"

Frankly, my dear, I don't give a damn.
—**GONE WITH THE WIND**

"

Nobody puts Baby in the corner.
—**DIRTY DANCING**

"

Carpe diem. Seize the day, boys.
Make your lives extraordinary.
—**DEAD POETS SOCIETY**

"

Gentlemen, you can't fight in here!
This is the War Room!
—**DR. STRANGELOVE**

Mama always said life was like
a box of chocolates. You never know
what you're gonna get.
—**FORREST GUMP**

You're gonna need a bigger boat.
—JAWS

Toto, I've got a feeling we're not in Kansas anymore.
—THE WIZARD OF OZ

I love the smell of napalm in the morning.
—APOCALYPSE NOW

We must all face the choice between what is right and what is easy.
—HARRY POTTER AND THE GOBLET OF FIRE

It doesn't take much to see that the problems of three little people don't amount to a hill of beans in this crazy world.
—CASABLANCA

I fart in your general direction. Your mother was a hamster and your father smelt of elderberries.
—MONTY PYTHON AND THE HOLY GRAIL

Leave the gun, take the cannoli.
—THE GODFATHER

> I like to crack the jokes
> now and again, but it's only because
> I struggle with math.
> —**TINA FEY**

A LAUGH A MINUTE

Keeping a sense of humor about life, the universe, and everything is essential to keeping sane. Laughter is immediate relief for whatever ails you, and we're lucky that there are so many notable people practicing the therapeutic art of comedy.

LAUGHTER, THE BEST MEDICINE

If there's one thing I know, it's that God does love a good joke.
—**HUGH ELLIOTT**

"

Laughter brings the swelling down on our national psyche.
—**STEPHEN COLBERT**

"

I am thankful for laughter, except when milk comes out my nose.
—**WOODY ALLEN**

"

Nothing to me feels as good as laughing incredibly hard.
—**STEVE CARELL**

"

I wake up laughing every day. I get a kick out of life.
—**BRUCE WILLIS**

"

Laughter is the shortest distance between two people.
—**VICTOR BORGE**

Good taste is the enemy of comedy.
—MEL BROOKS

Whoever established the high road, and how high it should be, should be fired.
—SANDRA BULLOCK

"

Tell me what you laugh at, and I'll tell you who you are.
—MARCEL PAGNOL

"

Laughter is an instant vacation.
—MILTON BERLE

"

You can't deny laughter. When it comes, it plops down in your favorite chair and stays as long as it wants.
—STEPHEN KING

"

Comedy is like catching lightning in a bottle.
—GOLDIE HAWN

"

I'm not funny. What I am is brave.
—LUCILLE BALL

"

The only way you can know where the line is, is if you cross it.
—DAVE CHAPPELLE

LIFE LESSONS

A synonym is a word you use when you can't spell the first word you thought of.
—BURT BACHARACH

"

It's only when the tide goes out that you learn who's been swimming naked.
—WARREN BUFFETT

"

The difference between fiction and reality? Fiction has to make sense.
—TOM CLANCY

"

When the winds of change blow, some people build walls, and others build windmills.
—CHINESE PROVERB

"

You should take your job seriously but not yourself. That is the best combination.
—DAME JUDI DENCH

"

Not being funny doesn't make you a bad person. Not having a sense of humor does.
—DAVID RAKOFF

There's no one way to dance.
And that's kind of my philosophy about everything.
—**ELLEN DEGENERES**

The trouble with having an open mind, of course,
is that people will insist on coming along and
trying to put things in it.
—**TERRY PRATCHETT**

Men don't care what's on TV.
They only care what else is on TV.
—**JERRY SEINFELD**

If there's a single lesson that life teaches us,
it's that wishing doesn't make it so.
—**LEV GROSSMAN**

You have to remember one thing about
the will of the people: It wasn't that long ago
that we were swept away by the macarena.
—**JON STEWART**

Without geography, you're nowhere.
—**JIMMY BUFFETT**

TECHNOLOGY

Because Google is so popular, it's conceited. Have you tried misspelling something lately? See the tone that it takes? "Um, did you mean . . . ?"
—ARJ BARKER

"

When I first heard about the campaign to get me to host *Saturday Night Live*, I didn't know what Facebook was. And now that I do know what it is, I have to say, it sounds like a huge waste of time!
—BETTY WHITE

"

So I'm reading a book on my new iPad, but can't the iPad read it for me? Do I have to do everything?
—MATTHEW PERRY

If it keeps up, man will atrophy all his limbs but the push-button finger.
—FRANK LLOYD WRIGHT

Personally, I'm waiting for caller IQ.
—SANDRA BERNHARD

E-mails are letters, after all,
more lasting than phone calls,
even if many of them r 2 cursory 4 u.
—ANNA QUINDLEN

"

To err is human, but to really foul things up
you need a computer.
—PAUL EHRLICH

"

Computers make it easier to do a lot of things,
but most of the things they make easier to do
don't need to be done.
—ANDY ROONEY

"

I don't believe in e-mail. I'm an old-fashioned girl.
I prefer calling and hanging up.
—SARAH JESSICA PARKER

THE PERFECT WORDS TO
OPEN WITH A LAUGH

The human brain starts working the moment you are born and never stops until you stand up to speak in public.
—GEORGE JESSEL

"

A dead-end street is a good place to turn around.
—NAOMI JUDD

"

I've had a perfectly wonderful evening, but this wasn't it.
—GROUCHO MARX

"

The problem is never how to get new, innovative thoughts into your mind, but how to get old ones out.
—DEE HOCK

"

It doesn't work to leap a twenty-foot chasm in two ten-foot jumps.
—PROVERB

"

Great ideas often receive violent opposition from mediocre minds.
—ALBERT EINSTEIN

YIDDISH FUN

Words should be weighed, not counted, goes the Yiddish proverb. Of the thousands of words English has borrowed from other languages, Yiddish loanwords are perhaps the weightiest. How many other nouns pack the precision, sarcasm, humor, and onomatopoeia into seven letters that schlump (sloppy dresser) does? For quiz answers, turn the page.

1. **kvetch** ('kvech) *v.*—A: cook. B: complain. C: boast.

2. **zaftig** ('zahf-tig) *adj.*—A: pleasantly plump. B: giddy. C: curious.

3. **chutzpah** ('hoot-spuh) *n.*—A: sudden attack. B: filled crepe. C: gall.

4. **yenta** ('yen-ta) *n.*— A: busybody. B: matchmaker. C: rabbi's wife.

5. **plotz** ('plots) *v.*—A: measure. B: figure out. C: collapse.

6. **meshuga** (muh-'shoog-uh) *adj.*— A: worthless. B: too sweet. C: daffy.

7. **nebbish** ('neb-ish) *n.*—A: elegantly dressed man. B: milquetoast. C: smart aleck.

8. **tchotchke** ('chach-kuh) *n.*— A: folk dance. B: bad memory. C: knickknack.

9. **schnorrer** ('shnor-ur) *n.*—A: loud sleeper. B: moocher. C: ladies' man.

10. **oy vey** ('oy 'vay) *interj.*— A: Happy birthday! B: Hip hip hooray! C: Oh, woe!

11. **kibitz** ('kib-its or kuh-'bits) *v.*—A: clean obsessively. B: tell jokes. C: offer opinions.

12. **mensch** ('mench) *n.*— A: coward. B: honorable person. C: ne'er-do-well.

13. **schlep** ('shlep) *v.*—A: haul. B: insult. C: weep.

14. **nudnik** ('nood-nik) *n.*—A: first-year student. B: bumpkin. C: bore.

15. **bubkes** ('bup-cuss) *n.*—A: stroke of luck. B: nothing. C: term of endearment.

16. **shamus** ('shah-mus or 'shay-) *n.*—A: detective. B: hoax. C: free-for-all.

17. **mazel tov** ('mah-zul 'tov) *interj.*—A: Sorry—my bad! B: Welcome home! C: Best wishes!

A Laugh a Minute   **167**

"Yiddish Fun" Answers

1. kvetch—[B] complain. If Bernice *kvetched* about her friends less, she might have more of them.

2. zaftig—[A] pleasantly plump. The *zaftig* beauty was the first plus-size contestant to win *America's Next Top Model*.

3. chutzpah—[C] gall. After jumping the light, the other driver had the *chutzpah* to blame me for the accident.

4. yenta—[A] busybody. The office romance provided irresistible fodder for the watercooler *yentas*.

5. plotz—[C] collapse. When my mom sees my report card, she'll *plotz*.

6. meshuga—[C] daffy. My *meshuga* neighbor has dressed his garden gnomes in flak jackets.

7. nebbish—[B] milquetoast. A *nebbish* in an ill-fitting suit, the accountant nervously said "excuse me" to the coworker blocking the fax machine.

8. tchotchke—[C] knickknack. Among the yard sale *tchotchkes*, there it was: Punchers the Lobster, one of the original Beanie Babies.

9. schnorrer—[B] moocher. That *schnorrer* Artie always forgets his wallet when we eat out.

10. oy vey—[C] Oh, woe! Dad got out of the car, looked at the flat tire, and said, "*Oy vey!*"

11. kibitz—[C] offer opinions. Jane does more *kibitzing* than helping.

12. mensch—[B] honorable person. The mayor is a *mensch*—respected even by those who disagree with him.

13. schlep—[A] haul. Lois *schlepped* the newspapers to the recycling center, realizing much later that she'd tossed her husband's prize baseball card collection.

14. nudnik—[C] bore. Don't look now, but here comes that *nudnik* from the IT department.

15. bubkes—[B] nothing. They went to Vegas with a bundle and came back with *bubkes*.

16. shamus—[A] detective. You don't have to be a *shamus* to figure out that the e-mail is a scam.

17. mazel tov—[C] Best wishes! You got the job? *Mazel tov!*

FUNNIEST ENGLISH WORDS

At long last, a quiz dedicated to plain ol' fun! Inspired by *The 100 Funniest Words in English*, by Robert Beard, these picks are all a mouthful, and some even sport serious definitions (others… well, not so much). Enjoy weaving them into your dinner-table conversation tonight. Answers on next page.

1. **flummox** ('fluh-muks) *v.*—A: laugh out loud. B: confuse. C: ridicule.

2. **crudivore** ('crew-dih-vor) *n.*—A: foulmouthed person. B: garbage can. C: eater of raw food.

3. **hoosegow** ('hoos-gow) *n.*—A: jail. B: scaredy-cat. C: strong liquor, usually moonshine.

4. **mollycoddle** ('mah-lee-kah-dl) *v.*—A: treat with an absurd degree of attention. B: mix unwisely. C: moo or imitate a cow.

5. **donnybrook** ('dah-nee-bruk) *n.*—A: rapid stream. B: wild brawl. C: stroke of luck.

6. **cantankerous** (kan-'tan-keh-res) *adj.*—A: very sore. B: hard to deal with. C: obnoxiously loud.

7. **codswallop** ('kahdz-wah-lep) *n.*—A: sound produced by a hiccup. B: rare rainbow fish. C: nonsense.

8. **doozy** ('doo-zee) *n.*—A: extraordinary one of its kind. B: incomprehensible song. C: double feature.

9. **discombobulate** (dis-kehm-'bah-byoo-layt) *v.*—A: take apart. B: fail. C: upset or frustrate.

10. **hootenanny** ('hoo-teh-na-nee) *n.*—A: group of owls. B: folksinging event. C: child's caregiver.

11. **yahoo** ('yah-hoo) *n.*—A: overzealous fan. B: pratfall. C: dumb person.

12. **kerfuffle** (ker-'fuh-fuhl) *n.*—A: failure to ignite. B: down pillow or blanket. C: disturbance.

13. **absquatulate** (abz-'kwah-chew-layt) *v.*—A: abscond or flee. B: stay low to the ground. C: utterly flatten.

14. **skullduggery** (skul-'duh-geh-ree) *n.*—A: Shakespearean prank. B: underhanded behavior. C: graveyard.

15. **flibbertigibbet** (flih-ber-tee-'jih-bet) *n.*—A: silly and flighty person. B: snap of the fingers. C: hex or curse.

A Laugh a Minute

"Funniest English Words" Answers

1. flummox—[B] confuse. Sarah is easily *flummoxed* by any changes to the schedule.

2. crudivore—[C] eater of raw food. To help boost my health, I'm declaring myself a *crudivore*.

3. hoosegow—[A] jail. After protesting a touch too loudly in court, Tara found herself in the *hoosegow*.

4. mollycoddle—[A] treat with an absurd degree of attention. "Lillie's my only grandchild—I'll *mollycoddle* her all I want!"

5. donnybrook—[B] wild brawl. It took four umps to quell the *donnybrook* at home plate.

6. cantankerous—[B] hard to deal with. The comic was greeted by a *cantankerous* crowd at his debut.

7. codswallop—[C] nonsense. "Oh, *codswallop*! I never went near that bowl of candy," Dad barked.

8. doozy—[A] extraordinary one of its kind. That was a *doozy* of a storm—luckily, we dodged the two downed trees.

9. discombobulate—[C] upset or frustrate. The goal of the simulator: *discombobulate* even the sharpest of pilots.

10. hootenanny—[B] folksinging event. After the concert, let's head up the hill for the informal *hootenanny*.

11. yahoo—[C] dumb person. Please try not to embarrass me at Sally's party, you big *yahoo*.

12. kerfuffle—[C] disturbance. I was referring to that minor *kerfuffle* called World War II.

13. absquatulate—[A] abscond or flee. Upon opening the door, Clare watched the new puppy *absquatulate* with her sneaker.

14. skullduggery—[B] underhanded behavior. The chairman was infamous for resorting to *skullduggery* during contract negotiations.

15. flibbertigibbet—[A] silly and flighty person. Do I have to spend the entire ride with that *flibbertigibbet* next to me?!

PIRATES IN THE HOUSE

Robert Beard's list of funny words also includes *filibuster*, which you probably know as a long political speech. But did you know it's also related to pirates? The Spanish *filibustero* means "freebooter," a pirate or plunderer. So you might say a *filibuster* in Congress is a way of stealing time—legislative piracy!

ABRACADABRA

A wave of our wand and presto! We conjure a page of magical words and phrases. Step right up and test your vocabulary—then transport yourself to the next page, where we reveal the answers.

1. **levitate** ('le-vih-tayt) *v.*—A: defy gravity. B: weave spells. C: disappear.

2. **clairvoyant** (klayr-'voy-ent) *adj.*—A: in a trance. B: ghostly. C: seeing beyond ordinary perception.

3. **planchette** (plan-'shet) *n.*—A: sorcerer's cloak. B: Ouija board pointer. C: mischievous fairy.

4. **mojo** ('moh-joh) *n.*—A: book of secrets. B: magical spell. C: mantra.

5. **telekinetic** (te-leh-kih-'neh-tik) *adj.*—A: predicting the future. B: calling on ghosts. C: using mind over matter.

6. **voilà** (vwah-'lah) *interj.*—A: "Begone!" B: "There it is!" C: "Open!"

7. **whammy** ('wa-mee) *n.*—A: trapdoor. B: illusion. C: hex or curse.

8. **soothsaying** ('sooth-say-ing) *n.*—A: prophecy. B: recitation of chants. C: revelation of a trick.

9. **mesmerized** ('mez-meh-riyzd) *adj.*—A: sawed in half. B: hypnotized. C: turned to pixie dust.

10. **augur** ('ah-ger) *v.*—A: serve as an omen. B: bend a spoon without touching it. C: chant in a monotone.

11. **shaman** ('shah-men) *n.*—A: fake psychic. B: healer using magic. C: genie in a bottle.

12. **occult** (uh-'khult) *adj.*—A: sinister. B: miraculous. C: secret.

13. **invoke** (in-'vohk) *v.*—A: transform. B: use ventriloquism. C: summon up, as spirits.

14. **sibyl** ('si-buhl) *n.*—A: séance. B: fortune-teller. C: black cat.

15. **pentagram** ('pen-teh-gram) *n.*—A: elixir. B: five-pointed star. C: enchanted staff.

A Laugh a Minute

"Abracadabra" Answers

1. levitate—[A] defy gravity. Before dunking the basketball, Michael *levitates* long enough to polish the backboard and rim.

2. clairvoyant—[C] seeing beyond ordinary perception. As a bookie, I find being *clairvoyant* really helps me call the races.

3. planchette—[B] Ouija board pointer. My *planchette* just spelled out "You're too gullible."

4. mojo—[B] magical spell. I've got my *mojo* working, but I still can't charm Angelina.

5. telekinetic—[C] using mind over matter. Chloe employs her *telekinetic* powers to make the trash empty itself.

6. voilà—[B] "There it is!" As he threw back the curtain, Houdini cried, "*Voilà!*"

7. whammy—[C] hex or curse. After the gypsy placed a *whammy* on Tex, he fell into the duck pond three times.

8. soothsaying—[A] prophecy. If Joe is so good at *soothsaying*, why does he always lose in Vegas?

9. mesmerized—[B] hypnotized. Since meeting Jenny, Paul has been stumbling around as though *mesmerized*.

10. augur—[A] serve as an omen. A flat tire on the first day surely *augurs* ill for our vacation.

11. shaman—[B] healer using magic. The local *shaman* recited a few incantations to heal my broken nose.

12. occult—[C] secret. At midnight, I was poring over an *occult* black-magic text.

13. invoke—[C] summon up, as spirits. While studying ancient Rome, I tried to *invoke* the ghost of Caesar to appear before me.

14. sibyl—[B] fortune-teller. My apprehension grew as the *sibyl* looked into her crystal ball and winced.

15. pentagram—[B] five-pointed star. David said his spells don't work unless he traces a *pentagram* with his wand.

DIVINING DICTIONARY

When predicting the future, the suffix we use is *-mancy*, which means "divination." *Pyromancy* involves reading the future in flames, *hydromancy* in water, and *chiromancy* in the lines on the palm of a hand. Another far-out example: *favomancy*, meaning "telling the future by reading beans scattered on the ground." Related to mantra and mania, the root *-mancy* is derived from mind.

USE YOUR WORDS

MASH-UPS

From brunch (breakfast + lunch) to Wi-Fi (wireless + fidelity), today's English language is full of hybrid words. Other examples include smog, sitcom, and Muppet, as well as those below. Enjoy the edutainment—or turn to the next page for the answers.

1. motorcade ('moh-ter-kaid) *n.*—A: breakdown. B: automatic response. C: procession of vehicles.

2. radome ('ray-dohm) *n.*—A: salad vegetable. B: antenna housing. C: all-night party.

3. digerati (di-juh-'rah-tee) *n.*—A: archaeologist. B: computer whizzes. C: screen pixels.

4. slurve ('slurv) *n.*—A: ice-cream drink. B: automobile stunt. C: baseball pitch.

5. telegenic ('te-li-je-nik) *adj.*—A: suitable manner and appearance for TV. B: having ESP. C: born on foreign soil.

6. meld ('meld) *v.*—A: liquefy. B: combine. C: harden with age.

7. bodacious (boh-'dey-shus) *adj.*—A: remarkable. B: interfering. C: part human, part machine.

8. chillax (chi-'laks) *v.*—A: ice fish. B: calm down. C: rudely insult.

9. agitprop ('ah-jit-prop) *n.*—A: political hype. B: building support. C: crowd control.

10. bromance ('bro-mans) *n.*—A: fraternity dwelling. B: gaseous element. C: close male friendship.

11. liger ('liy-ger) *n.*—A: liquid measure. B: midnight snack. C: big cat.

12. frenemy ('fre-nuh-mee) *n.*—A: false friend. B: opposition army. C: frantic movement.

13. Frankenfood ('fran-ken-food) *n.*—A: dangerous eats. B: genetically engineered food. C: fusion cuisine.

14. mockumentary (mok-yoo-'men-tah-ree) *n.*—A: simulated-trial manual. B: placebo. C: satirical film style.

15. sysop ('siys-op) *n.*—A: online administrator. B: photo shoot. C: music overdubbing.

A Laugh a Minute

"Mash-Ups" Answers

1. motorcade—[C] procession of vehicles (motor + cavalcade). How many insipid celebutantes are riding in the *motorcade*?

2. radome—[B] antenna housing (radar + dome). The plucky parasailer passed over the *radome* undetected.

3. digerati—[B] computer whizzes (digital + literati). Today's mathletes will become tomorrow's *digerati*.

4. slurve—[C] baseball pitch (slider + curve). A batter can only guesstimate where A.J.'s *slurve* will go.

5. telegenic—[A] suitable manner and appearance for TV (television + photogenic). Only the most *telegenic* dancers appear on the show *So You Think You Can Jazzercise*.

6. meld—[B] combine (melt + weld). Inventors *melded* two devices to create the camcorder.

7. bodacious—[A] remarkable (bold + audacious). Wasn't it *bodacious* of Bonnie to become a paratrooper?

8. chillax—[B] calm down (chill + relax). A puzzle addict, Daniel refused to *chillax* until he solved the cryptex.

9. agitprop—[A] political hype (agitation + propaganda). No one was persuaded by the *agitprop* promulgated in the newscast.

10. bromance—[C] close male friendship (brother + romance). Ben and Andy's *bromance* grew out of their mutual love of automobilia.

11. liger—[C] big cat (lion + tiger). I can't go to the Cineplex—I have to feed my *liger*.

12. frenemy—[A] false friend (friend + enemy). A true *frenemy*, Lisa poked fun at my bob before asking her hairstylist for one too.

13. Frankenfood—[B] genetically engineered food (Frankenstein + food). The food purists plotted ecotage against the *Frankenfood* conglomerate.

14. mockumentary—[C] satirical film style (mock + documentary). Kathy urged her Labradoodle-loving sister to watch *Best in Show*, a *mockumentary* about five dog owners.

15. sysop—[A] online administrator (system + operator). A savvy *sysop* knows how to detect malware.

THE I'S HAVE IT

What do whiz kids, fish sticks, miniskirts, and film critics have in common? Their only vowel is the letter i. So grab your skim milk, put on your string bikini, and hit this list. Then try hitchhiking to the next page for answers.

1. grissini (grih-'see-nee) *n.*—
A: Italian breadsticks. B: carved inscriptions. C: figure skating jump.

2. dirndl ('dern-duhl) *n.*—
A: needle for darning. B: full skirt. C: spinning top.

3. limpid ('lihm-pihd) *adj.*—
A: hobbling. B: perfectly clear. C: like a mollusk.

4. schism ('skih-zuhm) *n.*—
A: separation. B: pithy quotation. C: deep hole.

5. kimchi ('kihm-chee) *n.*—
A: logic puzzle. B: throw rug. C: pickled dish.

6. skinflint ('skihn-flihnt) *n.*—
A: scam artist. B: penny-pincher. C: fire starter.

7. insipid (ihn-'sih-pihd) *adj.*—
A: bland. B: just getting started. C: undrinkable.

8. fizgig ('fihz-gihg) *n.*—A: plan that fails. B: large swarm of bees. C: hissing firework.

9. jib ('jihb) *n.*—A: sharpened pencil point. B: bird's beak. C: triangular sail.

10. philippic (fih-'lih-pihk) *n.*—
A: international treaty. B: charitable gift. C: tirade.

11. viscid ('vih-sid) *adj.*—
A: sticky. B: transparent. C: wickedly cruel.

12. krill ('kril) *n.*—A: tiny crustaceans. B: peacock tail feathers. C: knitting pattern.

13. pippin ('pih-pihn) *n.*—A: apple. B: migrating songbird. C: thumbtack.

14. pidgin ('pih-juhn) *n.*—
A: trapshooter's target. B: toe turned inward. C: simplified language.

15. niblick ('nih-blihk) *n.*—
A: comic routine. B: iron golf club. C: pocket flask.

A Laugh a Minute

"The I's Have It" Answers

1. grissini—[A] Italian breadsticks. Daryl wished the child at the next table would stop playing drums with the *grissini*.

2. dirndl—[B] full skirt. For her role in the musical, Christina is donning a *dirndl* and learning to yodel.

3. limpid—[B] perfectly clear. The water in the bay was warm and *limpid*—ideal for an afternoon of snorkeling.

4. schism—[A] separation. There is quite a *schism* between your idea of good coffee and mine.

5. kimchi—[C] pickled dish. Annie used to hate Korean food, but now *kimchi* is her favorite snack.

6. skinflint—[B] penny-pincher. Our *skinflint* of an uncle never tips a dime.

7. insipid—[A] bland. No *insipid* love ballads for this band; we're here to rock!

8. fizgig—[C] hissing firework. The wedding reception ended with a celebratory *fizgig* display.

9. jib—[C] triangular sail. Harry is an amateur when it comes to sailing—he doesn't know the *jib* from the mainsail.

10. philippic—[C] tirade. We accidentally goaded Joaquin into one of his wild *philippics* about his ex-wife.

11. viscid—[A] sticky. The massive spider in my greenhouse has caught many a hapless fly in its *viscid* snare.

12. krill—[A] tiny crustaceans. One blue whale can consume up to four tons of *krill* each day.

13. pippin—[A] apple. "Ten bucks says I can knock that *pippin* right off your head!" said William Tell.

14. pidgin—[C] simplified language. Sean isn't afraid to travel to places where he doesn't speak the native tongue—he relies on *pidgin* to communicate.

15. niblick—[B] iron golf club. Emma cursed her *niblick* as her ball splashed down in the pond near the ninth hole.

WHY WIKI?
Ever wonder how the reference site Wikipedia got its name? In 1995, programmer Ward Cunningham called a user-editable website he'd created WikiWikiWeb, after the Wiki-Wiki shuttle buses he'd seen at the Honolulu airport. (*Wikiwiki* means "quickly" in Hawaiian.) That was the very first wiki—a site that allows contributions or corrections by its users.

BATTER UP

For rookies to old-timers, benchwarmers to all-stars, our national pastime is a rich field of vocabulary. Take a hefty swing at this quiz in honor of baseball. For answers, turn the page.

1. bandbox *n.*—A: warm-up area for pitchers. B: bleacher section. C: small stadium.

2. cleanup *adj.*—A: caught on the fly. B: fourth among batters. C: scoring zero runs.

3. pickle *n.*—A: hard-to-hold bat. B: bad umpire. C: play in which a runner is caught between bases.

4. rhubarb *n.*—A: heated argument. B: razzing from fans. C: thick infield grass.

5. shag *v.*—A: steal home. B: bobble a fly ball. C: practice catching in the outfield.

6. moxie *n.*—A: team mascot. B: extra spin on a pitch. C: skill and daring.

7. Texas leaguer *n.*—A: rookie player. B: double play. C: bloop hit.

8. Baltimore chop *n.*—A: high-bouncing ground ball. B: weak swing. C: ballpark hot dog.

9. fireman *n.*—A: relief pitcher. B: groundskeeper. C: third-base coach.

10. rubber game *n.*—A: blowout. B: deciding game of a series. C: poorly played game.

11. gun down *v.*—A: throw three straight strikes. B: throw out a runner. C: throw at a batter.

12. chin music *n.*—A: dispute with an umpire. B: high inside pitch. C: hometown cheers.

13. gopher ball *n.*—A: foul fly into the stands. B: hard-hit ground ball. C: easy pitch to slug.

14. bang-bang *adj.*—A: close, as a play at a base. B: ricocheting. C: requiring both hands.

15. fungo *n.*—A: exhibition game. B: catcher's mask. C: fly ball for practice.

16. blow smoke *v.*—A: taunt. B: throw fast. C: relax on an off day.

A Laugh a Minute **177**

"Batter Up" Answers

1. bandbox—[C] small stadium. No wonder Joe Bailey hit 50 homers last year—look at the dinky *bandbox* he calls a home park.

2. cleanup—[B] fourth among batters. Hinson, Rodriguez, and Pearson led off with walks, setting the stage for the Whammer, the league's top *cleanup* hitter.

3. pickle—[C] play in which a runner is caught between bases. Smalls escaped the *pickle* by taking a ball to the head.

4. rhubarb—[A] heated argument. Terry Durham and Jimmy Schnell went jaw-to-jaw in an ugly *rhubarb* at home plate.

5. shag—[C] practice catching in the outfield. How can Dugan text-message friends and *shag* flies at the same time?

6. moxie—[C] skill and daring. It took a lot of *moxie* for Buttermaker to pick the umpire's pocket like that.

7. Texas leaguer—[C] bloop hit. Our only base runner came courtesy of a *Texas leaguer* that plunked between two lazy fielders.

8. Baltimore chop—[A] high-bouncing ground ball. Porter is so quick, he can go from home to third before a *Baltimore chop* bounces twice.

9. fireman—[A] relief pitcher. We still think Walker is an odd name for our ace *fireman*.

10. rubber game—[B] deciding game of a series. But the southpaw did put out another fire to help us win the *rubber game* against the Knights.

11. gun down—[B] throw out a runner. Sent down to the minors, Kinsella managed to *gun down* only three out of 56 base stealers all season.

12. chin music—[B] high inside pitch. Savoy charged the mound after a little *chin music* from Wiggen.

13. gopher ball—[C] easy pitch to slug. Dutch looked more like Robert Redford in *The Natural* as he whacked my *gopher ball* into the mezzanine.

14. bang-bang—[A] close, as a play at a base. Another look in slo-mo clearly shows that the ump botched that *bang-bang* call at the plate.

15. fungo—[C] fly ball for practice. The Doc started second-guessing his rookie outfielder after watching him shag *fungoes* at spring training.

16. blow smoke—[B] throw fast. Icing down his hand, the catcher told reporters that Agilar was really *blowing smoke* tonight.

WORDS OF THE TIMES

Current events often dictate which words are looked up in online dictionaries. From merriam-webster.com, here are some terms that people frequently searched for in 2014. See the next page for answers.

1. wonk ('wonk) *n.*—A: nerdy expert. B: abject failure. C: double agent.

2. furlough ('fur-loh) *v.*—A: temporarily lay off from work. B: send long-distance. C: form a militia.

3. acerbic (a-'ser-bik) *adj.*—A: top secret. B: growing in a desert. C: sarcastic.

4. clemency ('kle-men-see) *n.*—A: petty crime. B: leniency. C: election of a pope.

5. vacuous ('va-kyoo-wus) *adj.*—A: in recess. B: empty-headed. C: irresistible.

6. austerity (aw-'ster-ih-tee) *n.*—A: heat wave. B: strict economizing. C: bitter disagreement.

7. cornucopia (kor-nuh-'koh-pee-uh) *n.*—A: trite comedy. B: abundance. C: fantastic dream.

8. bellicose ('be-lih-kohs) *adj.*—A: melodic. B: potbellied. C: warlike.

9. moniker ('mah-nih-ker) *n.*—A: milestone. B: nickname. C: stand-up comic.

10. curmudgeon (ker-'muh-jen) *n.*—A: dog breeder. B: grouch. C: knockout punch.

11. reconcile ('re-kon-siyl) *v.*—A: restore harmony. B: banish. C: put to extended use.

12. filibuster ('fi-lih-bus-ter) *v.*—A: meddle. B: round up allies. C: use tactics to delay or prevent an action.

13. capricious (ka-'prih-shus) *adj.*—A: fickle. B: wearing a hat. C: forming an island.

14. ignominious (ig-no-'mi-nee-us) *adj.*—A: disgraceful. B: lacking knowledge. C: using a false name.

15. indemnify (in-'dem-nih-fiy) *v.*—A: curse. B: imprison. C: pay for damages.

A Laugh a Minute

"Words of the Times" Answers

1. wonk—[A] nerdy expert. A known computer *wonk*, Mickey was recruited by a venerable tech company.

2. furlough—[A] temporarily lay off from work. Willy Wonka shut down the chocolate factory and *furloughed* the Oompa Loompas for two weeks.

3. acerbic—[C] sarcastic. On most news shows, there's more *acerbic* chitchat than there is insightful analysis.

4. clemency—[B] leniency. Bobby's lawyer asked the judge for *clemency* even though her client had been convicted of stealing billions.

5. vacuous—[B] empty-headed. As Joy gave her report on cryptozoology, she noticed a lot of *vacuous* stares.

6. austerity—[B] strict economizing. After she lost her job when her company downsized, Ann was forced to practice *austerity*.

7. cornucopia—[B] abundance. There's a *cornucopia* of coffee shops but not enough libraries.

8. bellicose—[C] warlike. Despite his *bellicose* demeanor, he's really a softy.

9. moniker—[B] nickname. Say, Woody, how did you get the *moniker* Mister Excitement?

10. curmudgeon—[B] grouch. In 12 years, that *curmudgeon* down the hall has never said good morning to me.

11. reconcile—[A] restore harmony. The Hatfields and McCoys decided to end their bitter feud and *reconcile*.

12. filibuster—[C] use tactics to delay or prevent an action. The president's opponents threatened to *filibuster* his nominee to the Supreme Court.

13. capricious—[A] fickle. Nothing is more *capricious* than New England weather.

14. ignominious—[A] disgraceful. After a promising start, the Mud Hens finished the season with an *ignominious* 100 losses.

15. indemnify—[C] pay for damages. "Somebody has to *indemnify* me for this broken window," Mr. Wilson told Dennis the Menace.

CHECK YOUR PRIDE

People often look up *hubris*, which means "overbearing pride." In ancient Greece, it conveyed an audacious attitude toward the gods. We see hubris in the story of the RMS *Titanic*, built with excessive grandeur and lost on her maiden voyage, and in Dr. Frankenstein, who presumed to acquire the power to create life. Hubris is foolish pride that leads to a fall.

AIN'T LOVE GRAND?

Love is a snowmobile racing across the tundra and then suddenly it flips over, pinning you underneath. At night, the ice weasels come.
—MATT GROENING

"

Put your hand on a hot stove for a minute, and it seems like an hour. Sit with a pretty girl for an hour, and it seems like a minute. That's relativity.
—ALBERT EINSTEIN

"

I was married by a judge. I should have asked for a jury.
—GROUCHO MARX

"

A girl phoned me the other day and said, "Come on over. There's nobody home." I went over. Nobody was home.
—RODNEY DANGERFIELD

QUOTABLE TWEETS

I got laid at IKEA this morning. Assembling the woman took a while though.
@JUDAHWORLDCHAMP (JUDAH FRIEDLANDER)

THE PERFECT WORDS FOR
ROASTS

His mother should have thrown him away and kept the stork.
—**MAE WEST**

"

[He was] one of the nicest old ladies I ever met.
—**WILLIAM FAULKNER**

"

He may look like an idiot and talk like an idiot, but don't let that fool you; he really is an idiot.
—**GROUCHO MARX**

"

I will always love the false image I had of you.
—**ASHLEIGH BRILLIANT**

"

A modest little person, with much to be modest about.
—**WINSTON CHURCHILL**

"

I've just learned about his illness. Let's hope it's nothing trivial.
—**IRVIN S. COBB**

I do desire we may be better strangers.
—**WILLIAM SHAKESPEARE**

She tells enough white lies to ice a wedding cake.
—**MARGOT ASQUITH**

In order to avoid being called a flirt, she always yielded easily.
—**CHARLES, COUNT TALLEYRAND**

He has no enemies, but is intensely disliked by his friends.
—**OSCAR WILDE**

That woman speaks eighteen languages and can't say no in any of them.
—**DOROTHY PARKER**

He loves nature in spite of what it did to him.
—**FORREST TUCKER**

There is nothing wrong with you that reincarnation won't cure.
—**JACK E. LEONARD**

Turn your wounds into wisdom.
—OPRAH

WORDS OF WISDOM

The insights of the greatest minds lead us to a deeper understanding of the world, humankind, and ourselves. Through the eyes of others we see new angles that can shape our own vision.

WISDOM

Wisdom outweighs any wealth.
—SOPHOCLES

"

There is a plan to this universe. There is a high intelligence, maybe even a purpose, but it's given to us on the installment plan.
—ISAAC BASHEVIS SINGER

"

Common sense is not so common.
—VOLTAIRE

"

I not only use all the brains that I have, but all that I can borrow.
—WOODROW WILSON

"

To understand a new idea, break an old habit.
—JEAN TOOMER

"

Common sense is wisdom with its sleeves rolled up.
—KYLE FARNSWORTH

"

It's the possibility of having a dream come true that makes life interesting.
—PAUL COELHO

The man who complains about the way
the ball bounces is likely the one who dropped it.
— **KENT HILL**

> You'll never have any mental muscle if you
don't have any heavy stuff to pick up.
— **DIANE LANE**

> Turn your face to the sun and the
shadows fall behind you.
— **JAN GOLDSTEIN**

> Never ask the barber if you need a haircut.
— **WARREN BUFFETT**

> Be open to learning new lessons even if they
contradict the lessons you learned yesterday.
— **ELLEN DEGENERES**

QUOTABLE TWEETS

True wisdom has a curious way
of revealing to yourself
your own true ignorance.
@NEILTYSON (NEIL DEGRASSE TYSON)

Words of Wisdom

LIFE

Think of life as a terminal illness, because if you do, you will live it with joy and passion, as it ought to be lived.
—**ANANA QUINDLEN**

> "

There are only two ways to live your life. One is as though nothing is a miracle. The other is as though everything is a miracle.
—**ALBERT EINSTEIN**

> "

There are no regrets in life, just lessons.
—**JENNIFER ANISTON**

> "

If you're quiet, you're not living. You've got to be noisy and colorful and lively.
—**MEL BROOKS**

> "

The first step to getting the things you want out of life is this: Decide what you want.
—**BEN STEIN**

> "

Big changes in our lives are more or less a second chance.
—**HARRISON FORD**

You don't have to have been near death to know…
what living is all about—but maybe it helps.
—**LANCE ARMSTRONG**

❝

Life's a roller coaster, and you never know
when it's going to take a turn.
—**TY PENNINGTON**

❝

Life is a series of commas, not periods.
—**MATTHEW MCCONAUGHEY**

❝

Keep moving if you love life, and keep
your troubles well behind you.
—**JOHN MCCAIN**

❝

I don't make plans, because life is short and
unpredictable—much like the weather!
—**AL ROKER**

🐦 QUOTABLE TWEETS

Find a spot on Earth that is
comfortable for you.
Keep that spot clean physically
or in your mind. Think about the spot
when you are away.
@YOKOONO

TRUTH

Truth may be stranger than fiction, goes the old saw, but it is never as strange as lies.
—**JOHN HODGMAN**

"

The truth needs so little rehearsal.
—**BARBARA KINGSOLVER**

"

Delete the adjectives and [you'll] have the facts.
—**HARPER LEE**

"

Bad taste is simply saying the truth before it should be said.
—**MEL BROOKS**

"

If you tell the truth, you don't need a long memory.
—**JESSE VENTURA**

"

The pursuit of truth is like picking raspberries. You miss a lot if you approach it from only one angle.
—**RANDAL MARLIN**

"

Lying makes a problem part of the future; truth makes a problem part of the past.
—**RICK PITINO**

KINDNESS

Do your little bit of good where you are; it is those little bits of good put together that overwhelm the world.
—**DESMOND TUTU**

>

You cannot do a kindness too soon, for you never know how soon it will be too late.
—**RALPH WALDO EMERSON**

>

A little kindness from person to person is better than a vast love for all humankind.
—**RICHARD DEHMEL**

QUOTABLE TWEETS

Every mental event has a neural correlate. Through mindfulness we can rewire the brain for peace, harmony, laughter, and love.
@DEEPAKCHOPRA

THE PERFECT WORDS FOR
PEP TALKS

It's a shallow life that doesn't give a person a few scars.
—GARRISON KEILLOR

"

If you are not criticized, you may not be doing much.
—DONALD RUMSFELD

"

He who limps is still walking.
—STANISLAW LEC

"

He who cannot forgive others destroys the bridge over which he himself must pass.
—GEORGE HERBERT

"

What does not kill him, makes him stronger.
—FRIEDRICH NIETZSCHE

"

Write injuries in sand, kindnesses in marble.
—FRENCH PROVERB

"

If we were born knowing everything, what would we do with all this time on this earth?
—NELLY

WORDS TO SHARE

We are a social species. Not only do we have thousands of words to use in conversation, we also have many to describe the very act of conversing. So the next time you're confabulating,[1] try out some of these words on your interlocutor.[2] For quiz answers, turn the page.

1. gainsay *v.*—A: repeat. B: add, as an afterthought. C: deny.

2. badinage (bad-uh-'nazh) *n.*—A: swearwords. B: playful back-and-forth. C: stern warning.

3. taciturn ('tass-uh-turn) *adj.*—A: chatty. B: quiet. C: afflicted with a lisp.

4. wheedle ('wee-dull) *v.*—A: tease. B: speak breathily. C: persuade with flattery.

5. loquacious (low-'kway-shus) *adj.*—A: quick to agree. B: talkative. C: to the point.

6. wag *n.*—A: unfair debater. B: joker. C: short digression.

7. polemic (puh-'lem-ick) *n.*—A: opinionated attack. B: off-the-cuff remark. C: awkward pause.

8. schmooze ('shmooz) *v.*—A: contradict oneself. B: chat. C: mispronounce.

9. maunder ('mawn-dur or 'mahn-) *v.*—A: ramble. B: squabble. C: gurgle.

10. rodomontade (rod-uh-mun-'tayd or -'tahd) *n.*—A: circular argument. B: talking while walking. C: bragging.

11. repartee (rep-ur-'tee or -ar-'tay) *n.*—A: verbal habit, as "like" and "you know." B: witty reply. C: rhetorical question.

12. bombastic (bahm-'bass-tick) *adj.*—A: shocking. B: pompous. C: given to interrupting.

13. prevaricate (prih-'var-uh-kate) *v.*—A: scream. B: emphasize. C: tell a half-truth.

14. colloquy ('coll-uh-kwee) *n.*—A: dialogue. B: slang usage. C: translation.

15. fustian ('fuss-chun) *adj.*—A: obscure. B: high-flown. C: mumbled.

16. tête-à-tête (tet-uh-'tet) *n.*—A: comeback. B: roundtable. C: private conversation.

17. insinuate (in-'sin-yoo-ate or -ya-wayt) *v.*—A: make hand gestures. B: embellish. C: artfully suggest.

1. chatting   2. participant in a dialogue

"Words to Share" Answers

1. gainsay—[C] deny. It cannot be *gainsaid* that the sign maker who spelled "Exit" wrong is an idiot.

2. badinage—[B] playful back-and-forth. The team's locker-room *badinage* is not for the squeamish.

3. taciturn—[B] quiet. The only *taciturn* member of a large and boisterous family, Mavis grew up to become a psychotherapist.

4. wheedle—[C] persuade with flattery. The saleswoman *wheedled* me into buying this dress.

5. loquacious—[B] talkative. My *loquacious* seatmate bent my ear all the way from LaGuardia to LAX.

6. wag—[B] joker. Ever the *wag*, Mike stood in the receiving line clutching a joy buzzer.

7. polemic—[A] opinionated attack. The meeting was interrupted by Jay's *polemic* against the copying machine.

8. schmooze—[B] chat. He doesn't know the difference between a driver and a putter—he just likes *schmoozing* at the country club.

9. maunder—[A] ramble. We listened to Uncle Horace's *maundering* stories, one right after another.

10. rodomontade—[C] bragging. The actress's Oscar acceptance speech came off as 45 seconds of unabashed *rodomontade*.

11. repartee—[B] witty reply. When Curly asked, "What's that monkey got that I ain't got?" Moe's *repartee* was "A longer tail."

12. bombastic—[B] pompous. The club president's speech would have seemed less *bombastic* without Tchaikovsky's "1812 Overture" playing in the background.

13. prevaricate—[C] tell a half-truth. When asked if he'd broken the window, the Little Leaguer *prevaricated*, claiming that as a southpaw, his aim couldn't have been that good.

14. colloquy—[A] dialogue. The professors' highbrow *colloquy* quickly turned into a slugfest.

15. fustian—[B] high-flown. The candidate's *fustian* oratory barely disguised his poor grasp of the issue.

16. tête-à-tête—[C] private conversation. After a quick *tête-à-tête* with his attorney, the defendant decided to change his plea.

17. insinuate—[C] artfully suggest. When my friends chipped in for my birthday present—a gift certificate for a housecleaning service—I had to wonder what they were *insinuating*.

SMARTY PANTS

Are you smarter than a 12th grader? We've been saving up these words—from the *Princeton Review's Word Smart: Genius Edition* test-prep guide—for our most confident quiz takers. Turn the page for answers.

1. **umbrage** ('um-brij) *n.*—
A: resentment. B: bright sunshine. C: utter confusion.

2. **sobriquet** ('soh-brih-kay) *n.*—
A: nickname. B: tight bandage. C: barbecue coal.

3. **feckless** ('fek-les) *adj.*—
A: bold and daring. B: of clear complexion. C: weak and ineffective.

4. **bailiwick** ('bay-lih-wik) *n.*—
A: special domain. B: holiday candle. C: dugout canoe.

5. **onus** ('oh-nus) *n.*—
A: proof of residency or status. B: burden. C: unique entity.

6. **ductile** ('duk-tuhl) *adj.*—
A: of plumbing. B: easily shaped or influenced. C: hard to locate or define.

7. **troglodyte** ('trah-glih-diyt) *n.*—
A: cave dweller or reclusive person. B: bird of prey. C: know-it-all.

8. **paean** ('pee-in) *n.*—
A: fervent prayer. B: lowly worker. C: song of praise.

9. **sangfroid** ('sahn-fwah) *n.*—
A: snooty attitude. B: coolness under pressure. C: French chef.

10. **redoubtable** (rih-'dau-te-bul) *adj.*—A: open to debate. B: famous. C: formidable.

11. **imprecate** ('im-prih-kayt) *v.*—
A: accuse. B: curse. C: pester or distract.

12. **modicum** ('mah-dih-kum) *n.*—
A: small portion. B: middle path. C: daily dosage.

13. **somnambulist** (sahm-'nam-byeh-list) *n.*—A: sleepwalker. B: hypnotizer. C: historian.

14. **restive** ('res-tiv) *adj.*—
A: comfortable. B: left over. C: fidgety.

15. **anomie** ('a-neh-mee) *n.*—
A: arch foe. B: mutual attraction. C: social instability.

Words of Wisdom

"Smarty Pants" Answers

1. umbrage—[A] resentment. Why did your team take such *umbrage* at being called the underdogs?

2. sobriquet—[A] nickname. Say, Paul, how did you get the *sobriquet* Grumpy?

3. feckless—[C] weak and ineffective. In formal debate, "Oh, yeah?" is a rather *feckless* rebuttal.

4. bailiwick—[A] special domain. "Ask me anything about grammar," the curmudgeonly copy editor said. "That's my *bailiwick*."

5. onus—[B] burden. "The *onus*," Mr. Peterson barked, "is on your boys to fix my broken window."

6. ductile—[B] easily shaped or influenced. Decisive? No. Tara's opinions are sometimes as *ductile* as Play-Doh.

7. troglodyte—[A] cave dweller or reclusive person. I wouldn't go so far as to call Jerry a *troglodyte*, but he's definitely on the shy side.

8. paean—[C] song of praise. Let us raise a toast and a rousing *paean* to Jay and Cathy's wedding!

9. sangfroid—[B] coolness under pressure. With unrelenting *sangfroid*, Andrea remained a pro at the poker table despite the high stakes.

10. redoubtable—[C] formidable. The pitcher shuddered as the *redoubtable* Albert Pujols strode to the plate.

11. imprecate—[B] curse. Before being banished, the witch ominously threatened to *imprecate* the town for five generations.

12. modicum—[A] small portion. All I ask is a *modicum* of cooperation with the housework.

13. somnambulist—[A] sleepwalker. For a *somnambulist*, Lady Macbeth is rather talkative.

14. restive—[C] fidgety. Peter got so *restive* during the SAT, he chewed his pencil almost to the lead.

15. anomie—[C] social instability. Apparently there's too much *anomie* in Congress for the bill to be passed.

A STROKE OF ...

Genius originally meant "guardian spirit," from the Latin *gignere* ("to beget, to produce"), and dates back to at least 1393. It's related to the words *genus, gender, generation*, and even *kin*—all suggestive of birth. The modern meaning, of a person endowed with a natural ability or talent, comes from Milton's *Iconoclastes* (1649).

ALL IN THE MIND

Don your thinking cap for this quiz on words about all matters cerebral. Feeling the brain strain? Turn the page for answers.

1. ken ('ken) *n.*—A: hunch. B: attention span. C: range of knowledge.

2. abstruse (ab-'stroos) *adj.*—A: scatterbrained. B: hard to comprehend. C: obvious to anyone.

3. cogent ('koh-jent) *adj.*—A: from a man's perspective. B: convincing. C: of two minds.

4. construe (kon-'strew) *v.*—A: interpret. B: baffle. C: refuse to believe.

5. erudition (er-uh-'di-shun) *n.*—A: clear speech. B: extensive learning through books. C: loss of memory.

6. nescient ('neh-shee- or 'neeh-see-unt) *adj.*—A: showing good judgment. B: having foresight. C: lacking knowledge.

7. sagacious (se-'gay-shus) *adj.*—A: beyond belief. B: showing insight. C: mentally stimulating.

8. métier ('me-tyay) *adj.*—A: measure of intelligence. B: doubt. C: area of expertise.

9. recondite ('re-kon- or ri-'kahn-diyt) *adj.*—A: triggering a memory. B: skeptical. C: deep or obscure.

10. untenable (un-'te-ne-bul) *adj.*—A: impossible to defend. B: not open to question. C: obtuse.

11. autodidact (aw-toh-'diy-dakt or '-dakt) *n.*—A: demanding teacher. B: complete thought. C: self-taught person.

12. empirical (im-'peer-ih-kul) *adj.*—A: all-knowing. B: widely accepted. C: from experience rather than theory.

13. polymath ('pah-lee-math) *n.*—A: teacher. B: person of great and varied learning. C: numerical puzzle.

14. cogitate ('kah-je-tayt) *v.*—A: think deeply. B: become confused. C: take a guess.

15. pundit ('pun-dit) *n.*—A: humorist. B: pupil. C: critic or airer of opinions.

Words of Wisdom

"All in the Mind" Answers

1. ken—[C] range of knowledge. Sorry, but the care and feeding of anything with eight legs is a little outside my *ken*.

2. abstruse—[B] hard to comprehend. Do you find the rules of British cricket a bit *abstruse*?

3. cogent—[B] convincing. Alice did not consider the Mad Hatter's reasoning to be all that *cogent*.

4. construe—[A] interpret. It's hard to *construe* a politician's real meaning through all the bluster.

5. erudition—[B] extensive learning through books. Despite her *erudition*, Jen was prone to commonsense blunders in her love life.

6. nescient—[C] lacking knowledge. "How can you offer the contract to that *nescient* neophyte?" Dan whined.

7. sagacious—[B] showing insight. Winning Fay's heart by reciting Persian poetry was Joe's *sagacious* plan.

8. métier—[C] area of expertise. Etiquette was Emily's purported *métier*, but it certainly didn't show at the state dinner last night.

9. recondite—[C] deep or obscure. Nothing, Jimmy's mom joked, is as *recondite* as the password for her son's tree house.

10. untenable—[A] impossible to defend. The row of dug-up flower beds put Andy's new puppy in a most *untenable* position.

11. autodidact—[C] self-taught person. In the field of foot-in-mouth, unfortunately, I'm an *autodidact*.

12. empirical—[C] from experience rather than theory. Jill has *empirical* evidence that microwaving a plate full of marshmallows is not a wise idea.

13. polymath—[B] person of great and varied learning. A true *polymath*, Randi was acing every question on *Jeopardy*!

14. cogitate—[A] think deeply. "To solve this case, Watson," said Sherlock Holmes, "one must *cogitate* over a pipeful of tobacco."

15. pundit—[C] critic or airer of opinions. I'm getting swamped by all the talking-head *pundits* on TV.

SOLID FOUNDATION

They say a good vocabulary is the foundation of learning. Master these terms related to architecture and construction, and you will build yourself a fine edifice. Answers on next page.

1. raze ('rayz) *v.*—A: build up. B: dig a foundation. C: tear down.

2. dexterous ('dek-ster-us) *adj.*—A: skillful. B: left-handed. C: turned clockwise.

3. jury-rig ('jur-ee-rig) *v.*—A: set up permanently. B: construct in a makeshift fashion. C: glaze.

4. stud ('stuhd) *n.*—A: slang for a good carpenter. B: leveling bar. C: upright post.

5. on spec (on 'spek) *adv.*—A: using blueprints. B: without a contract. C: ahead of schedule.

6. garret ('gar-it) *n.*—A: attic room. B: pantry or extra kitchen room. C: basement room.

7. annex ('a-neks) *n.*—A: supplementary structure. B: underground dwelling. C: foundation.

8. wainscot ('wayn-skoht) *n.*—A: intricate plasterwork. B: scaffolding. C: paneled part of a wall.

9. rotunda (roh-'tun-duh) *n.*—A: central column. B: circular room. C: revolving door.

10. plumb ('plum) *adj.*—A: not linked, as pipes. B: past its prime. C: vertical.

11. aviary ('ay-vee-ehr-ee) *n.*—A: house for birds. B: airport terminal. C: open lobby.

12. corrugated ('kor-eh-gayt-ed) *adj.*—A: with closed doors. B: rusted. C: having a wavy surface.

13. mezzanine ('meh-zeh-neen) *n.*—A: lowest balcony floor. B: domed ceiling. C: marble counter.

14. cornice ('kor-nes) *n.*—A: meeting of two walls. B: decorative top edge. C: steeple or spire.

15. vestibule ('ves-teh-buyl) *n.*—A: dressing room. B: lobby. C: staircase.

Words of Wisdom

"Solid Foundation" Answers

1. **raze**—[C] tear down. I hear they're going to *raze* the mall and build a greenhouse.

2. **dexterous**—[A] skillful. Charlotte spun her web with amazingly *dexterous* eight-handedness.

3. **jury-rig**—[B] construct in a makeshift fashion. The contractors were let go after they *jury-rigged* our home's first floor.

4. **stud**—[C] upright post. Don't start hammering the wall until you locate a *stud* behind it.

5. **on spec**—[B] without a contract. Dad is building the girls' dollhouse *on spec*.

6. **garret**—[A] attic room. I'm not fancy—a cozy *garret* is all I need to finish the novel.

7. **annex**—[A] supplementary structure. The children's *annex* was a welcome addition to the library.

8. **wainscot**—[C] paneled part of a wall. Marge's kids have treated the entire *wainscot* as an experimental crayon mural.

9. **rotunda**—[B] circular room. The conflicting blueprints for the *rotunda* have me going in circles!

10. **plumb**—[C] vertical. Our fixer-upper may need new floors, doors, and windows, but at least the walls are *plumb*.

11. **aviary**—[A] house for birds. "Your cat hasn't taken his eyes off that *aviary*," Sheryl noted.

12. **corrugated**—[C] having a wavy surface. All we have for a roof is a sheet of *corrugated* tin.

13. **mezzanine**—[A] lowest balcony floor. Sadly, our $165 seats in the *mezzanine* had an obstructed view.

14. **cornice**—[B] decorative top edge. You're going to need one heck of an extension ladder to reach that *cornice*.

15. **vestibule**—[B] lobby. Anxiety peaking, Claire waited over an hour in the *vestibule* for her interview.

GARDEN VARIETY

A *trellis* is a structure of crisscross slats on which vines or flowers may climb. An *espalier* is a trellis often set against a flat wall. An *arbor* makes an arch of that trellis, and a *pergola* puts the trellis above a frame made of posts. If the structure's roof is solid instead, you have a *gazebo*. And if the gazebo is high on a hill, it may be called a *belvedere* (Italian for "beautiful view").

SOLAR POWERED

The sun has long played a role in our celebrations, so we pay homage as the sun days cycle through the year. See next page for answers.

1. pantheism *n.*—A: crossing of social boundaries. B: burying of the dead. C: belief that God and the universe are identical.

2. propitiate *v.*—A: honor. B: appease. C: revive.

3. celestial *adj.*—A: ghostlike. B: fleeting. C: relating to the heavens.

4. ascension *n.*—act of …A: rising. B: offering. C: deferring.

5. perigee *n.*—A: layer of an atmosphere. B: point where an orbiting object is nearest to the earth. C: shift of seasons.

6. divination *n.*—A: split of harvest. B: immortality. C: supernatural insight into the future.

7. druid *n.*—A: Celtic priest. B: astrological society. C: blind follower.

8. hallowed *adj.*—A: mystical. B: respected. C: untouchable.

9. renascent *adj.*—A: warming. B: of the heart. C: rising again.

10. saltation *n.*—A: leaping or dancing. B: elaborate greeting. C: deep sleep.

11. declination *n.*—A: end of a season. B: diminished daylight. C: distance of a heavenly body from a point on the same plane as the earth's equator.

12. exuberate *v.*—A: plan precisely. B: eat with gusto. C: overflow.

13. bacchanal *n.*—A: wild, drunken revelry. B: monk's garment. C: inscription.

14. cache *n.*—A: storage place. B: prestige. C: awkward position.

15. synodic *adj.*—relating to … A: ancient writings. B: family bonds. C: alignment of stars and planets.

16. quondam *adj.*—A: formal. B: former. C: penitent.

Words of Wisdom

"Solar Powered" Answers

1. pantheism—[C] belief that God and the universe are identical. *Pantheism* demands a deep connection to nature.

2. propitiate—[B] appease. The villagers offered bushels of grain to *propitiate* the gods.

3. celestial—[C] relating to the heavens. The sparkling stars accentuated the evening's celestial majesty.

4. ascension—[A] act of rising. The morning crowd marveled at the sun's *ascension*.

5. perigee—[B] point where an orbiting object is nearest to the earth. With the moon at its *perigee*, the night sky was awash in light.

6. divination—[C] supernatural insight into the future. Lela's powers of *divination* proved eerily accurate.

7. druid—[A] Celtic priest. Mist swirled as the *druids* gathered near Stonehenge at daybreak.

8. hallowed—[B] respected. During the ceremony, even the wildest children quieted near the *hallowed* burial grounds.

9. renascent—[C] rising again. Every year, we suffer through a gray and bitter winter, eager for spring and its *renascent* light and warmth.

10. saltation— [A] leaping or dancing. Celebrants in the throes of *saltation* were silhouetted against the bonfire.

11. declination—[C] distance of a heavenly body from a point on the same plane as the earth's equator. Tiberius used astronomy and *declination* values for navigation.

12. exuberate—[C] overflow. Vegetables *exuberated* from storage cellars after the harvest.

13. bacchanal—[A] wild, drunken revelry. The streets were thronged as prayer gave way to *bacchanal*.

14. cache—[A] storage place. The townspeople stocked *caches* with grain in anticipation of a long winter.

15. synodic—[C] relating to alignment of stars and planets. Early calendars were based on the moon's *synodic* cycle.

16. quondam—[B] former. Spying her *quondam* beau at the party, she felt relieved that he was in her past.

USE YOUR WORDS

SHARP TALKER

You already know that staying in shape is a key to good health. But just as important: keeping your vocabulary finely tuned and toned. Try this quiz—about shapes of the literal sort—then hit the next page for answers.

1. gangling ('gan-gling) *adj.*—A: loose and lanky. B: bulging with muscles. C: short in stature.

2. helix ('hee-liks) *n.*—A: pointed tip. B: warped outline. C: spiral.

3. deltoid ('del-toyd) *adj.*—A: triangular. B: circular. C: squared off.

4. trefoil ('tree-foyl) *adj.*—A: pliable. B: having a three-leaf design. C: tapering narrowly.

5. conical ('kah-nih-kul) *adj.*—A: like an igloo. B: like a cone. C: like a tunnel.

6. pentacle ('pen-tih-kul) *n.*—A: star. B: crescent moon. C: square.

7. elliptical (ih-'lip-tih-kul) *adj.*—A: slanted. B: embossed. C: oval.

8. sigmoid ('sig-moyd) *adj.*—A: crossed like an X. B: curved like a C or an S. C: bent like an L.

9. whorl ('hworl) *n.*—A: well-rounded muscle. B: flat surface. C: circular pattern.

10. serrated ('seh-rayt-ed) *adj.*—A: interconnected, as with circles or rings. B: elongated. C: having notched edges.

11. cordate ('kor-dayt) *adj.*—A: stringlike. B: heart shaped. C: free-form.

12. svelte ('svelt) *adj.*—A: undulating. B: lean. C: in a checked or repeating pattern.

13. zaftig ('zaf-tig) *adj.*—A: pleasingly plump. B: moldable, like putty. C: seedlike, as in an avocado or a peach.

14. lozenge ('lah-zunj) *n.*—A: 90-degree angle. B: level used in architectural design. C: diamond.

15. ramify ('ra-meh-fiy) *v.*—A: become solid, as cement. B: jut out. C: split into branches or parts.

Words of Wisdom

"Sharp Talker" Answers

1. gangling—[A] loose and lanky. The protagonist of "The Legend of Sleepy Hollow" was the *gangling* pedagogue.

2. helix—[C] spiral. Judy is a DNA researcher, so she's getting a tattoo of a double *helix*.

3. deltoid—[A] triangular. The pyramids' architects obviously knew a thing or two about the stability of *deltoid* structures.

4. trefoil—[B] having a three-leaf design. The gardening club uses a *trefoil* symbol—a gilded clover—as its logo.

5. conical—[B] like a cone. My favorite *conical* item? Why, the ice-cream cone, of course, topped preferably with three scoops of chocolate.

6. pentacle—[A] star. Hey, this tarot deck is missing all the cards with *pentacles*!

7. elliptical—[C] oval. Just two times around the *elliptical* running track, and Rebecca was wiped out.

8. sigmoid—[B] curved like a C or an S. On Superman's chest sits a single scarlet *sigmoid* symbol.

9. whorl—[C] circular pattern. To find the treasure, take 50 paces east from the tree with the *whorl* in its trunk.

10. serrated—[C] having notched edges. "I'm not sure that old *serrated* knife is best for carving the turkey," Dad advised.

11. cordate—[B] heart shaped. Sarah is baking *cordate* cookies for her cardiologist boyfriend.

12. svelte—[B] lean. The holidays pose a serious challenge to my *svelte* frame!

13. zaftig—[A] pleasingly plump. Known for her *zaftig* figure, Caroline was a surprising choice for the fashion magazine's debut cover.

14. lozenge—[C] diamond. The boys dug up the grass to create a makeshift *lozenge* so they could play ball.

15. ramify—[C] split into branches or parts. "We need to *ramify* this department to keep productivity high!" Kerrie emphasized at yesterday's staff meeting.

WHAT'S THE ANGLE?

In geometry, you find various shapes called *polygons*, from the Greek *poly-* for "many" plus *gonia* for "angle." Hence, a pentagon has five angles (and sides), a hexagon has six, a heptagon has seven, an octagon has eight, and so on.

CHARACTER

If you don't have enemies, you don't have character.
—PAUL NEWMAN

Character—the willingness to accept responsibility for one's own life—is the source from which self-respect springs.
—JOAN DIDION

Great acting is being able to create a character. Great character is being able to be yourself.
—JOHN LEGUIZAMO

You grow up the day you have your first real laugh—at yourself.
—ETHEL BARRYMORE

Tension is who you think you should be. Relaxation is who you are.
—CHINESE PROVERB

The greatest conflicts are not between two people but between one person and himself.
—GARTH BROOKS

THE PERFECT WORDS TO
KEEP CALM & CARRY ON

God, grant me the serenity to accept the things I cannot change, the courage to change the things I can, and the wisdom to know the difference.
—**REINHOLD NIEBUHR**

"

The quieter you become, the more you can hear.
—**RAM DASS**

"

Be master of mind rather than mastered by mind.
—**ZEN PROVERB**

"

A crust eaten in peace is better than a banquet partaken in anxiety.
—**AESOP**

"

Take a deep breath and don't take any of it too seriously.
—**CHER**

"

Your mind will answer most questions if you learn to relax and wait for the answer.
—**WILLIAM S. BURROUGHS**

Nothing is permanent in this wicked world.
Not even our troubles.
—**CHARLIE CHAPLIN**

"

Slow down and everything you are chasing
will come around and catch you.
—**JOHN DE PAOLA**

"

I took a deep breath and listened to the
old bray of my heart. I am. I am. I am.
—**SYLVIA PLATH**

"

We shall not flag nor fail.
We shall go on to the end.
—**WINSTON CHURCHILL**

"

Serenity now!
—**FRANK COSTANZA (ON *SEINFELD*)**

Sitting quietly, doing nothing, spring comes, and the grass grows by itself.
—*ZENRIN*

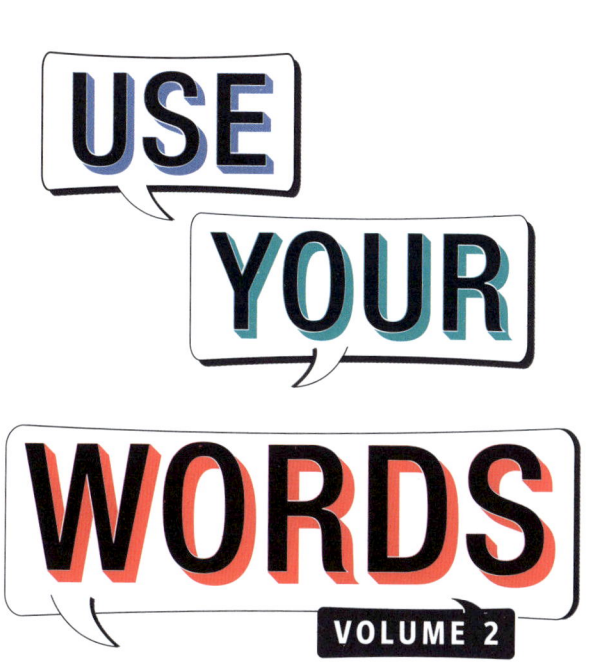

USE YOUR WORDS

VOLUME 2

CONTENTS

Introduction
vi

Working for a Living
1

This Land Is Our Land
27

Better with Age
55

Love Wins
81

Modern Family
107

Live It Up!
133

Belly Laughs
159

Wit & Wisdom
185

> The mind is not a vessel
> that needs filling
> but wood that needs igniting.
>
> **—PLUTARCH**

We know our readers love words—both learning new ways to express themselves and challenging their minds while learning the meaning of new words. In fact, we had such a positive response to *Use Your Words*—our very own hybrid of your favorite features, *Quotable Quotes* and *Word Power*—that we are pleased to offer another volume and another chance for readers to sharpen their word skills and wax poetic at social gatherings.

We've searched through the archives to find fresh new coinages from the movers, shakers, and influencers of today, as well as some long-forgotten words of wisdom from the past that never get stale. In this eclectic mix of quotes from voices old and new, young and old, conservative and progressive, we think we've found lots of gems for every occasion. Whether you're looking for the right words to congratulate someone on a work promotion, express your deep gratitude to a loyal friend, need to give voice to something painful that needs release, or just want to break the ice with a witty remark, you'll find the perfect *Quotable Quote* in these pages.

And while you'll look pretty smart quoting Cicero or Eleanor Roosevelt, you'll be even more impressive when your vocabulary matches the winners of the Scripps National Spelling Bee as highlighted in our selection of *Word Power* quizzes.

We've enjoyed curating these selections for you, and we hope you'll share your newfound knowledge with friends, family, coworkers, and acquaintances, and use your words to cheer, calm, teach, and inspire.

The Editors of *Reader's Digest*

> There's nothing you've ever been successful at that you didn't work on every day.
> —WILL SMITH

WORKING FOR A LIVING

We all have the capacity to forge our own futures and create our own success in life, but it never hurts to hear some sage advice from those who have paved the way for us.

SUCCESS

You cannot be really first-rate at your work
if your work is all you are.
—ANNA QUINDLEN

"

Inside of a ring or out, ain't nothing wrong with
going down. It's staying down that's wrong.
—MUHAMMAD ALI

"

There is no downside to winning.
It feels forever fabulous.
—PAT CONROY

"

The person who knows "how" will always have a job.
The person who knows "why" will always be his boss.
—DIANE RAVITCH

"

QUOTABLE TWEETS

Wow @serenawilliams plays so well,
so proud, but proud win lose or draw.
@VENUSESWILLIAMS

WORK FOR IT

When you're brought into this life,
you're given certain gifts,
and you have to use them.
—JANE GOODALL

"

If your ship doesn't come in, swim out to it.
—JONATHAN WINTERS

"

Doing anything less than something amazing
is squandering this whole reason that you're here.
—BRANDON STANTON

"

Thankfully, perseverance
is a great substitute for talent.
—STEVE MARTIN

"

A year from now you'll wish
you had started today.
—ANONYMOUS

Working for a Living

FAILURE

The best of us must sometimes eat our words.
—J.K. ROWLING

"

Be bold. If you're going to make an error, make a doozy.
—BILLIE JEAN KING

"

An inventor fails 999 times,
and if he succeeds once, he's in.
He treats his failures simply as practice shots.
—CHARLES KETTERING

"

Failure is just another way to learn
how to do something right.
—MARIAN WRIGHT EDELMAN

"

Failure is God's way of saying, "Excuse me,
you're moving in the wrong direction."
—OPRAH

"

Winning may not be everything,
but losing has little to recommend it.
—DIANNE FEINSTEIN

TALENT

Whoever said "It's not whether you win or lose that counts" probably lost.
—**MARTINA NAVRATILOVA**

"

Second place is just the first place loser.
—**DALE EARNHARDT**

"

I've missed more than 9,000 shots.
I've lost almost 300 games. I've failed over and over again in my life. And that is why I succeed.
—**MICHAEL JORDAN**

"

Genius is immediate, but talent takes time.
—**JANET FLANNER**

"

Talent is only a starting point.
—**IRVING BERLIN**

"

I want to thank my parents
for somehow raising me to have confidence that is disproportionate with my looks and abilities.
–**TINA FEY**

Working for a Living

Some are born great, some achieve greatness, and some hire PR officers.
—**DANIEL J. BOORSTIN**

"

Just because someone has fancy sneakers doesn't mean they can run faster.
—**JON BON JOVI**

"

You have to be first, different, or great. If you're one of them, you may make it.
—**LORETTA LYNN**

"

Persistence trumps talent and looks every time.
—**AARON BROWN**

"

A peacock that rests on his feathers is just another turkey.
—**DOLLY PARTON**

"

QUOTABLE TWEETS

The world is our office.
@KANYEWEST

PRACTICE

If you don't keep pushing the limits, you wake up one day and you're the "center square to block."
—**ROBIN WILLIAMS**

"

The talk you hear about adapting to change is not only stupid, it's dangerous. The only way you can manage change is to create it.
—**PETER DRUCKER**

"

Assume any career moves you make won't go smoothly.
They won't. But don't look back.
—**ANDY GROVE**

"

I don't know if I practiced more than anybody, but I sure practiced enough. I still wonder if somebody—somewhere—was practicing more than me.
—**LARRY BIRD**

THE PERFECT WORDS FOR
ENCOURAGEMENT

You never conquer a mountain. You stand on the summit a few moments; then the wind blows your footprints away.
—ARLENE BLUM

"

Success and failure. We think of them as opposites, but they're really not. They're companions—the hero and the sidekick.
—LAURENCE SHAMES

"

Success covers a multitude of blunders.
—GEORGE BERNARD SHAW

"

Failure is the condiment that gives success its flavor.
—TRUMAN CAPOTE

"

It takes as much courage to have tried and failed as it does to have tried and succeeded.
—ANNE MORROW LINDBERGH

"

Failure is an event, never a person.
—WILLIAM D. BROWN

MORNING PAPERS

Ever since 15th-century German printer Johannes Gutenberg invented the printing press and ushered in the era of the modern newspaper, the medium has been a part of everyday life. Today millions start their mornings poring over the papers. From the strange to the straightforward, newspaper names from around the world form this month's quiz. For answers, turn the page.

1. chronicle *n.*—A: daily ritual. B: widely held belief. C: account of events.

2. repository *n.*—A: paper shredder. B: medication-delivery device. C: container used for storage.

3. clarion *adj.*—A: high-pitched. B: partially obscured. C: loud and clear.

4. epitaph *n.*—A: editorial. B: clever headline. C: tombstone inscription.

5. ledger *n.*—A: accounting book. B: illustration. C: address book.

6. excelsior *adj.*—A: ever faithful. B: ever upward. C: ever changing.

7. flume *n.*—A: seabird with a wingspan four times its body length. B: narrow gorge with a stream running through it. C: warm summer wind.

8. Whig *n.*—A: staunch conservative. B: member of historical British political party. C: news editor appointed by the queen.

9. derrick *n.*—A: serif font. B: woody tropical plant. C: framework over an oil well.

10. gleaner *n.*—someone who...A: makes predictions. B: gathers information. C: classifies data.

11. dominion *n.*—A: control. B: large group of people. C: wisdom.

12. delta *n.*—A: high-altitude plain. B: triangular object. C: appointed officer.

13. laconic *adj.*—A: concise. B: weekly. C: circular.

14. hub *n.*—A: last-minute assignment. B: center of activity. C: funny caption.

DEEP ROOTS

Cyberspeak, geekspeak, California speak—we all indulge in jargon. The combining form -speak originated with *Newspeak*, the propagandistic language designed to "diminish the range of thought," in George Orwell's *1984*.

Working for a Living

"Morning Papers" Answers

1. chronicle—[C] account of events. Tom's election *chronicle* included an hourly time line.

2. repository—[C] container used for storage. Donnie kept photos of the house's history in a wooden *repository*.

3. clarion—[C] loud and clear. The pollution exposé was a *clarion* call to recycle.

4. epitaph—[C] tombstone inscription. Jed's *epitaph* made the mourners cry even more.

5. ledger—[A] accounting book. The auditor recorded the baker's expenses in his *ledger*.

6. excelsior—[B] ever upward. Climbing Mount Everest for an exclusive interview, Debbie exclaimed, "*Excelsior!*" to urge herself on.

7. flume—[B] narrow gorge with a stream running through it. Dejected, Doris watched the water rush down the *flume* and considered tossing in her failed first draft.

8. Whig—[B] member of historical British political party. His right-wing friends often joked that liberal-leaning John would have made a great *Whig*.

9. derrick—[C] framework over an oil well. Sunlight on the *derrick* cast a fitting shadow over the oil town.

10. gleaner—[B] someone who gathers information. A natural *gleaner* of racy details, Jane was the perfect choice for editor of the new gossip blog.

11. dominion—[A] control. As owner of both the newspaper and the bank, Morgan held the town under his *dominion*.

12. delta—[B] triangular object. The group of friends would often gather in secret at the sandy *delta* where the river splits.

13. laconic—[A] concise. *Laconic* yet creative: That was Colin's MO when he sat down to write captions.

14. hub—[B] center of activity. After sundown, the beach town's lone restaurant became the *hub* for tourists and locals alike.

BUILDING BLOCKS

Do you know your adze from your auger? And what exactly is a grommet? Sharpen your verbal edge by mastering these words related to construction and tools, then check the shed—or the next page—for answers.

1. serrated ('seh-ray-ted) *adj.*—A: primed for painting. B: toothed like a saw. C: waterproof.

2. vise (viys) *n.*—A: clamp that holds an object in place. B: mechanism to lift a car. C: flaw in building materials.

3. adze (adz) *n.*—A: ax-like tool with a curved blade. B: small rubber mallet. C: piece of scrap wood.

4. flanged (flanjd) *adj.*—A: sealed with wax. B: with a protruding rim. C: wound tightly.

5. torque (tork) *n.*—A: twisting force. B: mechanical failure. C: electrical current.

6. auger ('ah-ger) *n.*—A: master woodworker. B: spiral drill bit. C: sailor's knife.

7. dowel (dowl) *n.*—A: toilet plunger. B: peg. C: paint roller.

8. ferrule ('ferr-uhl) *n.*—A: beveled edge. B: tape measure. C: protective cap.

9. cambered ('kam-berd) *adj.*—A: encircled. B: arched. C: stained.

10. gauge (gayj) *n.*—A: deep groove. B: plumber's wrench. C: measuring instrument.

11. loupe (loop) *n.*—A: cutter. B: gripper. C: magnifier.

12. awl (all) *n.*—A: pointed tool for piercing holes. B: large wheelbarrow. C: system of pulleys.

13. casters ('kass-terz) *n.*—A: swiveling wheels. B: ball bearings. C: fishing reels.

14. grommet ('grah-meht) *n.*—A: ring that reinforces. B: copper pipe. C: gutter.

15. kludge (klooj) *n.*—A: blueprint. B: makeshift solution. C: tangled wire.

Working for a Living

"Building Blocks" Answers

1. serrated—[B] toothed like a saw. The fiery dragon's back was *serrated*, its claws razor-sharp.

2. vise—[A] clamp that holds an object in place. Before sanding the board, Louisa secured it in a *vise*.

3. adze—[A] ax-like tool with a curved blade. *Adzes* have been used to shape wood since the Stone Age.

4. flanged—[B] with a protruding rim. Bobby's model train has *flanged* wheels to keep it on the tracks.

5. torque—[A] twisting force. If you use the wrong *torque* setting on your drill, you could strip the screws.

6. auger—[B] spiral drill bit. To fish in the winter months, anglers use *augers* to bore holes in the ice.

7. dowel—[B] peg. Ethan decided to construct the birdhouse using wooden *dowels* instead of nails.

8. ferrule—[C] protective cap. Your hatchet's handle wouldn't have split if you'd braced it with a *ferrule*.

9. cambered—[B] arched. The highway is *cambered* in the middle to promote runoff of rain.

10. gauge—[C] measuring instrument. Christine used a homemade rain *gauge* to track the precipitation in her yard.

11. loupe—[C] magnifier. After examining the antique ring with his *loupe*, the appraiser determined the stone was glass.

12. awl—[A] pointed tool for piercing holes. Jerry used an *awl* to poke through the tough leather.

13. casters—[A] swiveling wheels. The heavy-duty *casters* on the dolly really helped make the move easier.

14. grommet—[A] ring that reinforces. Everything in Ashley's bathroom is pink, from the towels to the custom *grommets* she installed on the shower curtain.

15. kludge—[B] makeshift solution. I've patched together some of these cables; it's a bit of a *kludge*, but it just might work!

QUICK FIXES

What's the difference between *jury-rigged* and *jerry-built*? Not much—they both mean "hastily constructed." But *jury-rigged* suggests a clever makeshift, perhaps deriving from the Latin *adjutare* ("to aid") or the French *jour* ("day"), suggesting a short-term fix. *Jerry-built*, however, implies a shoddy job, though no one's quite sure who "Jerry" was.

STAYING CURRENT

The editors at Merriam-Webster added a whopping 850 words and definitions to the dictionary in 2018—including, appropriately, wordie ("lover of words"). Quiz yourself on these other newcomers, then look up the answers on the next page.

1. life hack ('life hak) *n.*—A: identity theft. B: short bio. C: clever tip.

2. chiweenie (chih-'wee-nee) *n.*—A: chewy noodle. B: Chihuahua/dachshund hybrid. C: crybaby.

3. demonym ('deh-muh-nim) *n.*—A: impish child. B: floor model. C: name for an inhabitant.

4. harissa (huh-'rih-suh) *n.*—A: spicy sauce. B: hair dye. C: brash woman.

5. cryptocurrency (krip-toh-'kuhr-en-see) *n.*—A: classified information. B: digital money. C: unpredictable events.

6. beach cruiser (beech 'croo-zer) *n.*—A: amateur surfer. B: bike with wide tires. C: migrating shorebird.

7. Wanderwort ('wahn-dur-wort) *n.*—A: daydreamer. B: tofu sausage. C: far-traveling word.

8. dumpster fire ('dump-ster fire) *n.*—A: total disaster. B: mass layoff. C: rumormonger.

9. poke (poh-'kay) *n.*—A: raw fish salad. B: online pest. C: rural town.

10. Silver Alert ('sil-ver uh-'lurt) *n.*—A: warning of a missing senior. B: notice of a price drop. C: ship's distress signal.

11. kombucha (kahm-'boo-chuh) *n.*—A: fermented tea. B: modular furniture. C: gorilla species.

12. mansplain ('man-splayn) *v.*—A: mooch off a friend. B: brag about money. C: explain condescendingly.

13. piloerection (py-loh-ih-'rek-shun) *n.*—A: demolished building. B: bristling of hairs. C: new website.

14. gastroplasty ('ga-stroh-pla-stee) *n.*—A: culinary customs. B: stomach surgery. C: horrible crime.

15. cotija (koh-'tee-hah) *n.*—A: hard Mexican cheese. B: ballroom dance. C: poisonous snake.

Working for a Living

"Staying Current" Answers

1. life hack [C] clever tip. Here's a simple *life hack:* Use dental floss to neatly slice up a cake.

2. chiweenie [B] Chihuahua/dachshund hybrid. My kids like Yorkie-poos, but I'm partial to *chiweenies.*

3. demonym [C] name for an inhabitant. As a Cleveland native, José prefers the *demonym* "Buckeye" over "Ohioan."

4. harissa [A] spicy sauce. After one bite of Marissa's lemon *harissa* chicken, my mouth was on fire.

5. cryptocurrency [B] digital money. I don't trust these *cryptocurrency* fads; I'd rather write a check than pay with Bitcoin.

6. beach cruiser [B] bike with wide tires. Did you hear that Bryce started a business renting *beach cruisers* to tourists?

7. Wanderwort [C] far-traveling word. The word *orange* is a classic *Wanderwort,* with roots in Sanskrit, Persian, and Arabic.

8. dumpster fire [A] total disaster. "Today was such a *dumpster fire*—I lost my wallet, I fought with my wife, and I got into a fender bender," Jess moaned.

9. poke [A] raw fish salad. With tzatziki, acai, and *poke* on this menu, I need a translator to order!

10. Silver Alert [A] warning of a missing senior. No need for a *Silver Alert;* we found Grandpa tinkering in the attic.

11. kombucha [A] fermented tea. The new health food store sells *kombucha* by the gallon.

12. mansplain [C] explain condescendingly. Ryan began to *mansplain* about film history to his date, even though she had a PhD in the subject.

13. piloerection [B] bristling of hairs. I dare you to read a Stephen King book without some serious *piloerection.*

14. gastroplasty [B] stomach surgery. "*Gastroplasty* can help some people lose weight, but it isn't right for everyone," cautioned Dr. Willis.

15. cotija [A] hard Mexican cheese. *Cotija* is often described as a cross between feta and Parmesan.

D'OH! GOOD ONE, HOMER

Also among Merriam-Webster's new words is *embiggen* ("to enlarge"). It was coined as a joke by the writers of *The Simpsons,* who had challenged themselves to invent two words that sounded real. The Springfield town motto is: "A noble spirit *embiggens* the smallest man." The other invented word was *cromulent* ("acceptable"), which has not had a life beyond the cartoon show—so far.

TAKE THE CHALLENGE

The challenge is on, Word Power fans! We canvassed the *Reader's Digest* editors for their favorite words, and they answered the call in top linguistic form. Are you game?
Answers on the next page.

1. antediluvian (an-tih-duh-'loo-vee-en) *adj.*—A: at dusk. B: nonalcoholic. C: developed a long time ago.

2. bamboozle (bam-'boo-zuhl) *v.*—A: get drunk. B: deceive. C: get quickly out of control.

3. blandish ('blan-dish) *v.*—A: coax with flattery. B: wave like a flag. C: tone down.

4. pellucid (puh-'loo-suhd) *adj.*—A: easy to understand. B: frozen solid. C: innocent of a crime.

5. debacle (dee-'bah-kuhl) *n.*—A: celebration. B: complete collapse. C: utter surprise.

6. blunderbuss ('bluhn-der-buhs) *n.*—A: sloppy kiss. B: careless person. C: pitfall.

7. onomatopoeia (ah-neh-mah-tuh-'pee-uh) *n.*—A: the use of words whose sound suggests the sense. B: repetition. C: speech impediment.

8. dreadnought ('dred-not) *n.*—A: braid of hair. B: medieval criminal. C: the largest of its kind.

9. spelunking (spe-'luhnk-ing) *n.*—A: racing on sleds. B: lifting weights. C: exploring caves.

10. sanguine ('san-gwen) *adj.*—A: confident. B: melodic. C: of or relating to the sun.

11. brouhaha ('brew-hah-hah) *n.*—A: group of witches. B: practical joke. C: uproar.

12. obfuscate ('ahb-fuh-skayt) *v.*—A: snatch away from. B: obscure. C: set on fire.

13. deride (dih-'riyd) *v.*—A: laugh at contemptuously. B: dismount. C: exterminate.

14. pusillanimous (pew-sih-'la-nuh-mus) *adj.*—A: catlike. B: odorous. C: cowardly.

15. detritus (dih-'triy-tuhs) *n.*—A: unpaid bills. B: debris. C: gap between two teeth.

Working for a Living

"Take the Challenge" Answers

1. antediluvian—[C] developed a long time ago. The cobbler used family-honored *antediluvian* methods to repair customers' shoes.

2. bamboozle—[B] deceive. Don't let the smooth car salesman *bamboozle* you.

3. blandish—[A] coax with flattery. Tom Sawyer could *blandish* his pals into painting a whole fence for him.

4. pellucid—[A] easy to understand. The physics professor had a knack for giving surprisingly *pellucid* lectures.

5. debacle—[B] complete collapse. The CFO took full responsibility for the tech company's financial *debacle*.

6. blunderbuss—[B] careless person. What kind of *blunderbuss* can't even remember to put the fire out before leaving camp?

7. onomatopoeia—[A] the use of words whose sound suggests the sense. With on-screen bursts like *kapow*, the original *Batman* TV series was famous for its use of *onomatopoeia*.

8. dreadnought—[C] the largest of its kind. That *dreadnought* of an SUV is a real gas hog.

9. spelunking—[C] exploring caves. Years of geology research led Andy to adopt *spelunking* as a favorite hobby.

10. sanguine—[A] confident. After studying the footprints, I am fairly *sanguine* that our cat is responsible for the mess in the kitchen.

11. brouhaha—[C] uproar. The ump's call at home plate led to quite a *brouhaha* with the Royals' catcher and manager.

12. obfuscate—[B] obscure. Could these instructions possibly *obfuscate* the desk's construction any further?

13. deride—[A] laugh at contemptuously. Know-it-all Alex *derided* his little sister for entering the spelling bee, but she got the last laugh after taking first place.

14. pusillanimous—[C] cowardly. Bert Lahr played the *pusillanimous* lion in *The Wizard of Oz*.

15. detritus—[B] debris. Vinnie photographed the *detritus* of the city streets for his abstract essay.

PRO AND CON

Pro and con don't just mean "for" and "against." That would be too easy, and English is anything but. Just to make things interesting (not to mention difficult for speakers native and new), as prefixes, pro sometimes means "before" and con often means "with." Here are some pros and cons that show there's no arguing with the sheer variety of the mother tongue. Answers on next page.

1. **protract** (pro-'trakt) *v.*—A: draw up a legal document. B: stick out. C: lengthen.

2. **contrite** (kun-'trite) *adj.*—A: boring. B: sorry for a wrong. C: twisted into strands, as rope.

3. **protuberant** (pro-'too-buh-rent) *adj.*—A: pointing upward. B: turned downward. C: bulging outward.

4. **consternation** (con-stur-'nay-shun) *n.*—A: inability to process sound. B: paralyzing dismay. C: puff of air.

5. **propinquity** (pro-'ping-kwuh-tee) *n.*—A: nearness in place or time. B: knowledge of all things. C: fussiness.

6. **consummate** ('con-suh-mutt) *adj.*—A: skilled. B: engrossing. C: born at the same time.

7. **profuse** (pruh-'fyoos) *adj.*—A: about to catch fire. B: easily agreeable. C: abundant.

8. **conflagration** (con-fluh-'gray-shun) *n.*—A: ceremonial banner folding. B: enormous fire. C: joining of rivers.

9. **prognosis** (prog-'no-sus) *n.*—A: nose job. B: state of half-sleep. C: forecast.

10. **convex** (con-'veks) *adj.*—A: curved inward. B: curved outward. C: broken in half.

11. **prostrate** ('pros-trate) *adj.*—A: lying at anchor. B: lying flat. C: lying through one's teeth.

12. **convivial** (kun-'viv-ee-ul) *adj.*—A: tangled. B: transparent. C: merry.

13. **probity** ('pro-buh-tee) *n.*—A: juvenile court. B: secret investigation. C: moral uprightness.

14. **consensus** (kun-'sen-sus) *n.*—A: blend of perfumes. B: group agreement. C: awareness of one's own surroundings.

15. **prolix** (pro-'liks) *adj.*—A: westward. B: wealthy. C: wordy.

Working for a Living 17

"Pro and Con" Answers

1. protract—[C] lengthen. The meal was *protracted* by Mary Lou's failure to take into account the three-and-a-half-hour cooking time for the turkey.

2. contrite—[B] sorry for a wrong. Then she dropped the bone china bowl full of mashed potatoes, but at least she was *contrite* about it.

3. protuberant—[C] bulging outward. Cousin Ida's naturally *protuberant* eyes make her seem perpetually surprised.

4. consternation—[B] paralyzing dismay. To our mother's *consternation*, Mr. Belvedere, Ida's Pekingese, was not housebroken.

5. propinquity—[A] nearness in place or time. "When deciding the Thanksgiving seating plan," Grandmother had warned me, "be vigilant for any unfortunate *propinquities*."

6. consummate—[A] skilled. A *consummate* parallel parker, Alfred somehow maneuvered the Winnebago into our crowded driveway.

7. profuse—[C] abundant. Joey dreaded the annual arrival of the aunts, with their *profuse* kisses and lipstick.

8. conflagration—[B] enormous fire. After last year's *conflagration*, we decided not to let Aunt Norma cook Thanksgiving dinner anymore.

9. prognosis—[C] forecast. Uncle Irv's confident *prognosis* that he'd be in shape for the 5K Turkey Trot turned out to be premature.

10. convex—[B] curved outward. His necktie clung to his *convex* belly like a snake sliding down a beach ball.

11. prostrate—[B] lying flat. *Prostrate* on the kitchen linoleum, Dad whimpered, "Who spilled the cranberry mold?"

12. convivial—[C] merry. My sister-in-law has a talent for making even the most *convivial* gathering seem like a funeral.

13. probity—[C] moral uprightness. When coffee was served, Grandpa produced a dozen sugar packets he had taken from various restaurants—a habit that, Grandmother said, demonstrated a lack of *probity*.

14. consensus—[B] group agreement. My nieces' and nephews' *consensus* was that pumpkin pie is technically a vegetable dish and that dessert should consist of double-chocolate brownies.

15. prolix—[C] wordy. Great-Uncle Cliff always puts us to sleep with his *prolix* tales of his youth in the old neighborhood.

STAY FOCUSED

Feeling lost? These vocabulary words are all about giving you directions: up or down, near or far, east or west, on and on. To locate the answers, navigate to the next page.

1. **starboard** ('star-berd) *n.*—A: ship's right side. B: ship's left side. C: ship's front.

2. **transpose** (trans-'pohz) *v.*—A: cut straight across. B: turn sharply. C: move to another place.

3. **nether** ('neh-ther) *adj.*—A: down low. B: overhead. C: spread out.

4. **anterior** (an-'teer-ee-er) *adj.*—A: at the midpoint. B: behind. C: in the front.

5. **juxtapose** ('juhk-stuh-pohz) *v.*—A: lay on top. B: put side by side. C: encircle.

6. **sinistral** ('sih-nih-struhl) *adj.*—A: from the south. B: underground. C: left-handed.

7. **periphery** (puh-'rih-fuh-ree) *n.*—A: great distance. B: close range. C: outer edges.

8. **apex** ('ay-peks) *n.*—A: clockwise motion. B: uppermost point. C: needle on a compass.

9. **aweigh** (uh-'way) *adj.*—A: over the side. B: off the bottom. C: trailing behind.

10. **egress** ('ee-gress) *n.*—A: entrance. B: exit. C: shortcut.

11. **recede** (rih-'seed) *v.*—A: pass underneath. B: lean to the right. C: move back.

12. **laterally** ('lat-uh-ruh-lee) *adv.*—A: sideways. B: backward. C: upward.

13. **polestar** ('pohl-star) *n.*—A: western route. B: North Star. C: southern tip.

14. **adjacent** (uh-'jay-sent) *adj.*—A: at the fore. B: neighboring. C: pressing down.

15. **abaft** (uh-'baft) *prep.*—A: to the rear of. B: on the border of. C: downstream from.

Working for a Living

"Stay Focused" Answers

1. starboard [A] ship's right side. Looking out over the ark's *starboard*, Noah scanned the horizon, hoping to spot land.

2. transpose [C] move to another place. Kyle's novel is a retelling of *Hamlet, transposed* to modern-day England.

3. nether [A] down low. "Why is my phone always lost in the *nether* reaches of my purse?" Rachel complained.

4. anterior [C] in the front. "I see that you've been flossing your *anterior* teeth, but you need to pay attention to your molars," said Dr. Kim.

5. juxtapose [B] put side by side. When you *juxtapose* the identical twins, it's impossible to tell them apart.

6. sinistral [C] left-handed. Did you know that the United States has had just eight *sinistral* presidents?

7. periphery [C] outer edges. My puppy is a bit shy—she tends to linger at the *periphery* of the dog park.

8. apex [B] uppermost point. The Hollywood actress had reached the *apex* of fame by age 18.

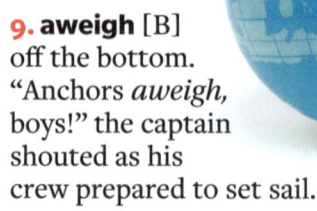

9. aweigh [B] off the bottom. "Anchors *aweigh*, boys!" the captain shouted as his crew prepared to set sail.

10. egress [B] exit. Are you sure this hedge maze has an *egress*?

11. recede [C] move back. When the floodwaters *recede* from our town, the cleanup will begin.

12. laterally [A] sideways. Good basketball players must be able to move well *laterally* as well as down the court.

13. polestar [B] North Star. "Once I catch sight of the *polestar*, I can get my bearings again," muttered the lost hiker.

14. adjacent [B] neighboring. The sisters lived in *adjacent* houses on Chestnut Drive for more than 50 years.

15. abaft [A] to the rear of. The private jet has a ritzy master suite *abaft* the main cabin.

GETTING ORIENTED

The Latin word *orientem,* meaning "the rising sun" or "the east," gave us the historical name for the world's eastern lands: the Orient. The Occident refers to the west, from the Latin *occidentem* ("sunset"). Things such as winds and auroras are *boreal* from the north and *austral* from the south—hence the name of that down-under continent.

WORD INVENTION

What do Mae West and the prophet Jeremiah have in common? They both inspired new words. World War II servicemen called their inflatable life jackets *Mae Wests*, after the voluptuous actress, and Jeremiah, who is traditionally credited with the book of Lamentations, gave us the word *jeremiad*, or complaint. But you don't have to be a famous sinner or saint to get your name in the dictionary. Sometimes the original namesake is forgotten today, but his or her word lives on. For quiz answers, turn the page.

1. **salchow** ('sow-cow) *n.*—A: heavy-coated dog breed. B: vegetable stew. C: figure skating jump.

2. **martinet** (mar-tuh-'net) *n.*—A: woodland songbird. B: gossipy neighbor. C: strict disciplinarian.

3. **mesmerize** ('mez-muh-rise) *v.*—A: stimulate with a shock. B: predict the future. C: spellbind.

4. **quisling** ('kwiz-ling) *n.*—A: medicinal tea. B: traitor. C: whim.

5. **Beaufort scale** ('bo-furt) *n.*—A: measure of wind force. B: measure of earthquakes. C: measure of rainfall.

6. **theremin** ('ther-uh-mun) *n.*—A: dome-topped house. B: iron-rich diet supplement. C: electronic musical instrument.

7. **Queensberry rules** ('kweenz-ber-ee) *n.*—A: principles of poker. B: boxing regulations. C: bylaws of diplomacy.

8. **bowdlerize** ('bode-luh-rise or bowd-) *v.*—A: talk in circles. B: develop land for commercial use. C: censor prudishly.

9. **Snellen chart** ('snel-un) *n.*—A: calorie-rating system. B: measure of bridge capacity. C: test for eyesight.

10. **draconian** (dray-'ko-nee-un) *adj.*—A: severe. B: affected by the full moon. C: unnecessarily complicated.

11. **maudlin** ('mawd-lun) *adj.*—A: sentimental. B: trendy. C: average.

12. **curie** ('cure-ee) *n.*—A: small fruit-filled pastry. B: unit of radioactivity. C: object provoking wonderment.

13. **Machiavellian** (mah-kee-uh-'vel-ee-un) *adj.*—A: traveling at the speed of sound. B: politically dishonest. C: ornate, as of architecture.

Working for a Living

"Word Invention" Answers

1. salchow—[C] figure skating jump. Swedish skater Ulrich Salchow. Uncle Larry's attempt at a double *salchow* ended with a broken tailbone.

2. martinet—[C] strict disciplinarian. French army officer Jean Martinet. My Latin teacher, a known *martinet*, made us conjugate the verb *esse* 50 times.

3. mesmerize—[C] spellbind. German physician Franz Anton Mesmer. The new reality show is stupid and offensive, but we were *mesmerized* anyway.

4. quisling—[B] traitor. Vidkun Quisling, pro-Nazi Norwegian politician. Ever since Johnny Damon left the Sox for the Yankees, Dad has called him a *quisling*.

5. Beaufort scale—[A] measure of wind force. British admiral Sir Francis Beaufort. I'm pretty sure that a 10 on the *Beaufort scale* is too high for kite flying.

6. theremin—[C] electronic musical instrument. Russian engineer Leon Theremin. The otherworldly sound in the Beach Boys' "Good Vibrations" was made by a *theremin*.

7. Queensberry rules—[B] boxing regulations. John Sholto Douglas, 9th Marquess of Queensberry. Pugsy wore cleats in the ring, in clear violation of the *Queensberry rules*.

8. bowdlerize—[C] censor prudishly. English editor Thomas Bowdler. The church group's *bowdlerized* version of *A Streetcar Named Desire* somehow lacked punch.

9. Snellen chart—[C] test for eyesight. Dutch ophthalmologist Herman Snellen. This book is so hard to read, it might as well be a *Snellen chart*.

10. draconian—[A] severe. Athenian lawmaker Draco. The *draconian* condo association bans window boxes.

11. maudlin—[A] sentimental. Mary Magdalene, traditionally depicted as a weeping penitent. Instead of a *maudlin* wedding song, the couple chose Led Zeppelin's "Whole Lotta Love."

12. curie—[B] unit of radioactivity. French chemists Pierre and Marie Curie. One *curie* is a relatively big amount, but Marie Curie didn't want the name associated with a tiny unit.

13. Machiavellian—[B] politically dishonest. Italian political philosopher Niccolò Machiavelli. The garden club president, in her *Machiavellian* rise to power, gave first place to an influential member's African violet.

MOTIVATION

Start by starting.
—MERYL STREEP

"

It's hard to lead a cavalry charge if you think you look funny on a horse.
—ADLAI STEVENSON

"

Treat a person as he is, and he will remain as he is. Treat him as he could be, and he will become what he should be.
—JIMMY JOHNSON

"

No pressure, no diamonds.
—MARY CASE

"

To be a champion, you have to believe in yourself when nobody else will.
—SUGAR RAY ROBINSON

"

As I like to say, take the shot, even if your knees are shaking.
—ROBIN ROBERTS

Working for a Living

THE PERFECT WORDS FOR
PROMOTIONS

Real success is finding your lifework in the work that you love.
—DAVID MCCULLOUGH

"
The work praises the man.
—IRISH PROVERB

"
Just as there are no little people or unimportant lives, there is no insignificant work.
—ELENA BONNER

"
One of the greatest sources of energy is pride in what you are doing.
—UNKNOWN

"
The more I want to get something done, the less I call it work.
—RICHARD BACH

"
Pleasure in the job puts perfection in the work.
—ARISTOTLE

Why not go out on a limb?
Isn't that where the fruit is?
—**FRANK SCULLY**

"

My father always told me, "Find a job you love and you'll never have to work a day in your life."
—**JIM FOX**

"

What isn't tried won't work.
—**CLAUDE MCDONALD**

"

What would life be if we had no courage to attempt anything?
—**VINCENT VAN GOGH**

"

You do your best work if you do a job that makes you happy.
—**BOB ROSS**

"

Genius begins great works;
labor alone finishes them.
—**JOSEPH JOUBERT**

Working for a Living

> The great arrogance of the present is to forget the intelligence of the past.
>
> **–KEN BURNS**

THIS LAND IS OUR LAND

As we work toward a future as a nation, it's important to remember the lessons of the past and to learn from the words of politicians, protestors, and patriots who have come before us.

ELECTIONS

You campaign in poetry; you govern in prose.
—MARIO CUOMO

"

An election is coming. Universal peace is declared, and the foxes have a sincere interest in prolonging the lives of the poultry.
—GEORGE ELIOT

"

Do you ever get the feeling that the only reason we have elections is to find out if the polls were right?
—ROBERT ORBEN

"

We pick politicians by how they look on TV and Miss America on where she stands on the issues. Isn't that a little backwards?
—JAY LENO

"

QUOTABLE TWEETS

Elections are when you have to make a choice. Perfection not often attainable!

@RUPERTMURDOCH

LEADERSHIP

Good leadership requires you to surround yourself with people of diverse perspectives who can disagree with you without fear of retaliation.
—DORIS KEARNS GOODWIN

"

You have to have a vision. It's got to be a vision you articulate clearly and forcefully. You can't blow an uncertain trumpet.
—REV. THEODORE HESBURGH

"

If you can affect someone when they're young, you are in their hearts forever.
—MARA WILSON

"

A leader takes people where they want to go. A great leader takes people where they don't necessarily want to go, but ought to be.
—ROSALYN CARTER

"

The day people stop bringing you their problems is the day you have stopped leading them.
—GEN. COLIN POWELL

"

Leaders don't create followers, they create more leaders.
—TOM PETERS

QUOTABLE TWEETS

True leadership is when you are willing to risk your power and voice so that ALL of ours can be heard.

@JTIMBERLAKE

> Even if I was king, I would do my own shopping.

—**HARRY, PRINCE OF WALES**

CHANGE

> If you want to make enemies, try to change something.

—**WOODROW WILSON**

> My parents told me, "Finish your dinner. People in China and India are starving." I tell my daughters, "Finish your homework. People in India and China are starving for your job."

—**THOMAS FRIEDMAN**

> The main dangers in this life are the people who want to change everything . . . or nothing.

—**LADY ASTOR**

Never doubt that a small group of thoughtful, committed citizens can change the world. Indeed, it is the only thing that ever has.
—**MARGARET MEAD**

Our dilemma is that we hate change and love it at the same time; what we really want is for things to remain the same but get better.
—**SYDNEY J. HARRIS**

A woman wasn't supposed to have a career. Today I'm convinced that there will be a woman president in my lifetime.
—**SHERRY LANSING**

The upside of painful knowledge is so much better than the downside of blissful ignorance.
—**SHERYL SANDBERG**

Unless someone like you cares a whole awful lot, nothing is going to get better. It's not.
—**DR. SEUSS, *THE LORAX***

PRESIDENTIAL ASPIRATIONS

There are advantages to being president.
The day after I was elected, I had my high school grades classified Top Secret.
—RONALD REAGAN

"
Frankly, I don't mind not being president.
I just mind that someone else is.
—EDWARD KENNEDY

"
My early choice in life was either to be a piano player in a whorehouse or a politician.
And to tell the truth, there's hardly any difference.
—HARRY TRUMAN

"
Being president is a lot like running a cemetery. You've got a lot of people under you and nobody's listening.
—BILL CLINTON

"
To those of you who received honours, awards, and distinctions, I say well done. And to the C students, I say you, too, can be president of the United States.
—GEORGE W. BUSH

Being president is like being a jackass in a hailstorm. There's nothing to do but stand there and take it.
—**LYNDON JOHNSON**

"

When the president does it, that means that it's not illegal.
—**RICHARD NIXON**

"

Any man who wants to be president is either an egomaniac or crazy.
—**DWIGHT D. EISENHOWER**

"

There are blessed intervals when I forget by one means or another that I am president of the United States.
—**WOODROW WILSON**

"

🐦 QUOTABLE TWEETS

I don't get the fuss about Presidents' Day. I spend my whole life not living up to promises, and nobody's giving me a holiday.
@HOMERJSIMPSON

This Land Is Our Land

HOME OF THE BRAVE

If we are to remain a free and viable society, we need to spend less time looking at screens and more time looking into each other's eyes.
—GLENN CLOSE

"

The difference between doing something and not doing something is doing something.
—JAMES CORDEN

"

We do not have to become heroes overnight.
Just a step at a time,
meeting each thing that comes up…
discovering we have the strength
to stare it down.
—ELEANOR ROOSEVELT

"

When you are actually powerful,
you don't need to be petty.
—JON STEWART

"

A vote is the great equalizer,
but only when it is cast.
—CHARLES M. BLOW

CURRENT EVENTS

When the winds of change blow,
some people build walls,
and others build windmills.
—**CHINESE PROVERB**

"
Social change is better achieved
by being for something
than against something.
—**HELENE GAYLE**

"
Times have not become more violent.
They have just become more televised.
—**MARILYN MANSON**

"
If we don't believe in free expression
for people we despise,
we don't believe in it at all.
—**NOAM CHOMSKY**

"
Activism is the rent I pay
for living on the planet.
—**ALICE WALKER**

THE PERFECT WORDS FOR
PROTEST CAMPAIGNS

You have the right to remain silent,
but I don't recommend it.
—PROTEST SIGN

Disobedience is the true foundation of liberty.
The obedient must be slaves.
—HENRY DAVID THOREAU

Never do anything against conscience
even if the state demands it.
—ALBERT EINSTEIN

As long as the world shall
last there will be wrongs, and
if no man objected and no man
rebelled, those wrongs
would last forever.
—CLARENCE DARROW

Man is not free unless government
is limited.
—RONALD REAGAN

HEAR HERE!

Words that sound alike are called *homophones*, and some—like oral (of speech) and aural (of hearing)—are trickier to differentiate than others. Take this ear-bending quiz, and then check your answers on the next page.

1. **gambol** ('gam-buhl) *v.*—A: frolic. B: take a risk. C: walk with a limp.

2. **humerus** ('hyoo-mer-us) *n.*—A: arm bone. B: comic. C: rich garden soil.

3. **discrete** (dis-'kreet) *adj.*—A: prudent. B: circular. C: separate.

4. **carrel** ('kayh-rel) *n.*—A: study alcove. B: Yuletide song. C: cattle pen.

5. **appellation** (ah-pel-'lay-shun) *n.*—A: mountain chain. B: name or title. C: sincere entreaty.

6. **pore** ('pohr) *v.*—A: read attentively. B: open slowly. C: rain down in buckets.

7. **dissent** (dih-'sent) *n.*—A: downward slope. B: cancellation. C: difference of opinion.

8. **straiten** ('strayt-in) *v.*—A: tidy up. B: hem in. C: become horizontal.

9. **martial** ('mahr-shul) *adj.*—A: of marriage. B: relating to war. C: upholding law.

10. **gild** ('gild) *v.*—A: form a trade union. B: cover with a thin layer of gold. C: feel remorse.

11. **complementary** (kom-pleh-'men-tuh-ree) *adj.*—A: given free as a courtesy. B: flattering with praise. C: having mutually completing parts.

12. **signet** ('sig-nit) *n.*—A: swan. B: seal. C: skunk.

13. **principle** ('prin-si-puhl) *n.*—A: school chief. B: rule or doctrine. C: sum earning interest.

14. **pallet** ('pal-lit) *n.*—A: sense of taste. B: bed. C: painter's board.

15. **augur** ('aw-ger) *n.*—A: drill bit. B: heat wave. C: reader of omens.

WHAT'S THAT SOUND?
The word *sound* has three different meanings. We're most familiar with *sound* meaning "noise," which is from the Latin sonus and is related to sonogram, song, sonnet, and even *swan* ("the sounding bird"). The *sound* meaning "unimpaired" comes from the German gesund ("healthy") and is related to gesundheit. And the *sound* meaning "body of water" makes a splashy connection to the Old English verb *swimman* ("to swim").

This Land Is Our Land

"Hear Here!" Answers

1. gambol—[A] frolic (sounds like: *gamble*). After Dorothy's house killed the Wicked Witch, the Munchkins *gamboled* and sang.

2. humerus—[A] arm bone (sounds like: *humorous*). To find your *humerus*, look between your shoulder and elbow.

3. discrete—[C] separate (sounds like: *discreet*). The king's men found Humpty Dumpty in a thousand *discrete* pieces.

4. carrel—[A] study alcove (sounds like: *carol*). I'll be cramming in a library *carrel*.

5. appellation—[B] name or title (sounds like: *Appalachian*). Ted prefers the *appellation* Sir Hugh Highcastle.

6. pore—[A] read attentively (sounds like: *pour* and *poor*). Jack Sparrow *pored* over the soggy treasure map.

7. dissent—[C] difference of opinion (sounds like: *descent*). Between Zoë and her mom, there is some *dissent* regarding bedtime.

8. straiten—[B] hem in (sounds like: *straighten*). Rodney was *straitened* by the cliff behind him and the lions in front of him.

9. martial—[B] relating to war (sounds like: *marshal*). We enjoy clapping to *martial* music on the Fourth of July.

10. gild—[B] cover with a thin layer of gold (sounds like: *guild*). The artist carefully *gilded* the mirror's ornate wood frame.

11. complementary—[C] having mutually completing parts (sounds like: *complimentary*). Count Dracula was wearing a tasteful black suit with a *complementary* cape.

12. signet—[B] seal (sounds like: *cygnet*). The deal isn't official until the queen stamps her *signet* on it.

13. principle—[B] rule or doctrine (sounds like: *principal*). As a *principle*, Dr. Frankenstein keeps spare parts in case his monster needs a tune-up.

14. pallet—[B] bed (sounds like: *palette*). The weary traveler gratefully slept on the straw-filled *pallet*.

15. augur—[C] reader of omens (sounds like: *auger*). Due to the home team's inexperience, I don't need an *augur* to predict this game will be a blowout.

ENGLISH COUSINS

Americans and Brits speak the same language—or do they? Test your knowledge of the Queen's English with this quiz, which features a bevy of British words. No need to hop across the pond for the answers; just turn the page.

1. fiddly ('fih-duh-lee) *adj.*—A: set to lively music. B: needing close attention. C: insignificant.

2. knackered ('na-kerd) *adj.*—A: clever. B: exhausted. C: cluttered.

3. brolly ('brah-lee) *n.*—A: umbrella. B: young man. C: streetcar.

4. pitch (pich) *n.*—A: northern county. B: playing field. C: stiff collar.

5. ta (tah) *interj.*—A: oh dear. B: to your health. C: thanks.

6. posh (pahsh) *adj.*—A: squishy. B: fancy. C: disdainful.

7. cack-handed ('kak-han-ded) *adj.*—A: guilty. B: clumsy. C: made-to-order.

8. aubergine ('oh-ber-zheen) *n.*—A: plum. B: zucchini. C: eggplant.

9. argy-bargy (ar-jee-'bar-jee) *n.*—A: pint of beer. B: argument. C: royal carriage.

10. chuffed (chuft) *adj.*—A: polished. B: discarded. C: delighted.

11. dog's breakfast (dahgz 'brek-fuhst) *n.*—A: confusing mess. B: savory pie. C: morning walk.

12. clanger ('klang-er) *n.*—A: church bell. B: copycat. C: blunder.

13. nick (nik) *v.*—A: shove. B: rush. C: steal.

14. chin-wag ('chin-wag) *n.*—A: close shave. B: friendly chat. C: goatee.

15. poppet ('pah-pet) *n.*—A: little one. B: bauble. C: tea biscuit.

This Land Is Our Land

"English Cousins" Answers

1. **fiddly** [B] needing close attention. I hate sewing on buttons—it's such *fiddly* work.

2. **knackered** [B] exhausted. *Knackered* after a long week, Giles ordered pizza and watched reruns instead of going to the gym.

3. **brolly** [A] umbrella. Bring your *brolly* and wear your boots—it's going to pour today!

4. **pitch** [B] playing field. The Reds dominated the game from the moment they stepped onto the *pitch*.

5. **ta** [C] thanks. "Ta, Dad!" Imogen yelled as she grabbed her lunch and ran out the door.

6. **posh** [B] fancy. My wife wants to go camping for our anniversary, but I'd prefer aweekend in a *posh* hotel.

7. **cack-handed** [B] clumsy. "Why am I always so *cack-handed?*" Susan grumbled, picking up shards of glass from the floor.

8. **aubergine** [C] eggplant. The chef chopped squash, *aubergine,* and garlic for the stir-fry.

9. **argy-bargy** [B] argument. "I don't agree with you, but let's not get into an *argy-bargy* about it," Rupert snapped.

10. **chuffed** [C] delighted. Arthur was *chuffed* when his painting won first place at the art show.

11. **dog's breakfast** [A] confusing mess. Dr. Cornwell's filing system is a complete *dog's breakfast*—I don't know how she finds anything.

12. **clanger** [C] blunder. After a series of on-air *clangers,* the newscaster was fired.

13. **nick** [C] steal. "I can't believe someone would *nick* my laptop!" Felicity cried.

14. **chin-wag** [B] friendly chat. George and Nigel meet at the pub for a *chin-wag* every Wednesday.

15. **poppet** [A] little one. "Give your granny a kiss, *poppet.*"

LET'S CONSULT SPELL-CHEQUE
Why do Brits and Yanks write some words differently? Because for his uniquely American dictionary, 19th-century lexicographer Noah Webster tweaked some terms to match our pronunciation—*colour* lost its *u, centre* became *center,* and *defence* switched to *defense.* Not all of his proposed alterations made their way into our books: He wanted to change tongue to tung.

MELTING POT

From aria to zucchini, Italian words add beauty and flavor to everyday English. Celebrate these words with Italian roots, and then take a gondola ride to the next page for answers.

1. **fiasco** (fee-'a-skoh) *n.*—A: rowdy celebration. B: complete failure. C: big fire.

2. **al dente** (all-'den-tay) *adj.*—A: seasoned with salt. B: eaten outdoors. C: cooked until firm.

3. **incognito** (in-kog-'nee-toh) *adv.*—A: well traveled. B: excessively complex. C: with a concealed identity.

4. **vendetta** (ven-'deh-tuh) *n.*—A: layered cake. B: blood feud. C: sales booth.

5. **patina** (puh-'tee-nuh) *n.*—A: high priest. B: lawn bowling. C: sheen produced by age.

6. **dilettante** ('dih-luh-tahnt) *n.*—A: coffee cup. B: dabbler. C: secret note.

7. **belvedere** ('bel-vuh-deer) *n.*—A: head butler. B: set of chimes. C: structure with a view.

8. **cameo** ('ka-mee-oh) *n.*—A: small role. B: almond cookie. C: sofa bed.

9. **sotto voce** ('sah-toh 'voh-chee) *adv.*—A: under one's breath. B: drunkenly. C: in the open.

10. **bravura** (bruh-'vyur-ah) *n.*—A: encore. B: battle cry. C: display of brilliance.

11. **amoretto** (a-muh-'reh-toh) *n.*—A: hazelnut flavoring. B: cherub. C: waistcoat.

12. **forte** ('for-tay) *adj.*—A: loud. B: masculine. C: built on a hill.

13. **bruschetta** (broo-'sheh-tuh) *n.*—A: grilled bread appetizer. B: thumbnail sketch. C: short story.

14. **campanile** (kam-puh-'nee-lee) *n.*—A: bell tower. B: army troop. C: best friend.

15. **brio** ('bree-oh) *n.*—A: cold spell. B: donkey. C: gusto.

This Land Is Our Land

"Melting Pot" Answers

1. fiasco—[B] complete failure. Though its premiere was a *fiasco*, the Broadway musical became the smash of the season.

2. al dente—[C] cooked until firm. I like my noodles *al dente*, but these are practically raw!

3. incognito—[C] with a concealed identity. The spy traveled *incognito*, using an assumed name.

4. vendetta—[B] blood feud. Romeo and Juliet's love affair was doomed by their families' *vendetta*.

5. patina—[C] sheen produced by age. "You can tell this writing desk is an antique by its beautiful *patina*," Marco explained.

6. dilettante—[B] dabbler. The maestro seeks a professional singer, not some weekend *dilettante*.

7. belvedere—[C] structure with a view. From the domed *belvedere*, we could watch Mount Etna erupting.

8. cameo—[A] small role. Francesca blew her audition for the lead, but she has a *cameo* as a taxi driver.

9. sotto voce—[A] under one's breath. "I always speak *sotto voce*," whispered Sophia, "to make sure people are listening."

10. bravura—[C] display of brilliance. The defense lawyer delivered the closing argument with *bravura*.

11. amoretto—[B] cherub. Why don't you paint a little *amoretto* above the kissing couple?

12. forte—[A] loud. In my opinion, a trombone serenade is too *forte* to be romantic.

13. bruschetta—[A] grilled bread appetizer. You can't order the *bruschetta* and the garlic knots; you're supposed to be watching your carbs!

14. campanile—[A] bell tower. The village's picturesque *campanile* has been standing since medieval times.

15. brio—[C] gusto. After just one sip of Chianti, I feel my *brio* returning.

NAME THAT NOODLE

Can you tell rigatoni from bucatini? You could if you knew that a noodle's name often tells you its shape—when you go back to its Italian-language roots. *Rigatoni*, from *riga*, or "line," has grooves; *bucatini*, from *buca*, or "hole," is hollow. Other varieties include bow-tie-shaped *farfalle* (*farfalla*, "butterfly"), pointed *penne* (*penna*, "quill"), spiraled *fusilli* (*fuso*, "spindle"), and long, thin *spaghetti* (*spago*, "string").

LATIN ROOTS

Latin is not the official language of any country today, but far from defunct, it's thriving in hundreds of our common English expressions. Whether it's alias ("somewhere else") or veto ("I forbid"), Caesar's language is entwined with ours. Pro bono (that is, "free") answers on next page.

1. **verbatim** (ver-'bay-tuhm) *adv.*—A: slowly and carefully. B: without stopping. C: word for word.

2. **mea culpa** (may-uh 'kul-puh) *n.*—A: congratulations. B: acknowledgment of fault. C: wavering decision.

3. **bona fide** ('boh-nuh fiyd) *adj.*—A: genuine. B: secret. C: at home.

4. **non sequitur** (nahn-'seh-kwuh-tuhr) *n.*—A: odd man out. B: comment that doesn't follow logically. C: failure to obey.

5. **ad infinitum** (ad in-fuh-'niy-tuhm) *adv.*—A: imitating. B: without end. C: making a bold display.

6. **status quo** (sta-tuhs 'kwoh) *n.*—A: good reputation. B: current state of affairs. C: complete sentence.

7. **magnum opus** ('mag-nuhm 'oh-puhs) *n.*—A: masterpiece. B: large debt. C: giant squid.

8. **per capita** (per 'ka-puh-tuh) *adv.*—A: financially. B: in block letters. C: for each person.

9. **ergo** ('er-goh) *adv.*—A: as soon as. B: therefore. C: otherwise.

10. **circa** (suhr-'kuh) *prep.*—A: about or around. B: after. C: between.

11. **persona non grata** (per-'soh-nuh nahn 'grah-tuh) *adj.*—A: fake. B: thankless. C: unwelcome.

12. **semper fidelis** (sem-per fuh-'day-luhs) *adj.*—A: at attention. B: innocent. C: always loyal.

13. **carpe diem** (kar-peh 'dee-uhm) *interj.*—A: happy anniversary! B: seize the day! C: listen, please!

14. **quasi** ('kwah-ziy) *adj.*—A: a bit seasick. B: having some resemblance. C: part time.

15. **quid pro quo** (kwid proh 'kwoh) *n.*—A: something given or received for something else. B: vote in favor. C: generous tip.

This Land Is Our Land 43

"Latin Roots" Answers

1. **verbatim**—[C] word for word. If you don't repeat the magic spell *verbatim*, the cave door won't open.

2. **mea culpa**—[B] acknowledgment of fault. Whenever Art misses a fly ball, he says, "*Mea culpa!*"

3. **bona fide**—[A] genuine. I was waiting for a *bona fide* apology after my argument with customer service.

4. **non sequitur**—[B] comment that doesn't follow logically. We were discussing the film when Taylor threw in a *non sequitur* about her new kitchen.

5. **ad infinitum**—[B] without end. Don't get my sister started on politics, or she'll start hurling her opinions *ad infinitum*.

6. **status quo**—[B] current state of affairs. The new CEO's structural moves have really changed the *status quo* for the better.

7. **magnum opus**—[A] masterpiece. I think of "Good Vibrations" as Brian Wilson's *magnum opus*.

8. **per capita**—[C] for each person. Ever the economist, Mom said, "Just one lollipop *per capita*, kids."

9. **ergo**—[B] therefore. The groom was late; *ergo*, the crowd—and the bride—appeared unsettled.

10. **circa**—[A] about or around. It was *circa* 1978 that Juliana first started collecting *Peanuts* memorabilia.

11. **persona non grata**—[C] unwelcome. After I dropped the ball and didn't call my best friend for years, he declared me *persona non grata*.

12. **semper fidelis**—[C] always loyal. Jack typically shortens the U.S. Marines motto to a yell of "*Semper fi!*"

13. **carpe diem**—[B] seize the day! Don't sit around procrastinating, you sluggard—*carpe diem*!

14. **quasi**—[B] having some resemblance. With a broom handle and three wires, I invented a *quasi* guitar.

15. **quid pro quo**—[A] something given or received for something else. Offer me trading advice, and I'll chip in some tech help; it's a *quid pro quo*.

> ### TRIVIAL PURSUIT
> The word *trivia* is Latin for "three roads" (*tri* + *via*). What's the connection? In ancient times, at a major crossroads, there was typically a kiosk listing regional information. Or you might find a group of local gossipers there. Travelers could learn local facts at these intersections—but the information might sometimes have seemed commonplace.

GETTING UP TO SPEED

No hurry—take your time ambling through this quiz on words about matters both slow and fast. Stumped? Hightail it to the next page for answers.

1. precipitate (pri-'si-pe-tet) *adj.*—A: gradual. B: inert. C: rash, hasty.

2. torpid ('tor-ped) *adj.*—A: sluggish. B: streamlined. C: explosive.

3. drogue ('drohg) *n.*—A: open speedboat. B: booster rocket. C: canvas parachute to slow a ship or plane.

4. tardigrade ('tar-de-grayd) *adj.*—A: restrained. B: rushed. C: slow in pace.

5. velodrome ('vee- or 'veh- or 'vay-leh-drohm) *n.*—A: nuclear accelerator. B: track for cycling. C: air-speed recorder.

6. paso doble ('pah-soh 'doh-blay) *n.*—A: quick march played at bullfights. B: shooting star. C: time-lapse motion.

7. dispatch (di-'spatch or 'di-spatch) *n.*—A: promptness or efficiency. B: postponement. C: impass.

8. baud ('bahd) *n.*— unit of ... A: film speed. B: data transmission speed. C: nautical speed.

9. hang fire (hang fyr) *v.*—A: delay. B: blast off. C: streak across the sky.

10. alacrity (uh-'lak-kre-tee) *n.*—A: ignition. B: cheerful readiness. C: pause before firing.

11. tout de suite (toot swyeet) *adv.*—A: immediately. B: at a given signal. C: not in time.

12. adagio (ah-'dah-jee-oh or -zhee-oh) *adv.*—A: fast. B: without stopping. C: at a slow tempo.

13. race runner (rays 'ruh-ner) *n.*—A: red fox. B: pronghorn antelope. C: North American lizard.

14. celerity (seh-'ler-eh-tee) *n.*—A: gear shift. B: rapidity of motion. C: snowballing effect.

15. catalytic (ka-teh-'li-tik) *adj.*—A: causing a slowdown. B: relating to an increase in a chemical reaction. C: precisely timed.

ENDURANCE TEST

A *marathon* is 26 miles and 385 yards. The word and that oddly specific distance date back to the 490 BC battle of Marathon, Greece, in which the Greeks defeated the Persians. A messenger carried news of the victory to Athens across some 26 miles. Centuries later, in the 1896 Olympics, the footrace debuted and adopted the name *marathon* in honor of the runner.

This Land Is Our Land

"Getting Up to Speed" Answers

1. precipitate—[C] rash, hasty. The hare made the *precipitate* decision to catch some z's during the race.

2. torpid—[A] sluggish. There is nothing more *torpid* than my 16-year-old daughter in the morning.

3. drogue—[C] canvas parachute to slow a ship or plane. "You're like a *drogue* on a rocket. Move it!" shouted the driver.

4. tardigrade—[C] slow in pace. The tortoise took great pride in his *tardigrade* gait.

5. velodrome—[B] track for cycling. Ever the biking enthusiast, Pete enjoyed training at the local *velodrome*.

6. paso doble—[A] quick march played at bullfights. The bullfighter grew anxious as the *paso doble* played before his debut.

7. dispatch—[A] promptness or efficiency. After clearing out the safe, the thief left the bank with *dispatch*.

8. baud—[B] unit of data transmission speed. "Mom, I could hand-deliver this message faster than your 300-*baud* dinosaur of a modem!"

9. hang fire—[A] delay. The driver beckoned, but we were *hanging fire* at the stage door, hoping for an autograph.

10. alacrity—[B] cheerful readiness. When Jo's brownies came out of the oven, the lazy twins suddenly moved with *alacrity*.

11. tout de suite—[A] immediately. The twins' older brother was on his feet *tout de suite* as the aroma wafted into his room.

12. adagio—[C] at a slow tempo. Either that violinist doesn't know *adagio* from allegro, or he can't keep time.

13. race runner—[C] North American lizard. I never saw Grandma Simmons as animated as the day our *race runner* escaped in her house.

14. celerity—[B] rapidity of motion. If a skunk stamps its feet and hisses, it's time to depart with *celerity*. Obviously, Grace's dog didn't know this.

15. catalytic—[B] relating to an increase in a chemical reaction. To see a *catalytic* reaction, apply a lit match to Gary's shoe from behind.

> ### SOUND SMARTER
> The adjectives *adverse* and *averse* are close cousins, but they are different. *Adverse* means "unfavorable, acting against or in a contrary direction" and typically refers to things, not people (an adverse reaction, for instance). *Averse* means "having an active feeling of distaste" and refers to a person's attitude (Sally is averse to all that adverse criticism).

NEXT GENERATION

Little-known fact: Students hoping to make the Scripps National Spelling Bee finals need to ace a multiple-choice vocabulary test much like this one. Word Power regulars can certainly outscore a bunch of kids, right? Here's your chance to find out, with words from the actual test. Check your answers on the next page.

1. **succinctly** (suhk-'sinkt-lee) *adv.*—A: concisely. B: vaguely. C: in a sneaky way.

2. **baneful** ('bayn-ful) *adj.*—A: prideful. B: harmful. C: fruitful.

3. **trenchant** ('tren-chent) *adj.*—A: always hungry. B: keenly perceptive. C: horizontal.

4. **beaucoup** ('boh-koo) *adj.*—A: lots of. B: handsome. C: imaginary.

5. **oblique** (oh-'bleek) *adj.*—A: muscular. B: translucent. C: slanting.

6. **gazetteer** (ga-zuh-'teer) *n.*—A: pirate. B: onlooker. C: dictionary of place-names.

7. **comestible** (kuh-'meh-stuh-buhl) *adj.*—A: easily mixed. B: edible. C: flammable.

8. **lenitive** ('leh-nuh-tiv) *adj.*—A: soothing. B: punishing. C: clairvoyant.

9. **plaudits** ('plah-dits) *n.*—A: approval. B: taxes. C: rice and beans.

10. **mountebank** ('moun-tih-bank) *n.*—A: wetland. B: horseback rider. C: quack.

11. **abstemious** (ab-'stee-mee-us) *adj.*—A: stylish. B: eating sparingly. C: inducing laughter.

12. **supercilious** (soo-per-'sih-lee-us) *adj.*—A: hairy. B: overly proud. C: like a clown.

13. **inscrutable** (in-'skroo-tuh-buhl) *adj.*—A: obvious. B: unbudging. C: hard to understand.

14. **abrogate** ('a-bruh-gayt) *v.*—A: wear down. B: skip over. C: annul.

15. **pennate** ('peh-nayt) *adj.*—A: written in ink. B: like a wing or feather. C: ring-shaped.

This Land Is Our Land

"Next Generation" Answers

1. succinctly—[A] concisely. "The answer," Mom said *succinctly*, "is no."

2. baneful—[B] harmful. It appears Kavya's cats have done *baneful* things to her brand-new sofa.

3. trenchant—[B] keenly perceptive. An op-ed writer should have a *trenchant* wit.

4. beaucoup—[A] lots of. That guy must be making *beaucoup* bucks with his Silicon Valley start-up.

5. oblique—[C] slanting. Corrie's painting style is very modern, full of dark colors and *oblique* lines.

6. gazetteer—[C] dictionary of place-names. You won't find "The Boondocks" in any official *gazetteer*.

7. comestible—[B] edible. That wedding cake was very pretty, but most of it wasn't even *comestible*.

8. lenitive—[A] soothing. You're going to need an ocean of *lenitive* ointment to treat that rash.

9. plaudits—[A] approval. Critics don't really understand the movie, but they're giving it *plaudits* anyway.

10. mountebank—[C] quack. Do you think that because Dr. Dwyer prescribes an hour of yoga every day she is a *mountebank*?

11. abstemious—[B] eating sparingly. Jack is a rather *abstemious* dinner guest.

12. supercilious—[B] overly proud. If you wear ripped jeans in that overpriced store, the salesperson will greet you with a *supercilious* sneer.

13. inscrutable—[C] hard to understand. "We'll never be able to build this bookcase. These instructions are *inscrutable*!"

14. abrogate—[C] annul. After a bitter argument, the two partners *abrogated* their contract.

15. pennate—[B] like a wing or feather. The detective's *pennate* mustache appeared stiffly waxed.

HOW DO YOU SPELL WISCONSIN?

How's this for an unusual spelling test? Google recently searched for the words people typed in most often to accompany the phrase "How to spell …" and then ranked the results by state. In Pennsylvania, it was *sauerkraut* that was most confusing. *Pneumonia* perplexed folks in Alabama, Maine, and Washington. And *Wisconsin* stumped the people of … Wisconsin!

ABCs

Here, we get down to the ABCs of words—the letters—with a quiz about their myriad faces, sounds, and symbols. Answers on next page.

1. serif ('ser-ef) *n.*—A: *X* to represent a kiss. B: lines at the ends of a letter. C: double letter.

2. zed ('zed) *n.*—A: dot over an *i*. B: British *Z*. C: underlined character.

3. cursive ('ker-siv) *adj.*—A: rounded, as *B* or *C*. B: in flowing penmanship. C: left-facing.

4. schwa ('shwah) *n.*—A: unstressed vowel. B: misspelled word. C: one-letter word.

5. aspirate ('as-peh-rayt) *v.*—A: end in *-ess*. B: start with an *A*. C: pronounce with an *H* sound.

6. majuscule ('ma-jes-kyewl) *n.*—A: italic letter. B: boldface letter. C: uppercase letter.

7. assonant ('a-suh-nunt) *adj.*—A: with the same vowel sound. B: using mixed fonts. C: hard to pronounce.

8. tilde ('til-duh) *n.*—A: squiggle over an *n*. B: two dots over an *o*. C: accent mark.

9. sigmoid ('sig-moyd) *adj.*—A: of an autograph. B: following a colon. C: shaped like an *S*.

10. decussate (de-'kuh-sayt) *v.*—A: slur. B: mispronounce. C: intersect, form an X.

11. logogram ('law-ge-gram) *n.*—A: picture writing. B: symbol standing for a word. C: set of initials.

12. burr ('ber) *n.*—A: rolled or trilled *r* sound. B: printing error. C: repeated vowel.

13. sibilant ('sih-bih-lent) *adj.*—A: similar in sound. B: in alphabetical order. C: having an *S* or hissing sound.

14. guttural ('guh-tuh-rel) *adj.*—A: from the throat. B: having a hard *G* sound. C: emphasized.

15. orthoepy ('or-theh-'weh-pee) *n.*—A: code. B: proper pronunciation. C: sign language.

This Land Is Our Land

"ABCs" Answers

1. serif—[B] lines at the ends of a letter. The words you're reading now use a *serif* font (note the embellishments). These use a sans serif ("without serif") font.

2. zed—[B] British Z. Since returning from London, Zooey has spelled her name out loud to us at least three dozen times using a *zed*.

3. cursive—[B] in flowing penmanship. I had to admire the lovely *cursive* of Mary's "Dear John" letter.

4. schwa—[A] unstressed vowel. In case you're wondering, the *e* in *vowel* is a *schwa*.

5. aspirate—[C] pronounce with an H sound. Eliza Doolittle didn't *aspirate* when she spoke of " 'Enry 'Iggins."

6. majuscule—[C] uppercase letter. Alex thinks he's so great, he signs his name in all *majuscules*.

7. assonant—[A] with the same vowel sound. The only thing Bob and Dot have in common is their names' *assonance*.

8. tilde—[A] squiggle over an *n*. Nuñez barked when the maître d' forgot the *tilde* in his name.

9. sigmoid—[C] shaped like an *S*. I tried to skate a figure 8 but slipped and left a *sigmoid* trail instead.

10. decussate—[C] intersect, form an X. The pirate let two strokes *decussate* on the map to mark his hidden treasure.

11. logogram—[B] symbol standing for a word. The Artist Formerly Known as Prince used a fancy *logogram* instead of his actual name.

12. burr—[A] rolled or trilled *r* sound. When Scotty says "rump roast," the *burrs* are like a purring motor.

13. sibilant—[C] having an *S* or hissing sound. Certain *sibilant* sounds struck Sussman as excessively snaky.

14. guttural—[A] from the throat. To illustrate *guttural* consonants, Professor Fenn literally growled at his students.

15. orthoepy—[B] proper pronunciation. Tongue-twisters like "rubber baby buggie bumper" are good exercises in *orthoepy*.

CONFUSED COUSINS

Here's a usage error that seems to be on the rise: *regiment* versus *regimen*. Despite the close spellings, the meanings are clear. A *regiment* is a military unit; a *regimen* is a systematic plan to improve health or skills (a diet regimen, a research regimen, for instance).

STRIVING FOR THE BEST

It's one thing to feel
that you are on the right path,
but it's another to think
that yours is the only path.
—PAULO COELHO

"

Injustice anywhere
is a threat to justice everywhere.
—REV. MARTIN LUTHER KING, JR.

"

Tomorrow belongs to those
who can hear it coming.
—DAVID BOWIE

"

The more you sweat in training,
the less you will bleed in battle.
—NAVY SEALS

"

Perfection is God's business,
I just try for excellence.
—MICHAEL J. FOX

This Land Is Our Land

THE PERFECT WORDS FOR
POLITICAL DEBATES

Change starts when someone sees the next step.
—WILLIAM DRAYTON

"

No person can be a great leader unless he takes genuine joy in the successes of those under him.
—W. A. NANCE

"

Determine that the thing can and shall be done, and then we shall find the way.
—ABRAHAM LINCOLN

"

Action may not always be happiness, but there is no happiness without action.
—BENJAMIN DISRAELI

"

All glory comes from daring to begin.
—EUGENE F. WARE

"

It is easy to sit up and take notice. What is difficult is getting up and taking action.
—AL BATT

Anyone can hold the helm when the sea is calm.
—**PUBLILIUS SYRUS**

> Well done is better than well said.
—**BENJAMIN FRANKLIN**

> Change will not come if we wait for some other person or some other time. We are the ones we've been waiting for. We are the change that we seek.
—**BARACK OBAMA**

> Dig the well before you are thirsty.
—**CHINESE PROVERB**

> Not everything that is faced can be changed. But nothing can be changed until it is faced.
—**JAMES BALDWIN**

> Nothing great was ever achieved without enthusiasm.
—**RALPH WALDO EMERSON**

> The most prominent place in hell is reserved for those who are neutral on the great issues of life.
—**REV. BILLY GRAHAM**

Who wants to reach
the end of their life
in a perfectly preserved body?
The scars and the crinkles and
the cracks are
what make us interesting.

—**BEAR GRYLLS**

BETTER WITH AGE

Embracing age—and all that goes with it—
may not be easy,
but it sure beats the alternative, as they say.
So take it all in and appreciate
the wisdom along with the wrinkles.

MAKING THE MOST OF IT

Life is too short to eat vanilla ice cream and dance with boring men.
—UNKNOWN

"
You don't get to choose how you're going to die. Or when. You can only decide how you're going to live. Now.
—JOAN BAEZ

"
I think it's a good health tip to say "I'm not a worrier."
—BILL MURRAY

"
I'm in the middle of my life, and I just don't have enough years left to spend a large proportion of them inside an iPhone.
—ZADIE SMITH

"
You know that old saying: "You're never too old to play. You're only too old for low-rise jeans."
—ELLEN DEGENERES

I'm learning in my old age
that the only thing you can do
to keep your sanity
is to stay in the moment.
—WILLEM DAFOE

"

If Joan of Arc could
turn the tide of an entire war
before her 18th birthday,
you can get out of bed.
—E. JEAN CARROLL

"

A diplomat is a man who
always remembers a woman's birthday
but never remembers her age.
—ROBERT FROST

"

Caesar—did he ever think
that he would end up as a salad?
—EDDIE IZZARD

"

I always say, on the day I die,
I hope I learn something new.
—KATHIE LEE GIFFORD

"

Hurry up. You're dying.
—MEGYN KELLY

THE TIME WE HAVE

I never think of the future. It comes soon enough.
— **ALBERT EINSTEIN**

"

How you spend your time is more important than how you spend your money. Money mistakes can be corrected, but time is gone forever.
— **DAVID B. NORRIS**

"

Time is an illusion. Lunchtime doubly so.
— **DOUGLAS ADAMS**

"

Time neither subtracts nor divides, but adds at such a pace it seems like multiplication.
— **BOB TALBERT**

"

Eternity is a terrible thought. I mean, where's it going to end?
— **TOM STOPPARD**

"

My doctor says if I don't drink, don't smoke, if I eat properly and take care of myself, I really should live until midnight.
— **MALACHY MCCOURT**

The future ain't what it used to be.
—**YOGI BERRA**

❝

Forever is a long time, but not as long as it was yesterday.
—**DENNIS H'ORGNIES**

❝

Yesterday is a canceled check; tomorrow is a promissory note; today is ready cash—use it.
—**KAY LYONS**

❝

For disappearing acts, it's hard to beat what happens to the eight hours supposedly left after eight of sleep and eight of work.
—**DOUG LARSON**

BEAUTY IN THE EYE OF THE BEHOLDER

Everybody needs beauty as well as bread, places to play in and pray in, where nature may heal and give strength to body and soul.
—**JOHN MUIR**

QUOTABLE TWEETS

Don't forget, for every drop of rain a flower grows! :)
@DOLLY_PARTON

❝

Unexpected intrusions of beauty. That is what life is.
—SAUL BELLOW

❝

The most beautiful thing in the world is, of course, the world itself.
—WALLACE STEVENS

❝

Creativity is allowing yourself to make mistakes. Art is knowing which ones to keep.
—SCOTT ADAMS

❝

If truth is beauty, how come no one has their hair done in the library?
—LILY TOMLIN

❝

Normal day, let me be aware of the treasure you are.
—MARY JEAN IRION

❝

Love beauty; it is the shadow of God on the universe.
—GABRIELA MISTRAL

Some people, no matter how old they get,
never lose their beauty—they merely move
it from their faces into their hearts.
—MARTIN BUXBAUM

"

Though we travel the world over to find the beautiful,
we must carry it with us or we find it not.
—RALPH WALDO EMERSON

"

People have the strength to overcome their
bodies. Their beauty is in their minds.
—PETER GABRIEL

"

Fashion is something that goes in one
year and out the other.
—DENISE KLAHN

NO ONE IS PERFECT

Your imperfections are what make you beautiful.
—SANDRA BULLOCK

"

Natural beauty takes at least two hours
in front of a mirror.
—PAMELA ANDERSON

Better with Age **61**

THE PERFECT WORDS FOR
GET-WELL CARDS

In a sick-room or a bed-room there should never be shutters shut.
—**FLORENCE NIGHTINGALE**

"
The only way to keep your health is to eat what you don't want, drink what you don't like, and do what you'd rather not.
—**MARK TWAIN**

"
Health is like money—we never have a true idea of its value until we lose it.
—**JOSH BILLINGS**

"
My own prescription for health is less paperwork and more running barefoot through the grass.
—**LESLIE GRIMUTTER**

"
Early to bed and early to rise, makes a man healthy, wealthy, and wise.
—**BENJAMIN FRANKLIN**

FACE IT!

Next time you take a look in the mirror, consider the many words that describe the face. Then see if you missed any in our quiz. For answers, and Deep Roots, turn to the next page

1. moue ('moo) *n.*—A: small grimace or pout. B: arch of an eyebrow. C: freckle or mole.

2. lingual ('ling-wool) *adj.*—A: located in the ears. B: about the tongue. C: having flared nostrils.

3. glower ('glau-er) *v.*—A: look radiantly happy. B: look bored or sleepy. C: look sullen or angry.

4. Vandyke (van-'dike) *n.*—A: short, pointed beard. B: wide, waxed mustache. C: bowl haircut.

5. buccal ('buh-cull) *adj.*—A: pertaining to the cheek. B: having a receding chin. C: having prominent front teeth.

6. rhinoplasty ('rye-no-plas-tee) *n.*—A: nose job. B: skin treatment for acne. C: lack of eyebrows.

7. nictitate ('nick-tuh-tate) *v.*—A: wiggle one's ears. B: wrinkle one's nose. C: wink one's eye.

8. proboscis (pruh-'boss-us or pruh-'boss-cuss) *n.*—A: forward-thrusting lower jaw. B: especially big nose. C: pronounced eyebrow ridge.

9. otic ('oh-tick) *adj.*—A: pertaining to the ear. B: pertaining to the eye socket. C: pertaining to the forehead.

10. maquillage (ma-kee-'yazh) *n.*—A: cosmetic makeup. B: gaping yawn. C: facial deformity.

11. palpebral (pal-'pee-brul) *adj.*—A: jug-eared. B: craggy. C: concerning the eyelids.

12. zygoma (zye-'go-muh) *n.*—A: cheekbone. B: chin. C: birthmark.

Better with Age 63

"Face It!" Answers

1. moue—[A] small grimace or pout. Lenny couldn't tell if Molly's lips were a pucker of desire or a *moue* of disgust.

2. lingual—[B] about the tongue. In *A Christmas Story,* Ralphie's classmate meets with a *lingual* accident when he licks a frozen flagpole.

3. glower—[C] look sullen or angry. Inadvertently seated at the same table, the Giants fan and the Patriots fan spent the entire wedding reception *glowering* at each other.

4. Vandyke—[A] short, pointed beard. He looks like a Beat poet with that *Vandyke* and beret.

5. buccal—[A] pertaining to the cheek. Gerard insisted he was the lost Dauphin even when a DNA analysis of his *buccal* cells proved he was not.

6. rhinoplasty—[A] nose job. Rudolph might have had a happier childhood if he'd had *rhinoplasty.*

7. nictitate—[C] wink one's eye. Molly couldn't tell if Lenny was *nictitating* because he was flirting with her or because he had something in his eye.

8. proboscis—[B] especially big nose. My uncle's got a *proboscis* that's the shape and size of Florida.

9. otic—[A] pertaining to the ear. She suffers from *otic* selectivity: She hears only what she wants to.

10. maquillage—[A] cosmetic makeup. Dress by Dior, *maquillage* by Bozo.

11. palpebral—[C] concerning the eyelids. As Justin slept, his frat brothers, with a little *palpebral* Magic Marker, gave him a look of wide-eyed surprise.

12. zygoma—[A] cheekbone. She has *zygomas* that could cut glass.

DEEP ROOTS

Supercilious means "haughty, disdainful, arrogant." It has two Latin roots: super ("over, above") and cilium ("eyelid"). Supercilious people since ancient Rome have been arching their eyebrows. A similar notion is behind *highbrow,* an intellectual snob.

BEAUTY OF WORDS

What makes a word beautiful? Is it a melodious sound? An exotic meaning? For whatever reason, the words below appeal to our sense of beauty—though their meanings may not all be *pellucid* (a pretty word for "clear"). Answers on next page.

1. **lavaliere** (lah-vuh-'leyr) *n.*—A: magma outflow. B: pendant on a chain. C: rider with a lance.

2. **flan** ('flan) *n.*—A: pizzazz. B: custard dessert. C: mirror reflection.

3. **panoply** ('pa-nuh-plee) *n.*—A: impressive array. B: bouquet. C: folded paper art.

4. **gambol** ('gam-buhl) *v.*—A: stake money on a horse. B: frolic about. C: sing in rounds.

5. **chalice** ('cha-luhs) *n.*—A: goblet. B: ankle bracelet. C: glass lamp.

6. **languorous** ('lan-guh-ruhs) *adj.*—A: of the tongue. B: in the tropics. C: lackadaisical or listless.

7. **pastiche** (pas-'teesh) *n.*—A: thumbnail sketch. B: fabric softener. C: artistic imitation.

8. **opulent** ('ahp-u-lehnt) *adj.*—A: right on time. B: pertaining to vision. C: luxurious.

9. **penumbra** (peh-'nuhm-bruh) *n.*—A: something that covers or shrouds. B: drowsiness. C: goose-feather quill.

10. **tendril** ('ten-druhl) *n.*—A: wooden flute. B: spiraling plant sprout. C: clay oven.

11. **imbroglio** (im-'brohl-yoh) *n.*—A: complicated mix-up. B: Asian palace. C: oil-painting style.

12. **dalliance** ('dal-lee-ents) *n.*—A: frivolous or amorous play. B: flourish on a trumpet. C: blinding light.

13. **mellifluous** (meh-'lih-fluh-wuhs) *adj.*—A: having broad stripes. B: milky white. C: sweet sounding.

14. **diaphanous** (diy-'a-fuh-nuhs) *adj.*—A: marked by a fine texture. B: having two wings. C: romantic.

15. **recherché** (ruh-sher-'shay) *adj.*—A: elegant or rare. B: well practiced. C: silent.

Better with Age **65**

"Beauty of Words" Answers

1. **lavaliere**—[B] pendant on a chain. The *lavaliere* around the princess's neck caught the eye of her suitor.

2. **flan**—[B] custard dessert. We went from one Mexican restaurant to another, searching for the perfect *flan*.

3. **panoply**—[A] impressive array. Eli was mesmerized by the *panoply* of dinosaur fossils at the museum.

4. **gambol**—[B] frolic about. In their downtime, North Pole elves are known to *gambol* in the snow.

5. **chalice**—[A] goblet. One *chalice* contains deadly poison; the other, an all-healing elixir—now choose!

6. **languorous**—[C] lackadaisical or listless. The winter chill made Sara long for the *languorous* hours of her summer at the lake house.

7. **pastiche**—[C] artistic imitation. You call his work a *pastiche*; I call it a knockoff.

8. **opulent**—[C] luxurious. During her first visit, Sally was overcome by the *opulent* entrance of Tiffany's.

9. **penumbra**—[A] something that covers or shrouds. Upon his first steps into the ancient chamber, the explorer fell under a *penumbra* of fear.

10. **tendril**—[B] spiraling plant sprout. The alien pod wrapped its *tendrils* around the captain's ankle.

11. **imbroglio**—[A] complicated mix-up. For my tastes, too many films these days are based around a much-expected *imbroglio*.

12. **dalliance**—[A] frivolous or amorous play. The couple's early *dalliance* was marked by subtle flirting and letter writing.

13. **mellifluous**—[C] sweet sounding. Nothing is so *mellifluous* as the jingle of a bell on our Christmas tree.

14. **diaphanous**—[A] marked by a fine texture. My wife wore a *diaphanous* veil on our wedding day.

15. **recherché**—[A] elegant or rare. Alison wondered if her grandmother's bejeweled shoes were too *recherché* for the office party.

CELLAR DOOR

Among others, the fantasy writer J. R. R. Tolkien maintained that the loveliest combination of sounds—with the *r*'s and *l*'s that people find lyrical—is the phrase *cellar door*. Try repeating it aloud. It ends with an open *o* sound, which Edgar Allan Poe called the "most sonorous" of the vowels (*sonorous* meaning "full sounding").

A IS FOR

The letter *A* is so much more than the alphabet's leader and a header for April: music note, blood type, Hawthorne favorite, mark of excellence, and even stardom vehicle for Mr. T. In its honor, a quiz devoted to words whose only vowel is *A*. Answers on the next page.

1. banal (buh-'nal or 'bay-nuhl) *adj.*—A: disallowed. B: uptight. C: trite.

2. annals ('a-nlz) *n.*—A: catacombs. B: chronicles. C: long johns.

3. arcana (ar-'kay-nuh) *n.*—A: mysterious or specialized knowledge. B: travel journal. C: rainbow.

4. masala (mah-'sah-la) *n.*—A: Chilean wine. B: Indian spice blend. C: Italian antipasto.

5. llama ('lah-muh) *n.*—A: beast of burden. B: heroic escape. C: priest or monk.

6. bazaar (buh-'zar) *n.*—A: weird event. B: marketplace. C: wailing siren.

7. paschal ('pas-kel) *adj.*—A: of computer languages. B: in a Gothic style. C: relating to Easter.

8. amalgam (uh-'mal-gum) *n.*—A: mixture. B: volcanic rock. C: back of the throat.

9. plantar ('plan-ter) *adj.*—A: vegetative. B: paved with asphalt. C: of the sole of the foot.

10. catamaran (ka-teh-meh-'ran) *n.*—A: Bengal tiger. B: black olive. C: boat with two hulls.

11. balaclava (ba-leh-'klah-vuh) *n.*—A: knit cap. B: Greek pastry. C: Russian mandolin.

12. avatar ('a-veh-tar) *n.*—A: mythological sibling. B: incarnation of a god. C: computer language.

13. spartan ('spar-tn) *adj.*—A: desertlike. B: marked by simplicity and lack of luxury. C: of classical theater.

14. allay (a-'lay) *v.*—A: refuse. B: take sides. C: calm.

15. lambda ('lam-duh) n.—A: Greek letter. B: Brazilian dance. C: college degree.

THEY MADE *THAT* A WORD?!

Speaking of all things "A," Merriam-Webster recently added to its *Collegiate Dictionary* the term *aha moment*—"an instance of sudden realization"—made popular by Oprah. Other modern lingo added to the latest iteration: *man cave* ("a room designed according to a man's tastes") and *earworm* ("a song that keeps repeating in one's mind" … thanks a lot, Carly Rae Jepsen).

Better with Age **67**

"A Is For" Answers

1. banal—[C] trite. Whenever the teacher says something too *banal,* Dorothy rolls her eyes.

2. annals—[B] chronicles. In the *annals* of sports idiocy, that was the biggest bonehead play I've ever seen!

3. arcana—[A] mysterious or specialized knowledge. I'd rather not know all the deep *arcana* of your arachnid research.

4. masala—[B] Indian spice blend. Easy on the *masala*—Sarah doesn't have the stomach for spicy dishes.

5. llama—[A] beast of burden. The llama is a domesticated South American camelid that has been used as a pack animal since the Pre-Columbian era.

6. bazaar—[B] marketplace. During her hunt at the *bazaar,* Sally found a turn-of-the-century compass that had belonged to her great-grandfather.

7. paschal—[C] relating to Easter. Terri spent hours on her *Paschal* bonnet—it started as a flowerpot!

8. amalgam—[A] mixture. Our team is a strong *amalgam* of raw youth and seasoned leadership.

9. plantar—[C] of the sole of the foot. "What do these *plantar* prints tell us, Holmes?" asked Watson.

10. catamaran—[C] boat with two hulls. Jack thinks he's Admiral Nelson now that he has won the marina's annual *catamaran* race.

11. balaclava—[A] knit cap. Hang your *balaclava* in the foyer and grab some stew.

12. avatar—[B] incarnation of a god. In Hindu mythology, Rama is the seventh *avatar* of the god Vishnu. (And yes, James Cameron, an *avatar* is also a being representing and controlled by a human.)

13. spartan—[B] marked by simplicity and lack of luxury. We didn't expect such *spartan* conditions in the honeymoon suite.

14. allay—[C] calm. Yesterday's board meeting did more than just *allay* our fears—it gave us an uptick of hope!

15. lambda—[A] Greek letter. Invert a *V,* and you've got a Greek *lambda*—or Bob's mustache.

68 USE YOUR WORDS, VOLUME 2

KEEP IT SIMPLE

You're busy at this time of year, so we made this quiz as easy as a, b, c. All these words include those letters—in order (ignoring some repeats). You'll find this aerobic mental exercise more fun if you don't fabricate the answers, which are on the next page.

1. **ambience** ('am-bee-ents) *n.*—A: act of listening. B: stroll. C: atmosphere.

2. **diabolical** (dy-uh-'bah-lih-kuhl) *adj.*—A: devilish. B: two-faced. C: acidic.

3. **sabbatical** (suh-'ba-tih-kuhl) *n.*—A: prayer shawl. B: strict command. C: extended leave.

4. **abject** ('ab-jekt) *adj.*—A: lofty. B: lowly. C: central.

5. **swashbuckler** ('swahsh-buh-kler) *n.*—A: studded belt. B: daring adventurer. C: threshing blade.

6. **abacus** ('a-buh-kuss) *n.*—A: sundial. B: magic spell. C: ancient counting tool.

7. **rambunctious** (ram-'bunk-shuss) *adj.*—A: goatlike. B: unruly. C: wide-awake.

8. **ambivalence** (am-'bih-vuh-lents) *n.*—A: medical aid. B: contradictory feelings. C: left-handedness.

9. **lambency** ('lam-ben-see) *n.*—A: meekness. B: desperation. C: radiance.

10. **abdicate** ('ab-dih-kayt) *v.*—A: give up. B: start. C: decline to vote.

11. **Malbec** (mal-'bek) *n.*—A: coffee blend. B: French pirate. C: red wine.

12. **abeyance** (uh-'bay-ents) *n.*—A: following orders. B: barking. C: temporary inactivity.

13. **shambolic** (sham-'bah-lik) *adj.*—A: misleading. B: disorganized. C: widely shunned.

14. **abscond** (ab-'skond) *v.*—A: steal away. B: trip and fall. C: fail to rhyme.

15. **sawbuck** ('saw-buk) *n.*—A: horse trainer. B: ten-dollar bill. C: tree trimmer.

Better with Age

"Keep It Simple" Answers

1. ambience [C] atmosphere. "Randy's Slop House" isn't much of a name, but the place actually has a nice *ambience*.

2. diabolical [A] devilish. Wile E. Coyote's *diabolical* schemes usually end as spectacular failures.

3. sabbatical [C] extended leave. Dr. Klein is taking a *sabbatical* this semester to finish her book.

4. abject [B] lowly. The sight of a spider in the bathtub made Big Joe act like an *abject* coward.

5. swashbuckler [B] daring adventurer. Robin Hood and Zorro are two famous fictional *swashbucklers*.

6. abacus [C] ancient counting tool. I couldn't do my homework, because my dog ate the beads off my *abacus*.

7. rambunctious [B] unruly. Is there anything more exhausting than babysitting a group of *rambunctious* five-year-olds?

8. ambivalence [B] contradictory feelings. I do have some *ambivalence* about trapping the chipmunks in my attic.

9. lambency [C] radiance. By the moon's *lambency*, the lovers staged their secret rendezvous.

10. abdicate—[A] give up. Having failed her accounting course, Paulina was forced to *abdicate* her role as class treasurer.

11. Malbec [C] red wine. Kendra savored a sip of *Malbec*, then took a bite of her filet mignon.

12. abeyance [C] temporary inactivity. The torrential rain seems to be in *abeyance*, but more storms are forecast.

13. shambolic [B] disorganized. Kyle's bachelor pad is always in a *shambolic* state, with dirty socks on the floor and dishes in the sink.

14. abscond [A] steal away. Where's that knave who *absconded* with the queen's tarts?

15. sawbuck [B] ten-dollar bill. "In the old days, you could buy dinner and a movie for just a *sawbuck*," Jean grumbled as she pulled out her wallet.

CHANGES

"Come autumn's scathe—come winter's cold—Come change—and human fate!" Elizabeth Barrett Browning writes in "Autumn," a reminder to embrace the changes that the seasons bring. In accord, a collection of words about change. Answers on next page.

1. ameliorate (uh-'meel-yuh-rayt) *v.*—A: make better or more tolerable. B: make worse. C: turn upside down.

2. tack ('tak) *v.*—A: switch horses. B: follow a zigzag course. C: tailor a suit.

3. ferment (fur-'mehnt) *n.*—A: state of unrest or disorderly development. B: improvement. C: evaporation.

4. synchronize ('sin-kreh-niyz) *v.*—A: cause to coincide. B: increase speed. C: move one's lips.

5. static ('sta-tik) *adj.*—A: in a frenzy. B: unchanging. C: moving through space.

6. flux ('fluhks) *n.*—A: series of failures. B: continued flow. C: rapid rise.

7. vicissitudes (vuh-'si-suh-toods) *n.*—A: exact opposites. B: minor adjustments. C: ups and downs.

8. fickle ('fih-kuhl) *adj.*—A: beginning to decay. B: marked by a lack of constancy. C: stuck in a rut.

9. immutable (ih-'myu-tuh-buhl) *adj.*—A: in motion. B: not susceptible to change. C: becoming a monster.

10. adapt (uh-'dapt) *v.*—A: spread gradually. B: become airborne. C: make fit, usually by alteration.

11. crescendo (kreh-'shen-doh) *n.*—A: sudden narrowing. B: gradual increase. C: change in color.

12. hiatus (hiy-'ay-tuhs) *n.*—A: growth spurt. B: interruption in time or continuity. C: change of season.

13. agitate ('a-juh-tayt) *v.*—A: replace. B: break into bits. C: disturb emotionally.

14. senescent (sih-'neh-snt) *adj.*—A: getting old. B: catching fire. C: developing a fragrance.

15. incorrigible (in-'kor-uh-juh-buhl) *adj.*—A: rustproof. B: spontaneous. C: not reformable.

Better with Age

"Changes" Answers

1. ameliorate—[A] make better or more tolerable. I find that just 15 minutes of yoga daily *ameliorates* my worries.

2. tack—[B] follow a zigzag course. Deftly, the captain *tacked* through the rocky shoals of the bay.

3. ferment—[A] state of unrest or disorderly development. Henry's writer's block was followed by a creative *ferment* in his poetry.

4. synchronize—[A] cause to coincide. Before we begin the 5K race, let's *synchronize* our watches.

5. static—[B] unchanging. Alyson found the novel's characters to be a bit *static* and one-dimensional.

6. flux—[B] continued flow. It's too soon to predict the election—everything's in *flux*.

7. vicissitudes—[C] ups and downs. One thing I've learned: Life is anything but constant, so enjoy its *vicissitudes*.

8. fickle—[B] marked by a lack of constancy. Tara described her niece as "*fickle* at best" after their visit to the toy store.

9. immutable—[B] not susceptible to change. Apparently, my upstairs tenant thinks loud, thumping music is his *immutable* right.

10. adapt—[C] make fit, usually by alteration. If you want to eat vegan, I can *adapt* the recipe.

11. crescendo—[B] gradual increase. The concerto ended with an unexpected yet effective *crescendo*.

12. hiatus—[B] interruption in time or continuity. The mayoral debate was marked by an uncomfortable *hiatus* before the incumbent responded.

13. agitate—[C] disturb emotionally. If you ask me, those therapy sessions just *agitate* Karyn even more.

14. senescent—[A] getting old. The rocking chair is gorgeous, but do you really see me as *senescent*?

15. incorrigible—[C] not reformable. I'm afraid our new puppy is simply *incorrigible* when it comes to sleeping on the couch.

JUST A PHASE?

The moon is a natural symbol of change, and its shape-shifting comes in phases. As it grows from invisibility (a new moon), it is *waxing*; when between half and full, it is called *gibbous* (literally, "humpbacked"). As it shrinks again, it is *waning*; and when it approaches a sliver of a fingernail in appearance, it is called a *crescent*.

SHORT ON TIME

There's never enough time—or words to describe it. See how long it takes you to do our quiz. For answers, turn the page.

1. anachronism (uh-'nak-ruh-niz-um) *n.*—A: brief interval. B: grandfather clock. C: thing misplaced in time.

2. concurrent (cun-'cur-unt) *adj.*—A: occasional. B: simultaneous. C: in the nick of time.

3. temporize ('tem-puh-rise) *v.*—A: evade in order to delay. B: get up-to-date. C: put on a schedule.

4. ephemeral (ih-'fem-uh-rul) *adj.*—A: short-lived. B: antique. C: improving with age.

5. dormancy ('door-mun-see) *n.*—A: incubation period. B: curfew. C: state of inactivity.

6. incipient (in-'sip-ee-unt) *adj.*—A: cyclical. B: just beginning. C: out of sync.

7. equinox ('ee-kwuh-nocks) *n.*—A: when day is longest. B: when day is shortest. C: when day and night are the same length.

8. pro tempore (pro-'tem-puh-ree) *adv.*—A: in good time. B: ahead of time. C: for the time being.

9. juncture ('junk-chur) *n.*—A: midyear. B: point in time. C: gap in the geologic record.

10. erstwhile ('urst-wile) *adj.*—A: past. B: present. C: future.

11. dilatory ('dill-uh-tor-ee) *adj.*—A: early. B: tardy. C: occurring at ever-widening intervals.

12. moratorium (more-uh-'tore-ee-um) *n.*—A: half a century. B: suspension of activity. C: clock tower.

13. perpetuate (pur-'peh-chuh-wate) *v.*—A: happen at the wrong moment. B: speed up. C: make everlasting.

14. horologe ('hore-uh-loje) *n.*—A: astronomical calendar. B: timepiece. C: dusk.

15. Olympiad (uh-'lim-pee-ad) *n.*—A: four-year interval. B: international date line. C: Greek sundial.

16. estivate ('es-tuh-vate) *v.*—A: speed. B: guess the time. C: pass the summer.

Better with Age

"Short on Time" Answers

1. anachronism—[C] thing misplaced in time. I'm pretty sure that the iPod earbuds Mona Lisa is wearing are an *anachronism*.

2. concurrent—[B] simultaneous. The soundings of the dinner bell and the fire alarm were *concurrent* in the house where we grew up.

3. temporize—[A] evade in order to delay. Asked what had happened to the plate of sugar cookies that had been on the counter, Jeremy *temporized* by telling his mother she looked beautiful.

4. ephemeral—[A] short-lived. The New England spring is as *ephemeral* as a mayfly.

5. dormancy—[C] state of inactivity. In the middle of the big sales meeting, Stanley emerged from *dormancy* with a loud snort.

6. incipient—[B] just beginning. Clem slathered on the herbal concoction and then examined his pate for any *incipient* hairs.

7. equinox—[C] when day and night are the same length. Arlene has the brownest of thumbs, but every spring *equinox*, she pores over all the nursery catalogs she can find.

8. pro tempore—[C] for the time being. They told me I could have the job *pro tempore*, until they find someone qualified.

9. juncture—[B] point in time. James realized he had come to an important *juncture* in his life when he lost his job and won the lottery on the same day.

10. erstwhile—[A] past. Our city's *erstwhile* mayor now makes his residence in the upstate penitentiary.

11. dilatory—[B] tardy. Stacy apologized for being *dilatory* in sending thank-you notes but was able to write one for our baby gift now that the baby is in college.

12. moratorium—[B] suspension of activity. My brother-in-law and I are observing a *moratorium* on political discussions.

13. perpetuate—[C] make everlasting. His self-flattery *perpetuates* the myth that he's actually competent.

14. horologe—[B] timepiece. Obsessed with *horologes*, my aunt stuffs her house with sundials, hourglasses, and cuckoo clocks.

15. Olympiad—[A] four-year interval. They're a very frugal couple; they eat out once an *Olympiad*.

16. estivate—[C] pass the summer. I am looking forward to *estivating* on the seashore.

ZZZZ

Here are some zippy words starting with the last letter of the alphabet. Proceed with zeal and zest, and when you need to check your answers, zoom over to the next page.

1. **zabaglione** (zah-buhl-'yo-nee) *n.*—A: canvas sack. B: stage villain. C: whipped dessert served in a glass.

2. **zaftig** ('zahf-tihg) *adj.*—A: charmingly witty. B: pleasingly plump. C: completely famished.

3. **zax** (zacks) *n.*—A: roofing tool. B: music synthesizer. C: caffeine pill.

4. **zephyr** ('zeh-fer) *n.*—A: ancient lute. B: gentle breeze. C: crown prince.

5. **zeta** ('zay-tuh) *n.*—A: prototype. B: sixth letter of the Greek alphabet. C: great beauty.

6. **zetetic** (zuh-'tet-ik) *adj.*—A: arid. B: investigative. C: made of hemp.

7. **ziggurat** ('zih-guh-rat) *n.*—A: lightning bolt. B: pyramidal tower. C: flying squirrel.

8. **zinfandel** ('zin-fuhn-del) *n.*—A: narrow valley. B: heretic. C: red wine.

9. **zircon** ('zer-kahn) *n.*—A: gas-powered blimp. B: gemstone. C: traffic cone.

10. **zloty** ('zlah-tee) *n.*—A: airhead. B: Polish currency. C: earphone jack.

11. **zoetrope** ('zoh-ee-trohp) *n.*—A: optical spinning toy. B: sun-loving flower. C: exaggeration.

12. **zori** ('zohr-ee) *n.*—A: antelope. B: flat sandal. C: seaweed wrap.

13. **zydeco** ('zy-deh-koh) *n.*—A: music of southern Louisiana. B: magnifying glass. C: secret password.

14. **zygomatic** (zy-guh-'mat-ik) *adj.*—A: related to the cheekbone. B: mysterious. C: of pond life.

15. **zyzzyva** ('ziz-uh-vuh) *n.*—A: type of weevil. B: tricky situation. C: fertilized cell.

Better with Age

"Zzzz" Answers

1. zabaglione—[C] whipped dessert served in a glass. I hate to waste a good *zabaglione*, but I'm on a diet.

2. zaftig—[B] pleasingly plump. The character in that film was a bit *zaftig*, thanks to her chocolate habit.

3. zax—[A] roofing tool. Kamal built this entire cabin himself, from laying every floorboard to trimming every roof tile with a *zax*.

4. zephyr—[B] gentle breeze. On stressful days, I like to fantasize I'm on a tropical beach with a cool *zephyr* blowing through my hair.

5. zeta—[B] sixth letter of the Greek alphabet. The up-and-coming tech firm uses a *zeta* as its logo.

6. zetetic—[B] investigative. "My *zetetic* methods," said Sherlock Holmes, "are quite elementary, my dear Watson."

7. ziggurat—[B] pyramidal tower. The king ordered his subjects to build a great *ziggurat* in his honor.

8. zinfandel—[C] red wine. "Do you think *zinfandel* pairs well with nachos?" Alyssa asked with a smirk.

9. zircon—[B] gemstone. She thought he gave her a diamond engagement ring, but those gems were just *zircons*.

10. zloty—[B] Polish currency. How's the *zloty* holding up against the euro?

11. zoetrope—[A] optical spinning toy. Before there were movies, people could get the illusion of motion from a *zoetrope*'s whirling images.

12. zori—[B] flat sandal. After the strap on her *zori* snapped, Joelle had to go barefoot for the rest of the day.

13. zydeco—[A] music of southern Louisiana. Ian became a big fan of *zydeco* on his last trip to New Orleans.

14. zygomatic—[A] related to the cheekbone. Many football players use a *zygomatic* stripe of greasepaint to reduce glare.

15. zyzzyva—[A] type of weevil. "I can't believe this—there are *zyzzyvas* in the organic quinoa I just bought!" Matthew exclaimed.

WHAT'S FUNNY ABOUT JOHNNY?

In Italian comedies of the 16th to 18th centuries, a clown named Giovanni was a stock figure. Typically a servant who cleverly mocked the other characters, this clown became known by the nickname Zanni. Eventually Zanni became the adjective *zany*, which we use today to mean kooky and madcap, like a screwball comedy.

MEMORY LANE

🐦 QUOTABLE TWEETS

They say memory is the
first thing to go.
The second thing to go is memory.

@GEORGETAKEI

❝

Memory is often less about the truth
than about what we want it to be.

—DAVID HALBERSTAM

❝

Anything that triggers good memories
can't be all bad.

—ADAM WEST

❝

A person without regrets is a nincompoop.

—MIA FARROW

❝

Happiness is nothing more than good health
and a bad memory.

—ALBERT SCHWEITZER

❝

It's surprising how much of memory is built
around things unnoticed at the time.

—BARBARA KINGSOLVER

THE PERFECT WORDS FOR
RETIREMENT SPEECHES

The key to retirement is to find joy in the little things.
—SUSAN MILLER

"
People ask how I feel about getting old. I tell them I have the same question. I'm learning as I go.
—PAUL SIMON

"
I'm not just retiring from the company, I'm also retiring from my stress, my commute, my alarm clock, and my iron.
—HARTMAN JULE

"
Retire? I can't spell the word. I'd play in a wheelchair.
—KEITH RICHARDS

"
Life begins at retirement.
—UNKNOWN

"
There's one thing I always wanted to do before I quit—retire!
—GROUCHO MARX

Retirement means no pressure, no stress, no heartache . . . unless you play golf.

—GENE PERRET

"

It is time I stepped aside for a less experienced and less able man.

—SCOTT ELLEDGE

"

The trouble with retirement is that you never get a day off.

—ABE LEMONS

"

Retirement, a time to enjoy life! A time to do what you want to do, when you want to do it, how you want to do it.

—CATHERINE PULSIFER

"

When a man retires and time is no longer a matter of urgent importance, his colleagues generally present him with a watch.

—RC SHERIFF

"

Don't simply retire from something; have something to retire to.

—HARRY EMERSON FOSDICK

In all the chaos that's going on, we need a little love and romance.
—DIANA KRALL

LOVE WINS

Love is hard and takes work, but a rewarding relationship is worth the effort. Reading words of wisdom about matters of the heart helps remind us how magical love can be.

ON MARRIAGE

Rituals are important.
Nowadays it's hip not to be married.
I'm not interested in being hip.
—JOHN LENNON

"

Here's the secret to a happy marriage:
Do what your wife tells you.
—DENZEL WASHINGTON

"

Most of my life, if a man did something
totally other than the way I thought it should be done,
I would try to correct him.
Now I say, "Oh, isn't that interesting?"
—ELLEN BURSTYN

"

I really do believe
if you can live through remodeling a home,
you can live the rest of your lives together.
—JENNIFER ANISTON

"

In the early years, you fight because
you don't understand each other. In later
years, you fight because you do.
—JOAN DIDION

ATTRACTION

I like to have nice conversations with a man that teach me something, make me mad, make me curious. Then I find him attractive.
—**RENEE ZELLWEGER**

Obviously I have this strange animal magnetism. It's very hard to take my eyes off myself.
—**MICK JAGGER**

"I've reached the age where competence is a turn-on."
—**BILLY JOEL**

To my eye, women get sexier around 35. They know a thing or two, and knowledge is always alluring.
—**PIERCE BROSNAN**

If you have good thoughts, they will shine out of your face like moonbeams, and you will always look lovely.
—**ROALD DAHL, *THE TWITS***

A LITTLE LOVE

🐦 QUOTABLE TWEETS

What matter is it where you find a real love that makes this life a little easier?

@ALECBALDWIN

"
Love is the net where hearts are caught like fish.
—**MUHAMMAD ALI**

"
Manners are love in a cool climate.
—**QUENTIN CRISP**

"
All our loves are first loves.
—**SUSAN FROMBERG**

"
What the world really needs is more love and less paperwork.
—**PEARL BAILEY**

"
When you fall in love, it doesn't matter how old you are. You always feel like a teenager.
—**AMY DICKINSON**

The perfect man? A poet on a motorcycle.
—LUCINDA WILLIAMS

"

I like a woman with a head on her shoulders.
I hate necks.
—STEVE MARTIN

"

Honesty is probably the sexiest thing
a man can give to a woman.
—DEBRA MESSING

"

Flirting is conversational chemistry.
—ISAAC MIZRAHI

"

Sex appeal is fifty percent what you've got and
fifty percent what people think you've got.
—SOPHIA LOREN

"

When you have no one in your life who you
can call and say, "I'm scared," then your life is
unfulfilling. You need somebody you can
trust enough to say, "I need help."
—STEVEN SODERBERGH

LOVE HURTS

Love is a great wrecker of peace of mind.
—SUSAN CHEEVER

"

Jealousy is all the fun you think they had.
—ERICA JONG

"

You don't need to be a heroin addict
or a performance poet to experience extremity.
You just have to love someone.
—NICK HORNBY

"

Tests of love always end badly.
—MELANIE THERNSTROM

"

Women are like the police. They could have all the
evidence in the world, but they still want the confession.
—CHRIS ROCK

"

Assumptions are the termites of relationships.
—HENRY WINKLER

"

What are the three words guaranteed to humiliate
men everywhere? "Hold my purse."
—FRANÇOIS MORENCY

QUOTABLE TWEETS

If you want to avoid heated arguments, never discuss religion, politics, or whether the toilet paper roll should go over or under.

—@ALYANKOVIC

"

Love is never as ferocious as when you think it's going to leave you.

—ANITA SHREVE

"

So many catastrophes in love are only accidents of egotism.

—HECTOR BIANCIOTTI

"

Four be the things I'd have been better without: love, curiosity, freckles and doubt.

—DOROTHY PARKER

"

Love is, or it ain't. Thin love ain't love at all.

—TONI MORRISON

"

It is often hard to bear the tears that we ourselves have caused.

—MARCEL PROUST

Love Wins

THE PERFECT WORDS FOR
WEDDING TOASTS

A journey is like marriage. The certain way to be wrong is to think you control it.
—JOHN STEINBECK

"

Love doesn't just sit there, like a stone; it has to be made, like bread, remade all the time, made new.
—URSULA K. LEGUIN

"

Let there be spaces in your togetherness / And let the winds of the heavens dance between you.
—KAHLIL GIBRAN

"

In marriage, being the right person is as important as finding the right person.
—WILBERT DONALD GOUGH

"

The key to a long and healthy marriage is that, honestly, there's nothing worth fighting about.
—JAY LENO

"

Marrying for love may be a bit risky, but it is so honest that God can't help but smile on it.
—JOSH BILLINGS

FEELING IT

Love is in the air every February 14, but why limit yourself to just one emotion? You'll experience a wide range of feelings in this vocabulary quiz. If you're in the mood, check the next page for answers.

1. **ebullient** (ih-'bull-yent) *adj.*—A: tranquil. B: haughty. C: enthusiastic.

2. **pique** (peek) *n.*—A: resentment. B: self-importance. C: whimsy.

3. **bonhomie** (bah-nuh-'mee) *n.*—A: nostalgia. B: friendliness. C: peace of mind.

4. **dour** ('dow-er) *adj.*—A: guilty. B: generous. C: gloomy.

5. **amatory** ('am-uh-tohr-ee) *adj.*—A: irritable. B: romantic. C: easygoing.

6. **timorous** ('tih-muh-rus) *adj.*—A: affectionate. B: fiery. C: fearful.

7. **wistfully** ('wist-fuh-lee) *adv.*—A: with sad longing. B: dreamily. C: in defiance.

8. **belligerent** (buh-'lij-uh-rent) *adj.*—A: hostile. B: regretful. C: sympathetic.

9. **fervor** ('fer-ver) *n.*—A: aggravation. B: strong preference. C: passion.

10. **compunction**. (kum-'punk-shun) *n*—A: remorse. B: exasperation. C: doubt.

11. **umbrage** ('uhm-brij) *n.*—A: indignant displeasure. B: destructive rage. C: meditative state.

12. **schadenfreude** ('shah-den-froy-duh) *n.*—A: tearfulness. B: timidity. C: joy at another's pain.

13. **querulous**. ('kwair-yuh-lus) *adj*—A: hyperactive. B: fretful. C: fickle.

14. **blithesome** ('blyth-sum) *adj.*—A: unconcerned. B: guarded. C: merry.

15. **lugubrious** (luh-'goo-bree-us) *adj.*—A: chatty. B: mournful. C: disgusted.

Love Wins

"Feeling It" Answers

1. ebullient [C] enthusiastic. Nina has such a bubbly, *ebullient* personality—I can't believe she was ever shy!

2. pique [A] resentment. After being passed over for a promotion, Manuel left the office in a fit of *pique*.

3. bonhomie [B] friendliness. There's an absence of *bonhomie* between the rival basketball teams.

4. dour [C] gloomy. How can you be so *dour* on this sunny morning?

5. amatory [B] romantic. Some people claim that chocolate can put you in an *amatory* mood, but I don't buy it.

6. timorous [C] fearful. Bernard is usually *timorous* around large dogs, but he seems to love our three golden retrievers.

7. wistfully [A] with sad longing. "I miss when my friends would call me on my birthday—now they just text!" Monica said *wistfully*.

8. belligerent [A] hostile. The sightseers were chased from the pond by a *belligerent* swan.

9. fervor [C] passion. Nicole's *fervor* for local honey inspired her to open a beekeeping business.

10. compunction [A] remorse. The con man showed no *compunction* about fleecing unsuspecting investors.

11. umbrage [A] indignant displeasure. Elvira took *umbrage* at being called a wicked witch.

12. schadenfreude [C] joy at another's pain. We all felt some *schadenfreude* when our boorish manager was finally fired.

13. querulous [B] fretful. I don't recommend traveling overseas with Aunt Lisa—she gets *querulous* and cranky on long flights.

14. blithesome [C] merry. "There is nothing so *blithesome* as a summer day at the beach with the children, is there?" Tim said.

15. lugubrious [B] mournful. This *lugubrious* violin solo isn't doing much to raise my spirits.

COME ON, FORGET YOUR TROUBLES
Our vote for the best emotion of them all: *happy*. It's certainly versatile, showing up in a number of quirky expressions. You might be *as happy as a clam* or *as happy as Larry*. An easygoing person is *happy-go-lucky,* while a reckless one is *trigger-happy*. And if you're still not feeling the joy, well, you can just head to *happy hour*—or some other *happy place*.

LOVE CONNECTION

This quiz is all about the language of love. We hope you'll feel ardor for these words of the heart. For answers, turn the page.

1. nuptial *adj.*—A: forced to elope. B: named after the mother. C: pertaining to a marriage.

2. Casanova *n.*—A: inn where honeymooners stay. B: man with many love affairs. C: nagging spouse.

3. rendezvous *n.*—A: meeting, as between lovers. B: formal engagement. C: romantic balcony view.

4. ardor *n.*—A: fierce heartbeat. B: heat of passion. C: garden with a love seat.

5. spoon *v.*—A: to fall deeply in love at first sight. B: go Dutch. C: kiss and caress.

6. rapture *n.*—A: secret love note. B: state of bliss. C: full bridal gown.

7. ogle *v.*—A: to stare at wolfishly. B: howl at the moon. C: rub noses affectionately.

8. coquette *n.*—A: young lady who flirts. B: heart-shaped pastry. C: lawn game for couples.

9. nubile *adj.*—A: hard to catch. B: of marrying age. C: posing while nude.

10. conjugal *adj.*—A: priestly. B: relating to a husband and wife. C: of a brassiere.

11. banns *n.*—A: music at weddings. B: announcement of marriage. C: divorce proceedings.

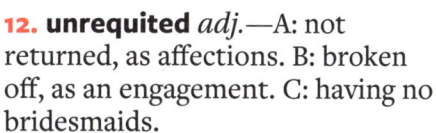

12. unrequited *adj.*—A: not returned, as affections. B: broken off, as an engagement. C: having no bridesmaids.

13. agape *n.*—A: spiritual love. B: endearing poem. C: openmouthed kiss.

14. shivaree *n.*—A: courtesy toward women. B: excited feeling. C: loud music played as a joke outside a newlywed couple's window.

Love Wins

"Love Connection" Answers

1. nuptial—[C] pertaining to a marriage. Everyone at the church was elated to see Matilda sob happily as she recited her *nuptial* vows.

2. Casanova—[B] man with many love affairs. The singer is such a playboy, just like his famous Italian ancestor Giovanni *Casanova*.

3. rendezvous—[A] meeting, as between lovers. Without telling their parents, Pierre and Marie arranged an ardent *rendezvous*.

4. ardor—[B] heat of passion. If two jurors fell in love, there would be *ardor* in the court.

5. spoon—[C] to kiss and caress. Under the moon in June, sweethearts *spoon* and swoon.

6. rapture—[B] state of bliss. After his first kiss, Woody walked around in a *rapture* for days.

7. ogle—[A] to stare at wolfishly. Dexter, an incorrigible lout, couldn't help but *ogle* the lady walking by.

8. coquette—[A] young lady who flirts. A winking *coquette* might distract even the most earnest croquet player.

9. nubile—[B] of marrying age. Felicity is not allowed to get engaged until she's *nubile*.

10. conjugal—[B] relating to a husband and wife. A *conjugal* deal may be sealed with a kiss.

11. banns—[B] announcement of marriage. The couple were going bananas waiting for the priest to read the *banns*.

12. unrequited—[A] not returned, as affections. My heart is ignited, but I'm blue because my love is *unrequited*.

13. agape—[A] spiritual love. I gape at the selfless purity of *agape*.

14. shivaree—[C] loud music played as a joke outside a newlywed couple's window. It may have been fun for their pals, but the earsplitting *shivaree* gave Erica and Ethan a honeymoon headache.

ALL THAT GLITTERS

Break out your bling—Word Power is going glam! We're shining the spotlight on glittery words related to jewelry. Will your score be as good as gold?
Turn the page for the answers.

1. bauble ('bah-bull) *n.*—A: showy trinket. B: flawed gemstone. C: set of bracelets.

2. gilt (gilt) *adj.*—A: silver-plated. B: finely carved. C: covered in gold.

3. carat ('kehr-uht) *n.*—A: unit of weight. B: measure of clarity. C: depth of color.

4. amulet ('am-yoo-let) *n.*—A: watchband. B: protective charm. C: adjustable clasp.

5. iridescent (eer-uh-'dess-ent) *adj.*—A: rustproof. B: having rainbow colors. C: made of glass.

6. alloy ('al-oy) *n.*—A: mixture of metals. B: gray pearl. C: precious mineral.

7. solitaire ('sah-luh-tayr) *n.*—A: loop in a chain. B: gem set alone. C: white metal.

8. girandole ('jeer-en-dohl) *n.*—A: pendant earring. B: rare moonstone. C: cuff link.

9. citrine. (sih-'treen) *n*—A: pink sapphire. B: yellow quartz. C: green topaz.

10. adorn (uh-'dorn) *v.*—A: determine value. B: make beautiful. C: bend into shape.

11. baguette (bag-'et) *n.*—A: beaded purse. B: cocktail ring. C: rectangular stone.

12. filigree ('fih-luh-gree) *n.*—A: vintage brass. B: impurity. C: delicate metalwork.

13. palladium (puh-'lay-dee-um) *n.*—A: fool's gold. B: pinkie ring. C: silver-white metal.

14. facet ('fass-et) *n.*—A: surface on a cut gem. B: nose stud. C: price per ounce.

15. rondelle (ron-'del) *n.*—A: heavy brooch. B: long necklace. C: jeweled ring.

Love Wins

"All That Glitters" Answers

1. bauble [A] showy trinket. Most of my accessories are *baubles* I found at yard sales.

2. gilt [C] covered in gold. Lenore slipped a *gilt* barrette into her long dark hair.

3. carat [A] unit of weight. The famous Hope Diamond weighs a whopping 45 *carats*!

4. amulet [B] protective charm. Clutching the *amulet* that hung around his neck, Rowen turned to face the evil sorcerer.

5. iridescent [B] having rainbow colors. Kelly's *iridescent* opal bracelet sparkled in the sunshine.

6. alloy [A] mixture of metals. Rose gold is actually an *alloy* of gold, silver, and copper.

7. solitaire [B] gem set alone. "Will you marry me?" asked the duke, slipping the diamond *solitaire* ring onto his beloved's finger.

8. girandole [A] pendant earring. In the 19th century, a fashionable lady might wear ornate *girandoles* to dinner.

9. citrine [B] yellow quartz. *Citrine's* distinctive color comes from traces of iron.

10. adorn [B] make beautiful. The fortune-teller's wrists were *adorned* with countless bangles, which clinked softly as she walked.

11. baguette [C] rectangular stone. "May I suggest a *baguette*, rather than an oval cut?" the salesperson said.

12. filigree [C] delicate metalwork. The queen's tiara features Victorian *filigree*.

13. palladium [C] silver-white metal. *Palladium* looks similar to platinum, but it's lighter and less expensive.

14. facet [A] surface on a cut gem. When a gem is expertly cut, *facets* create beautiful patterns on the stone.

15. rondelle [C] jeweled ring. Chaya's most prized possession is a sapphire *rondelle* that belonged to her great-grandmother.

ALL THAT GLITTERS

The names of gemstones often reflect their appearance—*ruby* comes from Latin's *rubeus* (meaning "red"), for example. Other inspiring qualities: *Diamond* is from the Latin *adamantem* ("hardest metal"), and *tanzanite* was discovered in Tanzania. Meanwhile, *amethyst* descended from the Greek *amethystos* ("not drunk"), as the purple stone was thought to prevent intoxication—if you drank out of an amethyst goblet.

ONLY U

Words with no vowels except u form a peculiar group—or, one might say, a rum bunch. Take a run (but not a bum's rush) through this quiz, featuring words with the vowel exclusively. Dumbstruck? Turn the page for answers.

1. fugu ('foo-goo) *n.*—A: African dance. B: flintstone. C: poisonous fish.

2. susurrus (su-'sir-us) *n.*—A: whispering sound. B: low layer of clouds. C: magic elixir.

3. tub-thump ('tub-thump) *v.*—A: challenge. B: support loudly. C: fail disastrously.

4. plumb ('plum) *adj.*—A: purplish-red. B: exactly vertical. C: exhausted.

5. mugwump ('mug-wump) *n.*—A: politically independent person. B: sad child. C: punch or fight.

6. kudzu ('kood- or 'kud-zoo) *n.*—A: two-masted ship. B: fast-growing vine. C: rabbit-like rodent.

7. luff ('luhf) *v.*—A: change your mind. B: deal a poker hand. C: turn a ship to the wind.

8. jumbuck ('juhm-buck) *n.*—A: Aus-tralian sheep. B: silver dollar. C: tangled mess.

9. succubus ('suc-cu-bus) *n.*—A: skin pore. B: double-decker trolley. C: female demon.

10. usufruct ('yoo-zuh- or 'yoo-suh-frukt) *n.*—A: stubborn person. B: legal right of use. C: light-bending prism.

11. chum ('chuhm) *n.*—A: gritty build-up. B: bait for fish. C: trill of a bird.

12. lutz ('luhtz) *n.*—A: ice-skating jump. B: unit of electric power. C: World War II bomber.

13. subfusc (sub-'fuhsk) *adj.*—A: using espionage. B: drab or dusky. C: too wet to ignite.

14. durum ('der-uhm) *n.*—A: wild bull. B: pause in poetry reading. C: kind of wheat.

15. pung ('pung) *n.*—A: military takeover. B: hole in a barrel. C: box-shaped sleigh.

DEEP ROOTS

When missionaries first arrived in sunny Polynesia, they distributed long dresses to the native women so they could cover up. Around 1923, these garments adopted the name *muumuu*—borrowed from the Hawaiian *mu'umu'u*, which means "cut off"—because the restrictive parts, particularly the yoke and the sleeves, were snipped away for comfort.

"Only U" Answers

1. fugu—[C] poisonous fish. Does Dad know he has to cut out the toxic parts of the *fugu* before he cooks it?

2. susurrus—[A] whispering sound. The *susurrus* of night winds lulled the sentry to sleep.

3. tub-thump—[B] support loudly. These pushy kids of ours are *tub-thumping* for a raise to their allowance.

4. plumb—[B] exactly vertical. Is it just me, or does that old tower in Pisa look not quite *plumb*?

5. mugwump—[A] politically independent person. Despite being a *mugwump*, Gary takes his civic duty very seriously come Election Day.

6. kudzu—[B] fast-growing vine. My roommate's stuff is taking over the dorm quicker than a *kudzu* in Dixie.

7. luff—[C] turn a ship to the wind. "A *real* yachtsman would know how to *luff* without suddenly knocking all the passengers overboard," Becky sniped under her breath.

8. jumbuck—[A] Australian sheep. In the song "Waltzing Matilda," it's a *jumbuck* that the swagman catches beside the billabong.

9. succubus—[C] female demon. According to folklore, a *succubus* often appears in dreams to seduce men (its male counterpart is an incubus).

10. usufruct—[B] legal right of use. Our lawyer friend David is often accused of taking work home: Last night, he asked his son, "Hey, who gave you the *usufruct* to play with my phone?"

11. chum—[B] bait for fish. "Chief, best drop another *chum* marker," Quint utters as the crew hunts down the famous predator in *Jaws*.

12. lutz—[A] ice-skating jump. Despite a less-than-perfect *lutz*, Carolann's program was strong enough to help her retain the regional title.

13. subfusc—[B] drab or dusky. Every year, Clarice waits for a *subfusc* winter morning to reread *Wuthering Heights*.

14. durum—[C] kind of wheat. I hate to tell you, but your all-*durum* diet is not gluten-free.

15. pung—[C] box-shaped sleigh. "Oh, what fun it is to ride in a… *pung*!" just doesn't have the same ring, does it?

SOUND SMARTER

Forming the negatives of words can be tricky, and often it's best to avoid our vowel of the month. Consider: *inadvisable* (not *unadvisable*), *infrequent* (not *unfrequent*), and *atypical* (not *untypical*). But sometimes the *u*'s have it: *uncontrollable* (not *incontrollable*) and *unalterable* (not *inalterable*).

ANIMAL INSTINCTS

Do you know your budgies from your whippets? Your alpacas from your yaks? Here, we separate the mice from the men by testing your knowledge of all creatures great and small. How many of these wild words can you tame? Answers on next page.

1. **ailurophile** *n.*—A: lover of cats. B: one who is afraid of animals. C: collector of snakes.

2. **leporine** *adj.*—of or relating to… A: a parrot. B: a goat. C: a hare.

3. **komondor** *n.*—A: Hungarian sheepdog. B: mythical lizard. C: trained falcon.

4. **Komodo dragon** *n.*—A: Chinese miniature dog. B: Indonesian lizard. C: North American toad.

5. **caudal** *adj.*—A: having pointed ears. B: born as twins. C: taillike.

6. **stridulate** *v.*—A: shed a coat. B: mate. C: make a shrill noise by rubbing together body structures, as a cricket does.

7. **clowder** *n.*—A: fish food. B: group of cats. C: old-fashioned wooden dog toy.

8. **brindled** *adj.*—A: streaky, as a coat. B: vaccinated. C: on end, as neck hairs.

9. **card** *v.*—A: breed for docility. B: brush or disentangle fibers, as of wool. C: demand to know a dog's pedigree.

10. **zoolatry** *n.*—A: animal worship. B: system for grouping animals. C: study of animal communication.

11. **vibrissa** *n.*—A: whisker. B: horse's hoof. C: tortoise's lower shell.

12. **grimalkin** *n.*—A: frog pond. B: hip injury in dogs. C: old female cat.

13. **feral** *adj.*—A: rabid or otherwise diseased. B: pregnant or in heat. C: not domesticated.

14. **cosset** *v.*—A: pamper or treat as a pet. B: selectively breed. C: grow more docile.

15. **ethology** *n.*—A: proper treatment of animals. B: science of genetics. C: study of animal behavior.

Love Wins **97**

"Animal Instincts" Answers

1. ailurophile—[A] lover of cats. Being an *ailurophile* is one thing, but building an entire wing for your feline friend is another.

2. leporine—[C] of or relating to a hare. "So much for the judges' *leporine* bias," boasted the tortoise as he studied the instant replay.

3. komondor—[A] Hungarian sheepdog. "Maybe I'll have your *komondor* do double duty as a kitchen mop!" Ms. Gulch growled.

4. Komodo dragon—[B] Indonesian lizard. The *Komodo dragon*'s name is justified: This carnivore is the heaviest living species of lizard in the world.

5. caudal—[C] taillike. Waving her arms in a ludicrously *caudal* fashion, Ann did her best to illustrate the puppy's excitement.

6. stridulate—[C] make a shrill noise by rubbing together body structures, as a cricket does. The insects continued to *stridulate*, forcing sleep-deprived Fran to don earplugs.

7. clowder—[B] group of cats. Testing a new catnip recipe, Leslie fled the room pursued by a crazed *clowder*.

8. brindled—[A] streaky, as a coat. Camouflaged in her costume, Marti hid among the *brindled* barnyard cows.

9. card—[B] brush or disentangle fibers, as of wool. At the rate Beth is *carding* that yarn, she'll have half a sweater by Easter!

10. zoolatry—[A] animal worship. Do you think naming your cocker spaniel Your Majesty is taking *zoolatry* too far?

11. vibrissa—[A] whisker. Constantly hurrying, the nervous White Rabbit still took time to fuss over each *vibrissa*.

12. grimalkin—[C] old female cat. We weren't sure who was creepier: the old lady or the bedraggled *grimalkin* that always sat on her lap.

13. feral—[C] not domesticated. When Liz said, "Smile for the camera," her son bared his teeth like a *feral* hound.

14. cosset—[A] pamper or treat as a pet. Uncle Paul *cossets* his nieces. They don't have to lift a finger.

15. ethology—[C] study of animal behavior. Natalie needs to complete her *ethology* degree before she can join the monkey expedition.

SOUND SMARTER

Here, we revisit *lay* and *lie*, specifically in the phrase *lay/lie low*. *Lie low* is the correct present-tense form. Why? Standard usage still applies: *Lie* doesn't require an object ("go lie down"); *lay* does ("lay your head down"). In the past tense, *lie* becomes *lay*; *lay* becomes *laid*. So a wily predator might lie low as it stalks its prey.

---

98   USE YOUR WORDS, VOLUME 2

LOVE DRAMA

Shakespeare's princely Hamlet is the character who mopes about muttering, "Words, words, words." Here, from the venerable play by the Bard, are some words (in their root form) you can actively employ today. If, tragically, you need answers, consult the next page.

1. impetuous (im-'peh-choo-wes) *adj.*—A: full of questions. B: scheming. C: rash.

2. traduce (truh-'doos) *v.*—A: shame using lies. B: parry with a sword. C: exchange for a profit.

3. whet ('wet) *v.*—A: sharpen or stimulate. B: moisten. C: hasten.

4. rub ('ruhb) *n.*—A: piece of gossip. B: difficulty. C: good-luck charm.

5. germane (jer-'mayn) *adj.*—A: poisonous. B: relevant. C: ghostly.

6. incorporeal (in-kor-'por-ee-uhl) *adj.*—A: using military might. B: having no body. C: full of tiny holes.

7. wax ('waks) *v.*—A: grow smaller. B: grow larger. C: grow a mustache.

8. paragon ('par-uh-gahn) *n.*—A: mounted soldier. B: five-sided figure. C: example of excellence.

9. calumny ('ka-luhm-nee) *n.*—A: row of pillars. B: disaster. C: character attack.

10. beguile (bih-'giyl) *v.*—A: bond or form a union. B: deceive. C: leave stranded.

11. felicity (fih-'lih-suh-tee) *n.*—A: ill fortune. B: faithful devotion. C: happiness.

12. sully ('suh-lee) *v.*—A: answer back smartly. B: drizzle. C: defile or tarnish.

13. malefactor ('ma-luh-fak-tuhr) *n.*—A: masculine quality. B: one who commits an offense. C: swear word.

14. exhort (ig-'zort) *v.*—A: dig up. B: overthrow or dethrone. C: urge strongly.

15. quintessence (kwin-'teh-sents) *n.*—A: most typical example. B: one fifth. C: fluidity in language or spoken word.

Love Wins

"Love Drama" Answers

1. **impetuous**—[C] rash. Jenny walks up and *impetuously* hugs complete strangers.

2. **traduce**—[A] shame using lies. Jed loves to watch politicians on TV *traducing* each other with bogus statistics.

3. **whet**—[A] sharpen or stimulate. The aroma of turkey was all I needed to *whet* my Thanksgiving appetite.

4. **rub**—[B] difficulty. Playing hooky is easy, but not getting caught—there's the *rub*.

5. **germane**—[B] relevant. Your Honor, my client's nickname—Light Fingers—is not *germane* to this case of theft.

6. **incorporeal**—[B] having no body. After supper, Grandfather sat us down by the fire for a tale of the *incorporeal* beings supposedly haunting his house.

7. **wax**—[B] grow larger. Noah's hopes *waxed* as the rain began to wane.

8. **paragon**—[C] example of excellence. The poet's debut collection was a *paragon* of eloquence.

9. **calumny**—[C] character attack. If you can't win a debate with reason, try outright *calumny*.

10. **beguile**—[B] deceive. Don't let the mermaids *beguile* you with their siren songs.

11. **felicity**—[C] happiness. Nothing could diminish the *felicity* of the family's first holiday together in years.

12. **sully**—[C] defile or tarnish. It would take only one blowhard to *sully* the mayor's reputation.

13. **malefactor**—[B] one who commits an offense. Upon seeing someone pulled over by a traffic cop, my dad used to announce, "There goes another *malefactor*!"

14. **exhort**—[C] urge strongly. The candidate *exhorted* the crowd to make the right choice come Election Day.

15. **quintessence**—[A] most typical example. The human rights speaker was the *quintessence* of humility.

> ### DARK DOINGS
> The moody Hamlet is often called the melancholy Dane. *Melancholy* means gloomy, but it literally refers to "black bile." You might recognize its root parts in *melan* (a dark pigment) and *chole* (gall or ill temper). In medieval times, bodily "humors" were thought to influence our moods, black bile being one of these fluids.

SNUGGLE UP

Button up your overcoat and put on your thinking cap.
This quiz is meant to keep you out in the cold.
See if you can keep your mind hot.
For answers, turn to the next page.

1. arctic *adj.*—A: like the North Pole. B: extremely windy. C: located at the top of an igloo.

2. hibernate *v.*—A: to hike in snowshoes. B: lie sleeping through the winter. C: come down as sleet.

3. rime *n.*—A: slush. B: frosty coating. C: thin outer layer of an Eskimo Pie.

4. tundra *n.*—A: powdery snow. B: hot Nordic drink. C: cold, treeless plain.

5. frappe *n.*—A: hockey slap shot. B: wool topcoat. C: milk shake with ice cream.

6. floe *n.*—A: flat mass of ice at sea. B: row of icicles on an eave. C: diner waitress who brings you ice water.

7. permafrost *n.*—A: outdoor thermometer. B: snowman's hairdo. C: ground that stays frozen all year.

8. gelato *n.*—A: Italian ice cream. B: large hailstone. C: hooded pullover jacket.

9. mogul *n.*—A: bump on a ski slope. B: figure skating jump. C: kinetic sculpture with suspended snowballs.

10. toboggan *n.*—A: sled without runners. B: mountain cabin in the Alps. C: indoor skating rink.

11. boreal *adj.*—A: frosted, as cornflakes. B: of the north. C: overcast.

12. sitzmark *n.*—A: blizzard. B: avalanche. C: depression left in snow by a skier falling backward.

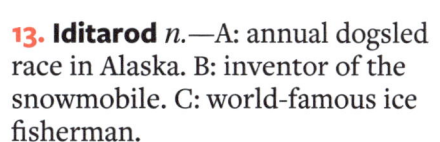

13. Iditarod *n.*—A: annual dogsled race in Alaska. B: inventor of the snowmobile. C: world-famous ice fisherman.

14. crampon *n.*—A: waterproof glove. B: ice climber's spiked footwear. C: frostbite.

Love Wins **101**

"Snuggle Up" Answers

1. arctic—[A] like the North Pole. Grandpa is always talking about how he trekked to school in *arctic* conditions.

2. hibernate—[B] lie sleeping through the winter. Many *hibernating* bears actually take a series of long naps.

3. rime—[B] frosty coating. After the ice storm, the *rime-encrusted tree branches* had an eerie look.

4. tundra—[C] cold, treeless plain. The explorer spotted a gray wolf across the *tundra*.

5. frappe—[C] milk shake with ice cream. In Boston you can order a *frappe*; in other parts of the country, this treat is a frosted, a velvet, or a cabinet.

6. floe—[A] flat mass of ice at sea. A *floe* may taste salty if you lick it because it's made of frozen seawater.

7. permafrost—[C] ground that stays frozen all year. Scientists worry that global warming is causing the Siberian *permafrost* to thaw and crumble.

8. gelato—[A] Italian ice cream. That hip new ice cream shop has all kinds of *gelato* flavors, including tomato-basil.

9. mogul—[A] ski slope bump. My brother went right from the bunny slope to the *mogul* field. Want to sign his cast?

10. toboggan—[A] sled without runners. The doomed lovers in the novel *Ethan Frome* steer their *toboggan* into a tree.

11. boreal—[B] of or located in the north. Billions of birds fly through the U.S. to the *boreal* forests to breed in the spring.

12. sitzmark—[C] indent left in snow by a skier falling backward. Uncle Harry said his ample *sitzmark* was a snow angel.

13. —[A] Alaskan dog-sled race. The winner of the *Iditarod* usually takes about ten days to finish the course.

14. crampon—[B] ice climber's spiked footwear. The mountaineer dug his *crampons* into the icy cliff face.

102   USE YOUR WORDS, VOLUME 2

TALK IT OUT

Having to explain it means you probably shouldn't have said it.
—**CARY CLACK**

"

Real listening is a willingness to let the other person change you.
—**ALAN ALDA**

"

When you don't know what you're talking about, it's hard to know when you're finished.
—**TOMMY SMOTHERS**

"

Eighty percent of all questions are statements in disguise.
—**DR. PHIL MCGRAW**

"

One thing I have learned is, if people tell you they had a "frank" discussion with someone, it is usually code for a yelling match with clenched fists.
—**LARRY KING**

"

When we criticize another person, it says nothing about that person; it merely says something about our own need to be critical.
—**RICHARD CARLSON**

THE PERFECT WORDS FOR
LOVE LETTERS

How in hell can you handle love without turning your life upside down? That's what love does; it changes everything.
—**LAUREN BACALL**

Love makes intellectual pretzels of us all.
—**SARAH BIRD**

Know that I love you and no matter what, I'll see you again.
—**BRIAN SWEENEY**

When the heart speaks, the mind finds it indecent to object.
—**MILAN KUNDERA**

In true love the smallest distance is too great, and the greatest distance can be bridged.
—**HANS NOUWENS**

In love, one and one are one.
—**JEAN-PAUL SARTRE**

This is the true measure of love: when we believe that we alone can love, that no one could ever have loved so before us, and that no one will ever love in the same way after us.
—JOHANN WOLFGANG VON GOETHE

❝

I love you, not only for what you are, but for what I am when I am with you.
—ROY CROFT

❝

As soon go kindle fire with snow, as seek to quench the fire of love with words.
—WILLIAM SHAKESPEARE

❝

There are a lot of things happening that show us that this, right now, is a time to love.
—STEVIE WONDER

❝

I was born when you kissed me. I died when you left me. I lived a few weeks while you loved me.
—HUMPHREY BOGART

If you want to walk fast,
walk alone.
If you want to walk far,
walk with others.
—**AFRICAN PROVERB**

MODERN FAMILY

Family is forever, and so are the friends
who become like family.
Today's family may look a little different
than in the past,
but the bonds that hold us together
are the same.

ROLE MODELS

The most remarkable thing about my mother
is that for 30 years she served the family
nothing but leftovers.
The original meal has never been found.
—**CALVIN TRILLIN**

"

Mother is a verb, not a noun.
—**SHONDA RHIMES**

"

They say our mothers really know how to push
our buttons—because they installed them.
—**ROBIN WILLIAMS**

"

🐦 **QUOTABLE TWEETS**

Being a mother is as beautiful and rewarding
as it is painful and devastating.
It is the highest of highs
and the lowest of lows.
@SARAHMCLACHLAN

"

I know enough to know that when
you're in a pickle . . . call Mom.
—**JENNIFER GARNER**

If pregnancy were a book, they would
cut the last two chapters.
— **NORA EPHRON**

"

No one else, ever, will think you're great
the way your mother does.
— **MARY MATALIN**

"

My perspective on my mother
has changed immensely.
She was a lot taller when I was younger.
— **HOWIE MANDEL**

"

It doesn't matter who my father was;
it matters who I remember he was.
— **ANNE SEXTON**

"

What's a good investment?
Go home from work early
and spend the afternoon
throwing a ball around with your son.
— **BEN STEIN**

"

You know what's cool?
My kids think I'm ordinary.
— **MICHAEL J. FOX**

Modern Family

PARENTAL ADVICE

My father used to say, "If you want to be different, do something different."
—**WYNTON MARSALIS**

"

My mom always said normal is just a cycle on the washing machine.
—**WYNONNA JUDD**

"

My father used to say, "Don't raise your voice. Improve your argument."
—**DESMOND TUTU**

"

It's never too late to have a happy childhood.
—**TOM ROBBINS**

"

My grandmother always used to say, "If you've got a dollar, there's plenty to share."
—**RIHANNA**

When your mother asks,
"Do you want a piece of advice?"
it is a mere formality. It doesn't matter
if you answer yes or no.
You're going to get it anyway.
—ERMA BOMBECK

"

My father said there were two kinds of people in the world: givers and takers. The takers may eat better, but the givers sleep better.
—MARLO THOMAS

"

I have found the best way to give advice to your children is to find out what they want and then advise them to do it.
—HARRY TRUMAN

"

We would worry less about what others think of us if we realized how seldom they do.
—ETHEL BARRETT

"

QUOTABLE TWEETS

I always dreamed about being
a pro QB, but more than anything,
I wanted to be like my dad.
@TIMTEBOW

Modern Family

FRIENDS FOR LIFE

Friends are the family you choose.
—**JENNIFER ANISTON**

"

What is it about friendship that makes being among friends so much richer than being among the most accomplished and interesting strangers?
—**SANDY SHEEHY**

"

One does not make friends. One recognizes them.
—**GARTH HENRICHS**

"

Ask friends about the people and places that shaped them, and summer springs up quickly when they tell their story: their first kiss, first beer, first job that changed everything.
—**NANCY GIBBS**

"

You don't have to have anything in common with people you've known since you were five. With old friends, you've got your whole life in common.
—**LYLE LOVETT**

"

The only way to have a friend is to be one.
—**RALPH WALDO EMERSON**

We love those who know the worst of us
and don't turn their faces away.
—WALKER PERCY

> No man can be called friendless when he has
God and the companionship of good books.
—ELIZABETH BARRETT BROWNING

WHAT FRIENDS ARE FOR

I value the friend who for me finds time
on his calendar, but I cherish the friend who
for me does not consult his calendar.
—ROBERT BRAULT

> Don't make friends who are comfortable to be with.
Make friends who will force you to lever yourself up.
—THOMAS J. WATSON SR.

> ## QUOTABLE TWEETS

A true #friend is someone
who thinks that you are a good egg even
though he knows you are slightly cracked.
—@CHR1STLIKE (RIGO CAMPOS)

Modern Family

THE PERFECT WORDS FOR
FRIENDSHIP

Before borrowing money from a friend, decide which you need most.
—**ADDISON H. HALLOCK**

"

The smile is the shortest distance between two people.
—**VICTOR BORGE**

"

A stranger rings. A friend knocks.
—**DAVE EGGERS**

"

How much love inside a friend? Depends how much you give 'em.
—**SHEL SILVERSTEIN,** *A LIGHT IN THE ATTIC*

"

It is when we are most lost that we sometimes find our truest friends.
—**WALT DISNEY'S** *SNOW WHITE AND THE SEVEN DWARFS*

"

If you have three people in your life that you can trust, you can consider yourself the luckiest person in the whole world.
— **SELENA GOMEZ**

A FAMILY GATHERING

Add some zest to your vocabulary with this feast of nutritious words and phrases. If you can't stand the heat in our kitchen, cool off with the answers on the next page.

1. gustatory ('guh-stuh-tohr-ee) *adj.*—A: full-bellied. B: relating to taste. C: rich and flavorful.

2. au gratin (oh 'grah-tin) *adj.*—A: cooked to medium rare. B: free of charge. C: covered with cheese and browned.

3. succulent ('suh-kyu-lent) *adj.*—A: sun-dried. B: juicy. C: sipped with a straw.

4. mesclun ('mess-klen) *n.*—A: mix of greens. B: shellfish. C: Cajun dipping sauce.

5. piquant ('pee-kent) *adj.*—A: in season. B: in small amounts. C: spicy.

6. chiffonade (shih-fuh-'nayd) *n.*—A: whipped margarine. B: shredded herbs or veggies. C: lemon pudding.

7. toothsome ('tooth-sum) *adj.*—A: chewy. B: delicious. C: hungry.

8. sous vide (soo 'veed) *adv.*—A: without salt. B: on the side. C: cooked in a pouch.

9. culinary ('kuh-lih-nehr-ee) *adj.*—A: of the kitchen. B: buttery. C: cage-free.

10. umami (ooh-'mah-mee) *n.*—A: oven rack. B: chopsticks. C: savory taste.

11. tempeh ('tem-pay) *n.*—A: part-time chef. B: soy cake. C: fondue pot.

12. fricassee ('frih-kuh-see) *v.*—A: cut and stew in gravy. B: deep-fry. C: sauté with mushrooms.

13. oenophile ('ee-nuh-fiyl) *n.*—A: wine lover. B: food critic. C: egg fancier.

14. poach (pohch) *v.*—A: cook in simmering liquid. B: fry in a small amount of fat. C: heat slowly in a covered pot.

15. fondant ('fahn-duhnt) *n.*—A: food lover. B: cake icing. C: large bib.

Modern Family **115**

"A Family Gathering" Answers

1. gustatory—[B] relating to taste. Here, try my new *gustatory* experiment—beet ice cream!

2. au gratin—[C] covered with cheese and browned. Is there anything better than onion soup *au gratin* on a cold, rainy day?

3. succulent—[B] juicy. For dessert, the chef served pound cake topped with *succulent* pears.

4. mesclun—[A] mix of greens. "You call this a salad? It's just a plate of wilted *mesclun*."

5. piquant—[C] spicy. The *piquant* smells from the Mexican restaurant wafted out onto the street.

6. chiffonade—[B] shredded herbs or veggies. If you add a *chiffonade* of fresh basil, this frozen pizza isn't half bad!

7. toothsome—[B] delicious. Hattie makes the most *toothsome* cherry pie I've ever tasted.

8. sous vide—[C] cooked in a pouch. Though preparing steak *sous vide* takes time, it will cook your meat evenly and retain the moisture.

9. culinary—[A] of the kitchen. Julia Child was a true *culinary* icon.

10. umami—[C] savory taste. *Umami* is one of the five basic tastes, along with sweet, sour, salty, and bitter.

11. tempeh—[B] soy cake. Ezra, a devoted vegan, serves *tempeh* burgers and tofu dogs at his cookouts.

12. fricassee—[A] cut and stew in gravy. Tired of turkey sandwiches and turkey soup, Hector decided to *fricassee* the leftovers from his Thanksgiving bird.

13. oenophile—[A] wine lover. A serious *oenophile*, Adrienne was horrified when her date added ice cubes to his pinot noir.

14. poach—[A] cook in simmering liquid. For breakfast, Sasha loves to *poach* an egg and pair it with avocado toast topped with tomato.

15. fondant—[B] cake icing. Kelly flunked her cake-making class when she slathered on too much *fondant*.

WHAT KIND OF FOOD PERSON ARE YOU?

If you appreciate fine dining, you might call yourself a *gourmet,* an *epicure,* or a *bon vivant*. If you have a healthy but unrefined appetite, you're a *gourmand* or a *trencherman*. And if you've done your homework on the history and rituals of haute cuisine, you're a *gastronome* (*gastronomy* is the art or science of good eating).

THERE'S NO PLACE LIKE HOME

Oh my! The 80th anniversary of *The Wizard of Oz* occurred in 2019. To celebrate, we're featuring words that include the enchanted *o* and *z* duo. If you've got a brain (or the nerve), follow the yellow brick road to the next page.

1. **woozy** ('woo-zee) *adj.*—A: fond of naps. B: mentally unclear. C: sneezy.

2. **lollapalooza** (lah-luh-puh-'loo-zuh) *n.*—A: mob scene. B: outstanding example. C: hammock.

3. **schmooze** (shmooz) *v.*—A: chat. B: mock. C: smear.

4. **protozoan** (proh-tuh-'zoh-uhn) *n.*—A: ancient times. B: one-celled creature. C: Greek sea god.

5. **schemozzle** (shuh-'mah-zuhl) *n.*—A: clumsy person. B: tiny pest. C: confused situation.

6. **cozy** ('coh-zee) *n.*—A: teapot cover. B: hidden nook. C: close friend.

7. **rebozo** (rih-'boh-zoh) *n.*—A: caboose. B: clown suit. C: long scarf.

8. **foozle** ('fooh-zuhl) *v.*—A: mess up. B: trick. C: lather.

9. **cocozelle** (kah-kuh-'zeh-lee) *n.*—A: type of zucchini. B: daring thief. C: small deer.

10. **lozenge** ('lah-zinj) *n.*—A: local pharmacy. B: medicated candy. C: afternoon cocktail.

11. **cryptozoology** (crip-tuh-zoh-'ah-luh-jee) *n.*—A: science of temperature. B: history of tombs. C: study of fabled animals.

12. **ooze** (ooz) *v.*—A: flow slowly. B: express discomfort. C: cover with mud.

13. **sozzled** ('sah-zuhld) *adj.*—A: infuriated. B: intoxicated. C: infatuated.

14. **arroz con pollo** (uh-'rohss kohn 'poh-yoh) *n.*—A: chicken dish. B: citizen's arrest. C: traditional dance.

15. **schnoz** (shnoz) *n.*—A: punch. B: nose. C: simpleton.

"There's No Place Like Home" Answers

1. woozy [B] mentally unclear. Ray felt slightly *woozy* after his dental surgery.

2. lollapalooza [B] outstanding example. The Hamiltons always throw a *lollapalooza* of a Halloween party.

3. schmooze [A] chat. Who wouldn't want to *schmooze* with Hollywood stars at a movie premiere?

4. protozoan [B] one-celled creature. Under the microscope, the tiny *protozoan* looks like a sci-fi monster.

5. schemozzle [C] confused situation. "This project has been a *schemozzle* from start to finish!" Billie complained.

6. cozy [A] teapot cover. "The pot stays nice and hot," said Aunt Em, "with a woolen *cozy* on it."

7. rebozo [C] long scarf. Judy bought *rebozos* in a few different colors on her trip to Mexico.

8. foozle [A] mess up. It was Henry's best round of golf ever—until he *foozled* a two-foot putt.

9. cocozelle [A] type of zucchini. Mama's sauce recipe calls for three ripe *cocozelles*, crushed tomatoes, and a whole lot of garlic.

10. lozenge [B] medicated candy. I can't seem to shake this cough; I've been popping throat *lozenges* for weeks.

11. cryptozoology [C] study of fabled animals. The *cryptozoology* website has a page dedicated to the Loch Ness Monster.

12. ooze [A] flow slowly. I love to watch the chocolate *ooze* out of a freshly baked molten lava cake.

13. sozzled [B] intoxicated. The keynote speaker was too *sozzled* to take the podium.

14. arroz con pollo [A] chicken dish. As a vegan, I'll take the *arroz* (rice) but skip the *pollo* (chicken).

15. schnoz [B] nose. "Watch out—you almost hit me right in the *schnoz*!" Bert exclaimed.

THE MERRY OLD LAND OF OZ
When author L. Frank Baum was wondering what to name the magical world where he set his stories, his eye fell upon his filing cabinet, whose drawers were alphabetically labeled *A–G, H–N, and O–Z*. Faster than you can say Toto, he had his book's title: *The Wonderful Wizard of Oz*. It was published in 1900.

TALK BIG

We are a social species. Not only do we have thousands of words to use in conversation, we also have many to describe the very act of conversing. So the next time you're confabulating,[1] try out some of these words on your interlocutor.[2] For quiz answers, turn the page.

1. gainsay *v.*—A: repeat. B: add, as an afterthought. C: deny.

2. badinage (bad-uh-'nazh) *n.*—A: swear-words. B: playful back-and-forth. C: stern warning.

3. taciturn ('tass-uh-turn) *adj.*—A: chatty. B: quiet. C: afflicted with a lisp.

4. wheedle ('wee-dull) *v.*—A: tease. B: speak breathily. C: persuade with flattery.

5. loquacious (low-'kway-shus) *adj.*—A: quick to agree. B: talkative. C: to the point.

6. wag *n.*—A: unfair debater. B: joker. C: short digression.

7. polemic (puh-'lem-ick) *n.*—A: opinionated attack. B: off-the-cuff remark. C: awkward pause.

8. schmooze ('shmooz) *v.*—A: contradict oneself. B: chat. C: mispronounce.

9. maunder ('mawn-dur or 'mahn-) *v.*—A: ramble. B: squabble. C: gurgle.

10. rodomontade (rod-uh-mun-'tayd or -'tahd) *n.*—A: circular argument. B: talking while walking. C: bragging.

11. repartee (rep-ur-'tee or -ar-'tay) *n.*—A: verbal habit, as "like" and "you know." B: witty reply. C: rhetorical question.

12. bombastic (bahm-'bass-tick) *adj.*—A: shocking. B: pompous. C: given to interrupting.

13. prevaricate (prih-'var-uh-kate) *v.*—A: scream. B: emphasize. C: tell a half-truth.

14. colloquy ('coll-uh-kwee) *n.*—A: dialogue. B: slang usage. C: translation.

15. fustian ('fuss-chun) *adj.*—A: obscure. B: high-flown. C: mumbled.

16. tête-à-tête (tet-uh-'tet) *n.*—A: comeback. B: roundtable. C: private conversation.

17. insinuate (in-'sin-yoo-ate or -ya-wayt) *v.*—A: make hand gestures. B: embellish. C: artfully suggest.

[1] chatting
[2] participant in a dialogue

Modern Family

"Talk Big" Answers

1. gainsay—[C] deny. It cannot be *gainsaid* that the sign maker who spelled "Exit" wrong is an idiot.

2. badinage—[B] playful back-and-forth. The team's locker-room *badinage* is not for the squeamish.

3. taciturn—[B] quiet. The only *taciturn* member of a large and boisterous family, Mavis grew up to become a psychotherapist.

4. wheedle—[C] persuade with flattery. The saleswoman *wheedled* me into buying this dress.

5. loquacious—[B] talkative. My *loquacious* seatmate bent my ear all the way from LaGuardia to LAX.

6. wag—[B] joker. Ever the *wag*, Mike stood in the receiving line clutching a joy buzzer.

7. polemic—[A] opinionated attack. The meeting was interrupted by Jay's *polemic* against the copying machine.

8. schmooze—[B] chat. He doesn't know the difference between a driver and a putter—he just likes *schmoozing* at the country club.

9. maunder—[A] ramble. We listened to Uncle Horace's *maundering* stories, one right after another.

10. rodomontade—[C] bragging. The actress's Oscar acceptance speech came off as 45 seconds of unabashed *rodomontade*.

11. repartee—[B] witty reply. When Curly asked, "What's that monkey got that I ain't got?" Moe's *repartee* was "A longer tail."

12. bombastic—[B] pompous. The club president's speech would have seemed less *bombastic* without Tchaikovsky's "1812 Overture" playing in the background.

13. prevaricate—[C] tell a half-truth. When asked if he'd broken the window, the Little Leaguer *prevaricated*, claiming that as a southpaw, his aim couldn't have been that good.

14. colloquy—[A] dialogue. The professors' highbrow *colloquy* quickly turned into a slugfest.

15. fustian—[B] high-flown. The candidate's *fustian* oratory barely disguised his poor grasp of the issue.

16. tête-à-tête—[C] private conversation. After a quick *tête-à-tête* with his attorney, the defendant decided to change his plea.

17. insinuate—[C] artfully suggest. When my friends chipped in for my birthday present—a gift certificate for a housecleaning service—I had to wonder what they were *insinuating*.

Q & A

Warning: This quiz—a question-and-answer session featuring the letters q and a—may leave you in a quagmire. So if you're stumped by our q's, just turn the page for the a's.

1. **qua** ('kwah) *prep.*—A: from top to bottom. B: beforehand. C: as, in the capacity of.

2. **quay** ('key) *n.*—A: wharf. B: game played with mallets. C: fox hunted by hounds.

3. **quaff** ('kwahf) *v.*—A: swing and miss. B: drink deeply. C: sing Christmas carols.

4. **quasi** ('kway- or 'kwah-zi) *adj.*—A: from a foreign country. B: having some resemblance. C: feeling seasick.

5. **quahog** ('co- or 'kwahhog) *n.*—A: edible clam. B: half penny. C: motorcycle sidecar.

6. **quantum** ('kwahn-tum) *n.*—A: type of comet. B: specified amount. C: Australian marsupial.

7. **quaver** ('kway-ver) *v.*—A: change your vote. B: sink down low. C: sound tremulous.

8. **quinoa** ('keen-wah or 'kee-no-eh) *n.*—A: grain from the Andes. B: beehive shape. C: chewable resin gum.

9. **quondam** ('kwahn-dem) *adj.*—A: enormous. B: former. C: backward or upside down.

10. **quetzal** (ket-'sall) *n.*—A: bow-shaped pasta. B: tropical bird. C: mica used in mirrors.

11. **quatrain** ('kwah-train) *n.*—A: end-of-semester test. B: underground railroad. C: four-line verse.

12. **quiniela** ('kwin-ye-la) *n.*—A: type of bet. B: porcupine's bristle. C: cheesy Mexican dish.

13. **quotidian** (kwoh-'ti-dee-en) *adj.*—A: janitorial. B: occurring every day. C: showing off one's knowledge.

14. **quacksalver** ('kwak-sal-ver) *n.*—A: ointment. B: glue. C: fraud or phony doctor.

15. **quinquennial** (kwin-'kw-en-nee-el) *adj.*—A: of thigh muscles. B: flowing freely. C: occurring every five years.

DEEP ROOTS

If you're a science enthusiast, you're likely familiar with the *quark,* a particle that's smaller than a proton or neutron. But do you know the word's origin? When physicist Murray Gell-Mann proposed the existence of the particle in 1964, he turned to a line from James Joyce's *Finnegans Wake* to name it: "Three quarks for Muster Mark!" The deeper root is perhaps the German *Quark, or curd,* slang for "nonsense."

Modern Family

"Q & A" Answers

1. qua—[C] as, in the capacity of. Try to judge the short stories *qua* short stories, not as landmarks of literature, the student pleaded.

2. quay—[A] wharf. The passengers moaned as the new captain tried to meet the *quay* in the storm.

3. quaff—[B] drink deeply. Make three wishes and then *quaff* this mysterious elixir.

4. quasi—[B] having some *resemblance*. The credit offer is from a *quasi* company—there's no address, no phone number, not even an employee.

5. quahog—[A] edible clam. As the crew team's lead vanished, the coach just sat there like a placid *quahog*.

6. quantum—[B] specified amount. Showing off after physics class, Carly said, "That's an extreme *quantum* of homework, don't you think?"

7. quaver—[C] sound tremulous. Every time you try to tell a lie, your voice *quavers*.

8. quinoa—[A] grain from the Andes. When the waiter said it was tilapia and arugula on a bed of *quinoa,* Lauren asked for an English translation.

9. quondam—[B] *former.* As soon as Harry's *quondam* girlfriend spotted him, she burst into a quasi fit of joy.

10. quetzal—[B] tropical bird. Thinking the affair was a costume party, Andy showed up with an eye patch, a peg leg, and a *quetzal* on his shoulder.

11. quatrain—[C] four-line verse. As a hardworking poet, Jill needs to rest and raid the refrigerator after every *quatrain.*

12. quiniela—[A] type of bet. To win a *quiniela,* you need to pick the first- and second-place horses, but you don't need to specify the order of the finish.

13. quotidian—[B] occurring every day. Set in her *quotidian* routine, the puppy begged for an extra treat after breakfast and dinner.

14. quacksalver—[C] fraud or phony doctor. That *quacksalver* I go to prescribes calamine lotion for every complaint.

15. quinquennial—[C] occurring every five years. Um, darling, I think it's time for your *quinquennial* bourbon and ginger.

SOUND SMARTER

Ensure and *insure* are often confused because their pronunciations are essentially the same. But their meanings are distinct: If you intend to say "make sure," go with *ensure*. But if you're taking out collision coverage for your car, you'd *insure* it. (So, for example, you might *ensure* that you *insure* a new vehicle before driving it off the lot.)

FAMILY GAME NIGHT

Whether your métier is crosswords, Scrabble, or Words with Friends, these terms—all short and sweet and vowel-powered—will help you (and your vocabulary) step it up when the game is on the line. Answers on the next page.

1. aerie ('eyr-ee) *n.*—A: sphere of knowledge. B: bird's nest. C: feeling of weirdness.

2. ennui (on-'wee) *n.*—A: boredom. B: group of nine experts. C: dispute or feud.

3. épée ('eh-pay) *n.*—A: traditional wedding dance. B: Southern word game. C: fencing sword.

4. erose (ih-'rohs) *adj.*—A: having an irregular margin, as a leaf. B: jaded. C: resembling Cupid.

5. alee (ah-'lee) *adv.*—A: as soon as possible. B: away from the wind. C: with great reluctance.

6. oryx ('or-iks) *n.*—A: African antelope. B: jet-black gemstone. C: highest point or achievement.

7. etui (ay-'twee) *n.*—A: small ornamental case. B: flightless bird. C: long-standing love affair.

8. aural ('or-uhl) *adj.*—A: reflecting light. B: related to the sense of hearing. C: occurring in the fall.

9. riata (ree-'a-tuh) *n.*—A: lasso. B: festival particular to the Southwest. C: break in the action.

10. wadi ('wah-dee) *n.*—A: shapeless lump. B: poisonous snake. C: stream bed.

11. olio ('oh-lee-oh) *n.*—A: butter substitute. B: terrible smell. C: hodgepodge.

12. arête (uh-'rayt) *n.*—A: South American cuckoo bird. B: sharp ridge. C: metrical foot in poetry.

13. outré (oo-'tray) *adj.*—A: hush-hush or illegal. B: bizarre. C: imported.

14. ogee ('oh-jee) *n.*—A: bishop's robe. B: S-shaped molding. C: wild party.

15. elide (ih-'liyd) *v.*—A: omit. B: speed along smoothly. C: embellish falsely.

THE CRUX OF IT

The fancy term for a crossword maker or fan is *cruciverbalist*. It has two main roots: *cruc,* from the Latin *crux* for "cross," and *verbal,* from the Latin *verbum* for "word." Originally from England, the crossword puzzle made its U.S. debut in December 1913 and was shaped like a diamond.

Modern Family

"Family Game Night" Answers

1. **aerie**—[B] bird's nest. Peering over the cliff, Ernie espied an erne's *aerie*.

2. **ennui**—[A] boredom. "Are we there yet?" moaned Lucy in inane *ennui*.

3. **épée**—[C] fencing sword. Swinging his *épée* overhead in grossly poor sportsmanship, Josh yelled, "You can never take our title!"

4. **erose**—[A] having an irregular margin, as a leaf. Intending an autumnal effect, the artist chose *erose* edges for the new sculpture.

5. **alee**—[B] away from the wind. The harbormaster kept his pipe lit *alee* and resumed his usual pose at the dock.

6. **oryx**—[A] African antelope. The horns of the *oryx* can be lethal and help to protect the animal from predators.

7. **etui**—[A] small ornamental case. Quite impressed with herself, Alice wandered around the crafts fair with her sewing kit in a handcrafted *etui*.

8. **aural**—[B] related to the sense of hearing. The speaker's voice, to put it politely, was an *aural* annoyance.

9. **riata**—[A] lasso. "Maybe I could use that *riata* to corral my kids!" said a weary Amy.

10. **wadi**—[C] stream bed. The dried-up *wadi* was a sad sight for the labored herd.

11. **olio**—[C] hodgepodge. A favorite among the neighbors, Grace's chili was known as the Outrageous *Olio*.

12. **arête**—[B] sharp ridge. Hoping to photograph the *arêtes* surrounding Alaska's Taku Glacier, Alison set out from Juneau.

13. **outré**—[B] bizarre. What's more *outré*: Hillary's hair color or her hot-pink cocktail dress?

14. **ogee**—[B] S-shaped molding. The designer demanded an *ogee* edge for the countertops throughout the expansive kitchen.

15. **elide**—[A] omit. In an apparent error, Liam *elided* a few key remarks from the now infamous speech.

SOUND SMARTER

How much difference can a letter or two make? Consider—and remember—these particular pairs: *peek* (to look) vs. *peak* (a summit); *obtuse* (describes a person who can't understand) vs. *abstruse* (describes an idea that's hard to understand); *flare* (a light) vs. *flair* (a talent); *attain* (accomplish through effort) vs. *obtain* (gain possession of).

MAKING FRIENDS

Whatever your personality type, you'll win friends and influence people with a good vocabulary. See which of these words related to character you can define—and perhaps which defines you—and then analyze the next page for answers.

1. **craven** ('kray-ven) *adj.*—A: reckless. B: fussy. C: cowardly.

2. **picaresque** (pi-kuh-'resk) *adj.*—A: like a daring rascal. B: good-looking on camera. C: standoffish.

3. **recluse** ('reh-kloos) *n.*—A: group leader. B: hermit. C: problem solver.

4. **narcissist** ('nar-suh-sist) *n.*—A: generous giver. B: self-absorbed sort. C: analytical type.

5. **ingratiate** (in-'gray-shee-ayt) *v.*—A: eat impulsively. B: attempt to control. C: try to gain favor.

6. **acolyte** ('a-kuh-liyt) *n.*—A: follower. B: braggart. C: daredevil.

7. **bon vivant** (bon-vee-'vahnt) *n.*—A: good listener. B: trusted ally. C: lover of fine dining.

8. **sanguine** ('san-gwin) *adj.*—A: optimistic. B: melancholy. C: shy.

9. **choleric** ('kah-luh-rik) *adj.*—A: logical. B: health-conscious. C: hot-tempered.

10. **congenial** (kuhn-'gee-nee-uhl) *adj.*—A: unreliable. B: given to gossip. C: friendly.

11. **bloviate** ('blo-vee-ayt) *v.*—A: get angry. B: rant pompously. C: commit petty crimes.

12. **venal** ('vee-nal) *adj.*—A: virtuous. B: corruptible. C: interfering.

13. **bumptious** ('bump-shus) *adj.*—A: pushy. B: countrified. C: roly-poly.

14. **altruistic** ('al-troo-is-tik) *adj.*—A: honest. B: kind to others. C: quick to change.

15. **bohemian** (bo-'hee-mee-in) *adj.*—A: macho guy. B: nonconformist. C: picker of arguments.

APPEALING ATTRIBUTES

Charm and *charisma* are similarly attractive traits. *Charm* comes from the Latin *carmen*, meaning "song," and is related to *chant*: A *charmer* magically enchants you. *Charisma* is even stronger; it comes from the Greek *charis*, meaning "grace"—a divine blessing, like a gift from the gods.

Modern Family

"Making Friends" Answers

1. **craven**—[C] cowardly. How *craven* to dump your beau via a text message!

2. **picaresque**—[A] like a daring rascal. Dashiell thinks wearing a cape makes him look more *picaresque*.

3. **recluse**—[B] hermit. You've never heard of Lady Gaga? You must be a *recluse*.

4. **narcissist**—[B] self-absorbed sort. What a *narcissist*, telling me every boring detail of his day!

5. **ingratiate**—[C] try to gain favor. To *ingratiate* herself with the pageant judges, Carla kept winking at them.

6. **acolyte**—[A] follower. No, I'm not with the band. I'm just one of the *acolytes*.

7. **bon vivant**—[C] lover of fine dining. If you need me, I'll be at the wine tasting with the other *bon vivants*.

8. **sanguine**—[A] optimistic. After a month of lessons, I feel *sanguine* about passing the road test.

9. **choleric**—[C] hot-tempered. The *choleric* judge pounded his gavel so hard that it broke.

10. **congenial**—[C] friendly. The catcher and the umpire seem too *congenial* to me.

11. **bloviate**—[B] rant pompously. To host a talk-radio show, it helps if you can *bloviate* on command.

12. **venal**—[B] corruptible. It's clear from the parade fiasco that your town supervisors are a bunch of *venal* crooks.

13. **bumptious**—[A] pushy. Becca only joined the choir because her *bumptious* mom nagged her into it.

14. **altruistic**—[B] kind to others. Piranhas are never described as *altruistic*.

15. **bohemian**—[B] nonconformist. Lulu's *bohemian* friends introduced her to edgy performance art.

> ### SUPERIORITY COMPLEX
> Someone with a *supercilious* air is stuck-up. In Latin, super is "above" and *cilium* is "eyelash," with "eyebrow" being *supercilium*—and when an ancient Roman asserted superiority, it was with an arched eyebrow, a gesture familiar enough today. A *haughty* person is high or acts like it (being height-y).

USE YOUR WORDS, VOLUME 2

SIGN LANGUAGE

Signs and symbols, our human shorthand, are all around us. And if you take the word of philosopher Charles Sanders Peirce, "We think only in signs." See how many you can think of. For answers, turn the page.

1. ampersand ('am-pur-sand) *n.*—A: the @ sign. B: the & sign. C: the # sign.

2. totem *n.*—A: signpost. B: emblem. C: figure of speech.

3. cachet (ka-'shay) *n.*—A: white flag of surrender. B: smoke signal. C: stamp of approval.

4. shibboleth ('shih-ba-leth) *n.*—A: figure burned in effigy. B: watchword. C: forbidden language.

5. stigma ('stig-muh) *n.*—A: religious rune. B: mark of disgrace. C: hieroglyph.

6. prognosticate (prog-'nos-tuh-kate) *v.*—A: foretell. B: serve as a badge or insignia. C: break a code.

7. Ameslan ('am-us-lan *or* 'am-slan) *n.*—A: American Sign Language. B: inventor of Braille. C: symbolic lion.

8. fusee (fyoo-'zee) *n.*—A: the % sign. B: warning flare. C: military tattoo.

9. logotype ('log-uh-type) *n.*—A: company emblem. B: ship captain's mark. C: condensed message.

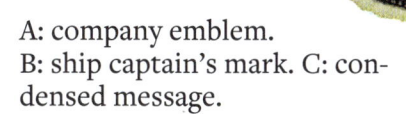

10. beck *n.*—A: design on a bottle cap. B: graffiti artist's signature. C: gesture.

11. tocsin ('tock-sun) *n.*—A: alarm bell. B: trumpet fanfare. C: symbol for poison.

12. auspicious (aw-'spih-shus) *adj.*—A: favorable. B: cryptic. C: bearing a signature.

13. diaphone ('dye-uh-fone) *n.*—A: directional blinker. B: signal amplifier. C: two-note foghorn.

14. metaphorical *adj.*—A: nonverbal. B: figurative. C: enciphered.

15. trefoil ('tree-foil) *n.*—A: symbol for aluminum. B: clover leaf symbol. C: the @ sign.

Modern Family

"Sign Language" Answers

1. ampersand—[B] the & sign. The pop diva uses an *ampersand* in her name—R&i—but her mother still calls her Randi.

2. totem—[B] emblem. That's Stanley, the pencil pusher in cubicle 2S-013; his personal *totem* is a hamster.

3. cachet—[C] stamp of approval. The fact that he was voted Most Popular by the senior class carried no *cachet* in the computer club.

4. shibboleth—[B] watchword. Shelley showed up in a wool-blend sweater, not knowing that "pashmina" was the fashion *shibboleth*.

5. stigma—[B] mark of disgrace. Botching the final question in Trivial Pursuit was a *stigma* she continued to bear at every family gathering.

6. prognosticate—[A] foretell. Seeing his shadow, Punxsutawney Phil *prognosticates* six more weeks of shoveling snow and scraping windshields.

7. Ameslan—[A] American Sign Language. This bar band is so loud, you have to use *Ameslan* to talk.

8. fusee—[B] warning flare. Rodney is a safety nut; he once set out *fusees* when his bike got a flat.

9. logotype—[A] company emblem. The hippie turned business executive likes to say that the Mercedes *logotype* is actually the peace symbol.

10. beck—[C] gesture. With a sidelong glance and a shy little *beck*, Yvette lured me toward the candy store.

11. tocsin—[A] alarm bell. Though he's been retired from the fire department for over 20 years, whenever Uncle Al hears a *tocsin*, he throws on a coat and slides down the banister.

12. auspicious—[A] favorable. "I thought a Valentine's Day wedding would be romantic," wailed the bride as she looked out the window, "but a blizzard is hardly an *auspicious* omen."

13. diaphone—[C] two-note foghorn. My brother-in-law thinks he's Enrico Caruso, but he sings like a *diaphone*.

14. metaphorical—[B] figurative. "When I said, 'Break a leg,'" the coach told the skier after the slalom, "I was being *metaphorical*."

15. trefoil—[B] clover leaf symbol. The architect wanted to ornament the arches of the junior high school with *trefoils* but had to settle for a fallout shelter symbol.

A FRIEND INDEED

The proper office of a friend is to side with you when you are in the wrong. Nearly anybody will side with you when you are right.
—MARK TWAIN

"

Lots of people want to ride with you in the limo, but what you want is someone who will take the bus with you when the limo breaks down.
—OPRAH

"

A loyal friend laughs at your jokes when they're not so good, and sympathizes with your problems when they're not so bad.
—ARNOLD H. GLASOW

"

We need old friends to help us grow old and new friends to help us stay young.
—LETTY COTTIN POGREBIN

THE PERFECT WORDS FOR
CARDS FOR MOM & DAD

I remember my mother's prayers and they have always followed me. They have clung to me all my life.
—ABRAHAM LINCOLN

"

The heart of a mother is a deep abyss at the bottom of which you will always find forgiveness.
—HONORÉ DE BALZAC

"

Mother love is the fuel that enables a normal human being to do the impossible.
—MARION C. GARRETTY

"

[A] mother is one to whom you hurry when you are troubled.
—EMILY DICKINSON

"

A mother is the truest friend we have . . .
—WASHINGTON IRVING

"

There's nothing like a mama-hug.
—ADABELLA RADICI

A father carries pictures where his money used to be.
—UNKNOWN

"
Directly after God in heaven comes a Papa.
—MOZART

"
Blessed indeed is the man who hears
many gentle voices call him father!
—LYDIA CHILD

"
One father is more than a hundred schoolmasters.
—GEORGE HERBERT

"
By the time a man realizes that maybe his father was right, he usually has a son who thinks he's wrong.
—CHARLES WADSWORTH

"
[My father] didn't tell me how to live;
he lived, and let me watch him do it.
—CLARENCE B. KELLAND

My rule is, if it's not more fun than surfing, I'm not gonna do it.
—SPIKE JONZS

LIVE IT UP!

Work hard, play hard
may sound like a cliché,
but rewarding ourselves
with the pursuit of happiness,
adventure, and fun
makes life worthwhile.

THE ROAD TO HAPPINESS

The most likely moment for something incredible to happen to me was the moment I was most certain nothing ever would.
—JANE PAULEY

"

The firsts go away—first love, first baby, first kiss. You have to create new ones.
—SARAH JESSICA PARKER

"

Sometimes when almost everything is wrong, one thing is so right you would do it all again.
—ALICE RANDALL

"

Let's face it, all the good stuff happens after midnight.
—MATT GROENING

"

Don't waste a minute not being happy. If one window closes, run to the next window—or break down a door.
—BROOKE SHIELDS

"

I have enjoyed life a lot more by saying yes than by saying no.
—RICHARD BRANSON

> Joy is one of the only emotions
> you can't contrive.
> **—BONO**

"

> There are some things in life where it's better to
> receive than to give, and massage
> is one of them.
> **—AL MICHAELS**

"

> A happy heart comes first,
> then the happy face.
> **—SHANIA TWAIN**

"

> I might not be famous one day.
> But I'd still be happy.
> **—SALMA HAYEK**

"

> The only way to have a life
> is to commit to it like crazy.
> **—ANGELINA JOLIE**

"

> Games are won by players who
> focus on the playing field—
> not by those whose
> eyes are glued to the scoreboard.
> **—WARREN BUFFETT**

BOOKS & STORIES

Not all those who wander are lost.
—J. R. R. TOLKIEN

"

Travel is fatal to prejudice, bigotry,
and narrow-mindedness.
—MARK TWAIN

"

I'm still ready to go to the moon, if they'll take me.
—WALTER CRONKITE

"

Life is always going to be stranger than fiction,
because fiction has to be convincing,
and life doesn't.
—NEIL GAIMAN

"

Books are no more threatened by Kindle
than stairs by elevators.
—STEPHEN FRY

"

My father always said,
"Never trust anyone whose TV
is bigger than their bookshelf."
—EMILIA CLARKE

🐦 QUOTABLE TWEETS

@x_elenatheresa Books should always be open.

@CORMACMCCARTHYS

❝

Reading gives us someplace to go when we have to stay where we are.
—**MASON COOLEY**

❝

The first lesson reading teaches is how to be alone.
—**JONATHAN FRANZEN**

❝

A good book is like an unreachable itch. You just can't leave it alone.
—**LAURA BUSH**

❝

I've written 17 novels, and I've found out that fiction can't keep up with real life.
—**JOHN GRISHAM**

❝

Don't judge a book by its cover 'til you've read the book.
—**JAMIE LEE CURTIS**

MUSIC

Jazz is democracy in music.
—**WYNTON MARSALIS**

"
What in the world would I sing for if I had it all?
—**DAVE MATTHEWS**

"
Rock is so much fun. That's what it's all about—filling up the chest cavities and empty kneecaps and elbows.
—**JIMI HENDRIX**

"
Music is the shorthand of emotion.
—**LEO TOLSTOY**

"
Without music, life is a journey through a desert.
—**PAT CONROY**

"
QUOTABLE TWEETS

@WesleyStace Well try to finish before the show.
The best music is recorded before 7pm, so your muse can replenish itself drinking at night.
@EUGENEMIRMAN

ART

The practice of art isn't to make a living.
It's to make your soul grow.
—KURT VONNEGUT

"
Art is so wonderfully irrational, exuberantly
pointless, but necessary all the same.
—GÜNTER GRASS

"
I feel strongly that the visual arts are of vast importance.
Of course I could be prejudiced. I am a visual art.
—KERMIT THE FROG

"
All great art comes from a sense of outrage.
—GLENN CLOSE

"
Art doesn't reproduce the visible but
rather makes it visible.
—PAUL KLEE

"
Art extends each man's short time on earth
by carrying from man to man the whole
complexity of other men's lifelong experience,
with all its burdens, colors and flavor.
—ALEKSANDR SOLZHENITSYN

Live It Up!

THE PERFECT WORDS FROM
QUOTABLE BOOKS

It is a truth universally acknowledged
that a single man in possession of a good fortune
must be in want of a wife.
—*PRIDE AND PREJUDICE*, JANE AUSTEN

"

You better not never tell nobody but God.
—*THE COLOR PURPLE*, ALICE WALKER

"

The snow in the mountains was melting
and Bunny had been dead for several weeks
before we understood
the gravity of our situation.
—*THE SECRET HISTORY* BY DONNA TARTT

"

We slept in what had once been the gymnasium.
—*THE HANDMAID'S TALE* BY MARGARET ATWOOD

"

Mr. and Mrs. Dursley,
of number four Privet Drive,
were proud to say that they were perfectly normal,
thank you very much.
—*HARRY POTTER AND THE PHILOSOPHER'S STONE*,
BY J.K. ROWLING

GOING PLACES

If you have a touch of wanderlust this quiz might help: The theme is toponyms, words derived from place-names both real and fictional. Bon voyage! Answers on next page.

1. **balkanize** *v.*—A: divide into factions. B: coat with rubber. C: prevent from entering.

2. **Byzantine** *adj.*—A: artificial. B: complicated. C: dangerous.

3. **sybarite** *n.*—seeker of… A: knowledge. B: power. C: pleasure.

4. **lilliputian** *adj.*—A: highly fragrant. B: very small. C: wondrous.

5. **madras** *n.*—A: colorful light-cotton fabric. B: hearty lentil soup. C: large, noisy crowd.

6. **Dixieland** *n.*—style of… A: country music. B: country gospel. C: jazz.

7. **tabby** *n.*—A: type of silk taffeta. B: variety of wine grape. C: type of wallcovering.

8. **El Dorado** *n.*—A: symbol of peace. B: place of great wealth and opportunity. C: dance to celebrate life.

9. **lyceum** *n.*—A: trellised pathway. B: hall for public lectures. C: ornate display.

10. **solecism** *n.*—A: minor blunder in speech. B: expression of disgust. C: statement of worth.

11. **jodhpurs** *n.*—A: leather boots. B: riding breeches. C: protective gloves.

12. **magenta** *n.*—A: light pink. B: purplish red. C: dark blue.

13. **Boeotian** *adj.*—A: heavy. B: witty. C: dull or obtuse.

14. **fescennine** *adj.*—A: silent. B: loud. C: obscene.

15. **canopic jar** *n.*—jar for… A: preserving food. B: storing embalmed entrails. C: keeping medicine.

> **SOUND SMARTER**
> Want to prove yourself a true grammarian? Take care to use *proved* and *proven* correctly. *Proved* is the verb form (a past participle, as in "Red with shame, Leah was proved wrong"). Use *proven* only as an adjective ("A trip to the tropics is a proven remedy for the winter blues"). Legalese exception: "innocent until proven guilty."

Live It Up!

"Going Places" Answers

1. balkanize—[A] divide into factions (the Balkan Peninsula was split into small warring nations). The policies *balkanized* the already troubled nation.

2. Byzantine—[B] complicated (the bureaucracy of Byzantium was complex). Confused by the *Byzantine* map, Jo was three hours late.

3. sybarite—[C] seeker of pleasure (the ancient Greek city Sybaris was known for wealth and luxury). A *sybarite,* Tom favored costly, rare Italian reds.

4. lilliputian—[B] very small (in Gulliver's Travels, the inhabitants of Lilliput were tiny). The *lilliputian* minnows slid through Puck's netting.

5. madras—[A] colorful light-cotton fabric (the style originated in Madras, India). Elsie begged Mom for the pricey orange-and-yellow *madras* top.

6. Dixieland—[C] style of jazz (Dixie is a nickname for the U.S. South, where the style originated). They sat for hours in awe of the *Dixieland* band.

7. tabby—[A] type of silk taffeta (the fabric was first made in Al-'Attabiya, Baghdad). Carol's elegant *tabby* scarf didn't suit her tattered tee.

8. El Dorado—[B] place of great wealth and opportunity (the city was said to hold fabulous riches). Eli labeled Silicon Valley his *El Dorado.*

9. lyceum—[B] hall for public lectures (Aristotle taught in Lyceum, a gymnasium near Athens). The professor feared the *lyceum's* massive scale.

10. solecism—[A] minor blunder in speech (a substandard form of language was spoken in Soloi, a city in ancient Cilicia). The groom's *solecism* led to the couple's first big tiff.

11. jodhpurs—[B] riding breeches (they were designed in Jodhpur, India). Lillie wore her old *jodhpurs* for the race.

12. magenta—[B] purplish red (the color's dye was discovered the year of the Battle of Magenta, Italy, 1859). At sunset, the sky turned a stunning *magenta.*

13. Boeotian—[C] dull or obtuse (Greek Boeotians were labeled bores by Athenians). Mae struggled to explain performance art to her *Boeotian* cousin.

14. fescennine—[C] obscene (the ancient Italian town Fescennia was noted for offensive verse). "Those lyrics are *fescennine!*" Will's mom cried.

15. canopic jar—[B] jar for storing embalmed entrails (it was mistakenly associated with Canopus, Egypt). King Tut's tomb holds four *canopic* jars.

ELEMENTARY

This quiz is for fans of the BBC series and Netflix favorite *Sherlock*, as well as readers of the original mystery tales by Sir Arthur Conan Doyle. Sleuth out the meanings—or follow the trail to the next page for answers.

1. **connoisseur** (kah-neh-'sir) *n.*—A: swindler. B: expert. C: paid informant.

2. **faculties** ('fa-kuhl-teez) *n.*—A: powers. B: intricate details. C: sudden insights.

3. **infallible** (in-'fa-leh-buhl) *adj.*—A: never wrong. B: remaining questionable or unsolved. C: carefully balanced.

4. **minatory** ('min-uh-tor-ee) *adj.*—A: unethical. B: with a menacing quality. C: subversive.

5. **furtive** ('fer-tiv) *adj.*—A: nervous. B: sneaky. C: tall and thin.

6. **untoward** (uhn-'toh-uhrd) *adj.*—A: illogical. B: strongly opinionated. C: not favorable.

7. **facilitate** (fuh-'sih-luh-tayt) *v.*—A: make easier. B: confront. C: unravel.

8. **incisive** (in-'siy-siv) *adj.*—A: urgent. B: doubtful. C: impressively direct.

9. **tenacious** (tuh-'nay-shus) *adj.*—A: persistent. B: well concealed. C: supremely rational.

10. **desultory** ('deh-suhl-tor-ee) *adj.*—A: yielding no clues. B: hot and humid. C: having no plan.

11. **proficiency** (pruh-'fih-shun-see) *n.*—A: right-handedness. B: likelihood. C: great skill.

12. **illustrious** (ih-'luhs-tree-uhs) *adj.*—A: graphic. B: eminent. C: deceiving.

13. **injunction** (in-'junk-shun) *n.*—A: order. B: coincidence. C: shot of medicine or drugs.

14. **truculent** ('truh-kyuh-luhnt) *adj.*—A: cruel or harsh. B: puzzled. C: of few words.

15. **sardonic** (sahr-'dah-nik) *adj.*—A: carelessly dressed. B: threatening. C: mocking.

Live It Up!

"Elementary" Answers

1. connoisseur—[B] expert. "Can you recommend an art *connoisseur?*" the detective asked after the robbery at the museum.

2. faculties—[A] powers. The prosecution set out to test the full *faculties* of the defense team.

3. infallible—[A] never wrong. "Not to worry—our key witness has an *infallible* memory," the lawyer said.

4. minatory—[B] with a menacing quality. The thief gave his victim a *minatory* gaze before leaving her in the alley.

5. furtive—[B] sneaky. I didn't for one second trust the suspect—he has a cruel and *furtive* look.

6. untoward—[C] not favorable. "Barring *untoward* circumstances," said the judge, "we'll have a decision by week's end."

7. facilitate—[A] make easier. The sergeant needed at least one more lead to *facilitate* the investigation.

8. incisive—[C] impressively direct. "Guilty," the juror offered in a most *incisive* tone.

9. tenacious—[A] persistent. Though not very personable, Officer Bluntley can be as *tenacious* as a bulldog.

10. desultory—[C] having no plan. After finding no clues at the crime scene, the police began what felt like a *desultory* search for evidence.

11. proficiency—[C] great skill. "I claim no *proficiency* at lab work—but I am a huge *CSI* fan!"

12. illustrious—[B] eminent. After an *illustrious* 30-year career, Detective Klein finally decided to step down.

13. injunction—[A] order. For failing to follow the *injunction,* Thomas was ordered to serve 90 days of community service.

14. truculent—[A] cruel or harsh. The witness was unscathed by the prosecutor's *truculent* remarks.

15. sardonic—[C] mocking. "Catch me if you can!" cried the felon with a *sardonic* laugh.

CALLING ALL DETECTIVES

The term *private eye* alludes simply to *private i* (short for *investigator*). You may also call such a person a *tec* (short for *detective*), a *gumshoe* (from quiet, rubber-soled footwear), a *sleuth* (from an Old Norse word for "trail"), a *shamus* (of Yiddish origin), or a *hawkshaw* (from a detective in the 1863 play *The Ticket of Leave Man*).

CURIOUSER & CURIOUSER

The year 2015 marked the 150th anniversary of Lewis Carroll's *Alice's Adventures in Wonderland*. Carroll (aka Charles Lutwidge Dodgson) invented words like *boojum* and *jabberwocky*, and his works abound with more terms worth knowing. In celebration of Alice, here's a sampling. Answers, next page.

1. **hookah** ('hu-kuh) *n.*—A: staff of a shepherdess. B: chess queen's crown. C: smoking pipe.

2. **platitudes** ('pla-tih-tewds) *n.*—A: trite sayings. B: temperate climates. C: heaping servings.

3. **welter** ('wel-tur) *v.*—A: toss among waves. B: droop in the sun. C: shrink in size.

4. **lory** ('lor-ee) *n.*—A: tall tale. B: type of parrot. C: atmospheric phenomenon, as the northern lights.

5. **impertinent** (im-'pur-tuh-nunt) *adj.*—A: late for a meeting. B: talking rapidly. C: rude.

6. **languid** ('lan-gwed) *adj.*—A: speaking fluently. B: sluggish or weak. C: slightly tilted.

7. **ungainly** (un-'gayn-lee) *adj.*—A: not attractive. B: clumsy or awkward. C: sickly thin.

8. **livery** ('lih-vuh-ree) *n.*— A: model boat. B: uniform. C: long, boring speech.

9. **antipathies** (an-'tih-puh-thees) *n.*—A: miracle cures. B: sudden storms, usually in the tropics. C: feelings of dislike.

10. **will-o'-the-wisp** (will-uh-thuh-'wisp) *n.*—A: fast speaker. B: rare plant. C: misleading goal or hope.

11. **sally** ('sa-lee) *n.*—A: female rabbit. B: white smock or robe. C: witty remark.

12. **griffin** ('grih-fun) *n.*—A: monster with wings. B: horn. C: cranky man.

13. **cravat** (kruh-'vat) *n.*—A: game similar to croquet. B: scarf-like necktie. C: two-person rowboat.

14. **hansom** ('hant-sum) *n.*—A: horse-drawn carriage. B: knight or nobility. C: chimney flue.

15. **sagaciously** (suh-'gay-shus-lee) *adv.*—A: wisely. B: dimly or foolishly. C: ambitiously.

Live It Up! **145**

"Curiouser & Curiouser" Answers

1. hookah—[C] smoking pipe. Gerry found a shop downtown that offers supplies for his antique *hookah*.

2. platitudes—[A] trite sayings. Our coach offered a dozen peppy *platitudes* like "No pain, no gain."

3. welter—[A] toss among waves. Heading for shore, Karyn stayed focused on the buoy *weltering* in the distance.

4. lory—[B] type of parrot. Mitch set off for Australia to study and photograph the *lory* in the wild.

5. impertinent—[C] rude. "Would it be too *impertinent* to point out that I can hear you snoring six rows back?"

6. languid—[B] sluggish or weak. By three in the afternoon, I am too *languid* to think about anything but coffee and a couch.

7. ungainly—[B] clumsy or awkward. Is it me, or is he the most *ungainly* mime you've ever seen?

8. livery—[B] uniform. The butler's rumpled *livery* made him a prime suspect in the disappearance of our dinner host.

9. antipathies—[C] feelings of dislike. I'd say there were some mild *antipathies* between the two speakers at the city hall meeting.

10. will-o'-the-wisp—[C] misleading goal or hope. You might follow the *will-o'-the-wisp* of bipartisanship regarding the new law, but you'd be foolish.

11. sally—[C] witty remark. Aside from the occasional *sally*, the sportscasters had little to offer.

12. griffin—[A] monster with wings. Felix was fascinated by the illustrations of the *griffin* in his mythology book.

13. cravat—[B] scarf-like necktie. I'm going to the party as James Bond—would he wear a *cravat*?

14. hansom—[A] horse-drawn carriage. The producer of Cinderella was troubled by the plan to transform the *hansom* into a pumpkin onstage.

15. sagaciously—[A] wisely. The critic *sagaciously* pointed out the logic holes in Tara's dense first novel.

A PUZZLE FROM WONDERLAND

Here is one of Lewis Carroll's small riddles in rhyme. Can you solve it?

Dreaming of apples on a wall,
And dreaming often, dear,
I dreamed that, if I counted all,
How many would appear?

Answer: Ten would appear, as he is dreaming "[of ten], dear."

PERCHANCE TO DREAM

If your bed is calling you, snuggle up with this relaxing quiz on sleep-related terms. Answers on next page.

1. **somniloquist** *n.*—A: sleep talker. B: loud snorer. C: story reader.

2. **eiderdown** *n.*—A: hotel turndown service. B: organic sleeping pill. C: duck-feather-filled comforter.

3. **hypnopompic** *adj.*—A: brought about by hypnosis. B: prewaking. C: coma-like.

4. **pandiculation** *n.*—A: undressing. B: closing one's eyes. C: stretching.

5. **tenebrous** *adj.*—A: dark. B: prone to sleeplessness. C: exhausted.

6. **torpor** *n.*—state of… A: sluggishness. B: wakefulness. C: reverie.

7. **quiescent** *adj.*—A: at rest. B: lacking sleep. C: silent.

8. **bruxism** *n.*—A: sudden waking. B: teeth grinding. C: bed-wetting.

9. **coverlet** *n.*—A: bathrobe for royalty. B: sleeping mask. C: bedspread.

10. **siesta** *n.*—A: mug for warm milk. B: afternoon nap. C: Spanish lullaby.

11. **soporific** *adj.*—A: sleep-inducing. B: nightmarish. C: restless.

12. **REM sleep** *n.*—stage of sleep during which… A: you're most likely to dream. B: sleep is the deepest. C: you're least likely to dream.

13. **negligee** *n.*—A: sleep attire sometimes worn by women. B: someone who ignores the need for sleep. C: extra-plush slippers.

14. **languish** *v.*—A: pretend to sleep. B: breathe shallowly. C: lose vitality.

15. **boudoir** *n.*—A: woman's bedroom. B: four-poster bed. C: decorative pillow.

16. **davenport** *n.*—A: fuzzy nightcap. B: pullout sofa. C: pleasant daydream.

SOUND SMARTER

Here's a grammar rule not worth losing sleep over but certainly worth heeding: the difference between *compare* with and *compare* to. *Compare with* means "to place side by side, noting differences and similarities," as in: "Warren's boss noted his inconsistency as she *compared* his goals *with* his yearly performance." Use *compare* to when you want to note only similarities, usually between unlike objects, as Shakespeare did: "Shall I *compare* thee *to* a summer's day?"

Live It Up!

"Perchance to Dream" Answers

1. somniloquist—[A] sleep talker. He married a *somniloquist* and never lacked for nighttime conversation.

2. eiderdown—[C] duck-feather-filled comforter. Noting the hotel's firm mattress and soft, fluffy *eiderdown*, a weary Josie anticipated a cozy night.

3. hypnopompic—[B] prewaking. After watching *Monday Night Football,* the students floated into class the next morning in a *hypnopompic* state.

4. pandiculation—[C] stretching. Frank's lengthy yawn and *pandiculation* gave his dinner guests the hint to call it a night.

5. tenebrous—[A] dark. Donna tripped over the skates as she groped for the light switch in the *tenebrous* room.

6. torpor—[A] state of sluggishness. After playing in the sun all morning, John lazed about in a *torpor*.

7. quiescent—[A] at rest. The rowdy kids were finally *quiescent* after the TV was switched on.

8. bruxism—[B] teeth grinding. Kyla's nightlong *bruxism* sounded like a chain saw.

9. coverlet—[C] bedspread. Stephanie chose a bright purple *coverlet* to match the room's garish decor.

10. siesta—[B] afternoon nap. Rob lay down for a postlunch *siesta*.

11. soporific—[A] sleep-inducing. The *soporific* play caused many audience members to run for coffee during intermission.

12. REM sleep—[A] stage of sleep during which you're most likely to dream (REM is short for "rapid eye movement," characteristic of this stage). Waking suddenly from her *REM sleep,* Jesse could recall her dreams in perfect detail.

13. negligee—[A] sleep attire sometimes worn by women. Lisa donned her *negligee* and waited for her groom in the honeymoon suite.

14. languish—[C] lose vitality. After a long day at the office, Sonja *languished* on the sofa and fell asleep.

15. boudoir—[A] woman's bedroom. Stressed about her interview the next day, Sonja wandered to her lavender-scented *boudoir* for a good night's rest.

16. davenport—[B] *pullout sofa.* Cormac invited his guest to sleep on the *davenport*.

> **DEEP ROOTS**
> Can you spot ways in which the Greek *nárkē,* meaning "numbness," appears in modern sleep terms? It's the basis (along with *lêpsis,* "seizure") for *narcolepsy,* a disorder characterized by uncontrollable spells of sleep. It's also at the root of *narcotic,* a drug that can induce sleep or produce a dull, pain-free (sleeplike) condition.

A WONDERFUL WORLD

How well do you know the peaks and valleys of planet Earth? Can you tell a bluff (that's a cliff) from a gulch (a narrow ravine)? Circumnavigate your way through this list of words, and then turn the page for answers.

1. **biosphere** ('by-uh-sfeer) *n.*—A: gases around Earth. B: parts of Earth that support life. C: planet's outer crust.

2. **strata** ('stray-tuh) *n.*—A: rock layers. B: low clouds. C: seabed.

3. **bayou** ('by-oo) *n.*—A: tropical island. B: deep cavern. C: marshy waterway.

4. **arroyo** (uh-'roy-oh) *n.*—A: gully. B: grassland. C: coral island.

5. **cartography** (kar-'tah-gruh-fee) *n.*—A: study of glaciers. B: art of mapmaking. C: science of erosion.

6. **seismic** ('siyz-mihk) *adj.*—A: prone to floods. B: related to earthquakes. C: covered in lava.

7. **scree** (skree) *n.*—A: loose rocks. B: peninsula. C: magma flow.

8. **ecology** (ih-'kah-luh-jee) *n.*—A: relationship of organisms to their environment. B: cycle of ocean currents. C: composting.

9. **terra firma** ('ter-uh 'fur-muh) *n.*—A: natural dam. B: sandbar. C: dry land.

10. **aquifer** ('a-kwuh-fur) *n.*—A: geyser. B: waterfall. C: underground water bed.

11. **flora** ('flohr-uh) *n.*—A: animal life. B: plant life. C: minerals.

12. **tarn** (tarn) *n.*—A: mountain lake. B: sinkhole. C: fossilized wood.

13. **latitude** ('la-tih-tood) *n.*—A: distance east or west from the prime meridian. B: imaginary line through Earth's center. C: distance north or south from the equator.

14. **primordial** (pry-'mohr-dee-uhl) *adj.*—A: densely forested. B: on highest ground. C: from earliest times.

15. **hogback** ('hahg-back) *n.*—A: U-turn in a river. B: steep-sided ridge. C: tributary.

Live It Up!

"A Wonderful World" Answers

1. biosphere—[B] parts of Earth that support life. The *biosphere* is home to a stunning variety of species, from tiny microbes to enormous whales.

2. strata—[A] rock layers. Did you know the *strata* of the Grand Canyon are hundreds of millions of years old?

3. bayou—[C] marshy waterway. Marie often paddles down the *bayou* in her canoe at sunrise.

4. arroyo—[A] gully. That's my car at the bottom of the *arroyo*, Officer.

5. cartography—[B] art of mapmaking. "Why would anyone study *cartography* in the age of Google Maps?" Dora asked.

6. seismic—[B] related to earthquakes. After moving out west, Nick got used to regular *seismic* activity.

7. scree—[A] loose rocks. Petra had to scramble through piles of ankle-wrenching *scree* to reach the summit.

8. ecology—[A] relationship of organisms to their environment. Scientists are studying the effect of oil spills on deep-sea *ecology*.

9. terra firma—[C] dry land. After a week on the rickety sailboat, Alex couldn't wait to return to *terra firma*.

10. aquifer—[C] underground water bed. The Ogallala *Aquifer* stretches all the way from South Dakota to Texas.

11. flora—[B] plant life. Walt's art is inspired by the *flora* of Cape Cod.

12. tarn—[A] mountain lake. A dip in a *tarn* is just as bracing as a shot of espresso.

13. latitude—[C] distance north or south from the equator. Lines of *latitude* are also called parallels.

14. primordial—[C] from earliest times. This *primordial* forest looks like something straight out of *Game of Thrones*.

15. hogback—[B] steep-sided ridge. Honey, I'm not sure you should take a selfie so close to the *hogback's* rim!

POLAR OPPOSITES

When you were a kid, did you ever try digging to China or Australia—or whatever was down there? Points on Earth that are opposite each other (such as the North and South Poles) are called *antipodes* (an-'tih-poh-deez). The word comes from the Greek *anti* ("opposite") and *pod* ("foot"), meaning "people who have their feet against our feet." So whose feet are pressed against yours? Probably no one's. In most of America, your antipode is in the Indian Ocean.

TALKING HOOPS

Suit up… it's time to see how you play word games in the clutch! We've picked 15 everyday words and phrases that do double duty on the court or in other sports. Answers on next page.

1. **downtown** *adv.*—A: far from the basket. B: right under the basket. C: at the end of the bench.

2. **scratch** *adj.*—A: arranged with little selection, as a team. B: extra or reserve, as a player. C: injured.

3. **dish** *v.*—A: trash-talk. B: pivot on one foot. C: pass to a teammate.

4. **brick** *n.*—A: solid defender. B: ungraceful shot. C: outdoor court.

5. **waltz** *n.*—A: easy victory. B: smooth move or scoring attempt. C: man-to-man defense.

6. **key** *n.*—A: penalty area. B: lane in front of the basket. C: player in the center position.

7. **weak side** *n.*—A: area away from the ball. B: left hand or foot. C: tournament underdog.

8. **cage** *n.*—A: dugout. B: batting-practice area in baseball. C: opposing players' locker room.

9. **rock** *n.*—A: ten-year veteran. B: lopsided victory. C: the basketball.

10. **Sweet Sixteen** *n.*—A: Big East teams. B: NCAA tournament round. C: all-star selectees.

11. **pine** *n.*—A: slang for bus. B: broken bat. C: players' bench.

12. **platoon** *v.*—A: spread out widely. B: combine squads. C: alternate at a position.

13. **chippy** *adj.*—A: avidly devoted. B: rough, aggressive. C: exhausted.

14. **squeaker** *n.*—A: close game. B: winning shot. C: final match.

15. **scrimmage** *n.*—A: practice game. B: starting lineup. C: point spread.

16. **rubber** *n.*—A: game with flexible rules. B: game that breaks a series tie. C: game postponed, or "bounced," because of weather.

DEEP ROOTS

The Georgetown Hoyas may be the most mysteriously named college team in the country. Over a century ago, a Georgetown student invented the cheer "Hoya Saxa!" from the Greek *hoia* for "such" or "what" and the Latin *saxa* for "rocks." The cheer meant simply "What rocks!" and was likely a reference to either the football team's defense or the baseball team, nicknamed the Stonewalls. But it caught on, and soon all the school's teams adopted the name.

Live It Up!

"Talking Hoops" Answers

1. downtown—[A] far from the basket. Max bet Harry that he couldn't hit five baskets in a row from *downtown*.

2. scratch—[A] arranged with little selection, as a team. As the strike loomed, Coach Barnes was forced to assemble a *scratch* group of local amateurs.

3. dish—[C] pass to a teammate. Pivoting on one foot, Julia *dished* the casserole to Marco, who slammed it into the oven.

4. brick—[B] ungraceful shot. I flipped my token at the coin slot, but it was a *brick* and clanged off the turnstile.

5. waltz—[A] easy victory. When it comes to roping, Tex usually wins in a *waltz*.

6. key—[B] lane in front of the basket. Whenever I linger by Kate's desk, she yells, "Three-second limit in the *key*!"

7. weak side—[A] area away from the ball. Kyle ran to the *weak side*, hollering to his teammate, "Get in the game!"

8. cage—[B] batting-practice area in baseball. After going five for five in the Little League contest, Dean was given a day off from the batting *cage*.

9. rock—[C] the basketball. Tell Alison to quit being such a show-off and pass the *rock* already!

10. Sweet Sixteen—[B] NCAA tournament round. Art picked the Toledo Mud Hens to make the *Sweet Sixteen*, even though they're a baseball team.

11. pine—[C] players' bench. Albert makes the most of his time riding the *pine* in the bullpen—he steals the other team's pitching signs.

12. platoon—[C] alternate at a position. Andy and I *platoon* at the reception desk; I've got mornings.

13. chippy—[B] rough, aggressive. When it's the last subway car, things can get *chippy* on the platform.

14. squeaker—[A] close game. My knuckles were white after that 100–99 *squeaker* against the Nets.

15. scrimmage—[A] practice game. That kid goes all-out even in a shirts-versus-skins *scrimmage*.

16. rubber—[B] game that breaks a series tie. "Do you know who's pitching in tomorrow's *rubber* game?" the anxious manager asked.

SOUND SMARTER

A couple of *redundancies* have crossed our desks recently: *new recruit* and *refer back*. A rookie forward is simply a *recruit*, who by definition is new—and if you're *referring* to the 2010 NBA draft for info on him, of course you're looking back. So *recruit* and *refer* should both stand on their own.

SPELL CHECK

The 2013 Scripps National Spelling Bee, won by 13-year-old Arvind Mahankali on May 30, was the first to feature vocabulary quizzes as qualifiers. Below is a sampling of the words tackled by the kids, with fresh definitions to challenge you. Take your turn to see if you'd qualify for the bee—then check the next page for answers.

1. dearth ('durth) *n.*—A: fireplace. B: value. C: shortage.

2. flooey ('floo-ee) *adj.*—A: open and breezy. B: like jam. C: askew.

3. egregious (ih-'gree-jus) *adj.*—A: very bad. B: very small. C: fond of company.

4. infinitesimal (in-fi-nih-'te-suh-mul) *adj.*—A: uncountable. B: of prime numbers. C: tiny.

5. capitulate (kuh-'pi-chuh-layt) *v.*—A: surrender. B: amass cash. C: start a new sentence.

6. lassitude ('las-i-tood) *n.*—A: femininity. B: permanence. C: lethargy.

7. mercurial (mer-'kyur-ee-ul) *adj.*—A: running errands. B: obscured. C: quick to change.

8. prodigal ('prah-di-gul) *adj.*—A: spending unwisely. B: giving unwanted advice. C: arrogant.

9. discern (dih-'sern) *v.*—A: detect. B: have trouble understanding. C: get rid of.

10. volatile ('vah-la-tihl) *adj.*—A: explosive. B: willing. C: spoken aloud.

11. flamboyant (flam-'boi-ent) *adj.*—A: showy. B: young and foolish. C: on fire.

12. fandango (fan-'dan-go) *n.*—A: wild dog. B: lively dance. C: bleacherite.

13. eradicate (ih-'rah-di-kayt) *v.*—A: plant deeply. B: destroy completely. C: bring to light.

14. fusillade ('fyoo-si-lahd) *n.*—A: candlewick. B: barrage of shots. C: strong glue.

15. campestral (kam-'pes-tral) *adj.*—A: of open fields. B: toward evening. C: buggy.

SPELLING FOR SMARTY-PANTS
When you spell correctly, you're practicing *orthography,* which is a word with Greek roots. *Ortho* means "correct" or "right" and is found in words like *orthodox* ("right opinion") and orthodonture ("correct teeth"). The suffix *-graphy* means "writing" and is found in words like *biography* ("life writing") and *geography* ("the writing of the earth").

Live It Up!

"Spell Check" Answers

1. **dearth**—[C] shortage. There is a *dearth* of Darth Vader costumes at this convention.

2. **flooey**—[C] askew. Your tie is crooked, your socks don't match—your whole outfit is *flooey*.

3. **egregious**—[A] very bad. Your deportment, sir, is reprehensible and *egregious*.

4. **infinitesimal**—[C] tiny. When we say we're perfect, we don't count *infinitesimal* flaws.

5. **capitulate**—[A] surrender. Don't *capitulate* to his whims—stick to your guns.

6. **lassitude**—[C] lethargy. An adolescent in the morning is a case study in *lassitude*.

7. **mercurial**—[C] quick to change. Her *mercurial* taste in clothes keeps everyone guessing.

8. **prodigal**—[A] spending unwisely. Since winning the lottery, he's been a *prodigal* fool.

9. **discern**—[A] detect. Squinting through the spyglass, I was able to *discern* a pirate ship.

10. **volatile**—[A] explosive. Be careful; Nick has a rather *volatile* temper.

11. **flamboyant**—[A] showy. Oscar Wilde was nothing if not *flamboyant*.

12. **fandango**—[B] lively dance. After a touchdown, it's not necessary to dance a *fandango* in the end zone.

13. **eradicate**—[B] destroy completely. To *eradicate* my termites, I've purchased an aardvark.

14. **fusillade**—[B] barrage of shots. A *fusillade* of hailstones banged down on our windshield.

15. **campestral**—[A] of open fields. Even the most devoted city lovers can appreciate the beauty of a *campestral* milieu.

FIX OUR MISTAKE!

Here are eight words from the 2013 National Spelling Bee. Are they all correct, or have we misspelled one or more?

gesundheit
trattoria
brewhaha
inocuous

surveillance
belligerent
poinsettia
sarsaparilla

Answer: We misspelled three of the words: *brouhaha, innocuous,* and *belligerent.*

SPORTS

Everything at a baseball game is a little brighter, a little sharper, a little more in focus. It's a magical break from the worries and cares of everyday life.
—**LARRY KING**

"

If I'm winning, I have to act like I'm not bored. If it's a tough match, I act like I'm having a good time. I'm a drama queen.
—**SERENA WILLIAMS**

"

There's more to boxing than hitting. There's not getting hit, for instance.
—**GEORGE FOREMAN**

"

Baseball, it is said, is only a game. True. And the Grand Canyon is only a hole in Arizona.
—**GEORGE WILL**

"

QUOTABLE TWEETS

I'm starting to think that Jesus does love football.
@APLUSK (ASHTON KUTCHER)

Live It Up!

THE PERFECT WORDS FOR
CELEBRATIONS

Life is not dated merely by years.
Events are sometimes the best calendars.
—BENJAMIN DISRAELI

"

You only live once. But if you work
it right, once is enough.
—FRED ALLEN

"

We are all mortal until the first kiss and
the second glass of wine.
—EDUARDO GALEANO

"

Is not life a hundred times too short
for us to bore ourselves?
—FRIEDRICH NIETZSCHE

"

Dance till the stars come down from the rafters!
Dance, Dance, Dance till you drop!
—W. H. AUDEN

Karaoke is the great equalizer.
—**AISHA TYLER**

We're fools whether we dance or not,
so we might as well dance.
—**JAPANESE PROVERB**

When wine goes in strange things come out.
—**FRIEDRICH SCHILLER**

Drink, and dance and laugh and lie,
Love the reeling midnight through,
For tomorrow we shall die!
(But, alas, we never do.)
—**DOROTHY PARKER**

Spend the afternoon. You can't take it with you.
—**ANNIE DILLARD**

There is no cure for birth and death,
save to enjoy the interval.
—**GEORGE SANTAYANA**

All my life I've wanted to be somebody, but now I see I should have been more specific.
—LILY TOMLIN

BELLY LAUGHS

As we like to say around here, laughter is the best medicine, so we hope you'll always keep your sense of humor, even (or especially) in the tough times.

LAUGHTER, THE BEST MEDICINE

Humor is a rubber sword—it allows you to make a point without drawing blood.
—MARY HIRSCH

I'd rather be funny than wise.
—DENNIS MILLER

My daughter started making fart noises with her mouth and then laughing. And I was like, Oh well, I've taught her everything I know.
—ANDY SAMBERG

Wit is the key, I think, to anybody's heart. Show me the person who doesn't like to laugh and I'll show you a person with a toe tag.
—JULIA ROBERTS

Laughter and tears are both responses to frustration and exhaustion . . . I myself prefer to laugh, since there is less cleaning up to do afterward.
—KURT VONNEGUT

You can't stay mad at somebody who makes you laugh.
—JAY LENO

🐦 QUOTABLE TWEETS

Thought I found a snake in my garage. Turns out it was a bunch of spiders in a snake costume going to a party. Thank god. Hate real snakes.

@NICKSWARDSON

"

I was street-smart, but unfortunately the street was Rodeo Drive.

—CARRIE FISHER

"

Never be afraid to laugh at yourself. After all, you could be missing out on the joke of the century.

—DAME EDNA EVERAGE

"

I've been very lucky in my life in terms of people who are able to tolerate me.

—PATTON OSWALT

"

I couldn't tell a joke if my life depended on it.

—DIANE KEATON

"

One doesn't have a sense of humor. It has you.

—LARRY GELBART

PERSONALLY SPEAKING

I haven't the slightest idea how to change people, but still I keep a long list of prospective candidates just in case I should ever figure it out.
—DAVID SEDARIS

Great people talk about ideas, average people talk about things, and small people talk about wine.
—FRAN LEBOWITZ

The difference between Sly Stallone and me is that I am me and he is him.
—ARNOLD SCHWARZENEGGER

There's nothing like a gleam of humor to reassure you that a fellow human being is ticking inside a strange face.
—EVA HOFFMAN

A narcissist is someone better-looking than you are.
—GORE VIDAL

I'm better off not socializing. I make a better impression if I'm not around.
—CHRISTOPHER WALKEN

QUOTABLE TWEETS

Just taught my kids about taxes by eating 38% of their ice cream.
@CONANOBRIEN

> There's something very powerful about looking in the mirror and asking yourself a question. Because I think it's really hard to lie.
> **—KRISTEN WIIG**

> The world can't end today, because it's already tomorrow in Australia.
> **—CHARLES M. SCHULZ**

> In real life, I assure you, there is no such thing as algebra.
> **—FRAN LEBOWITZ**

> Instructions for living a life:
> Pay attention.
> Be astonished.
> Tell about it.
> **—MARY OLIVER**

KEEPING IT REAL

There's power in looking silly and not caring that you do.
—AMY POEHLER

"

The beaten path is the safest, but the traffic's terrible.
—JEFF TAYLOR

"

The safest way to double your money is to fold it over once and put it in your pocket.
—KIN HUBBARD

"

The only thing worse than beating a dead horse is betting on one.
—RELIENT K

"

You can't get spoiled if you do your own ironing.
—MERYL STREEP

"

They say you only go around once, but with a muscle car you can go around two or three times.
—TIM ALLEN

"

I am old enough to know that a red carpet is just a rug.
—AL GORE

HEALTH AND FITNESS, SO TO SPEAK

Cross-country skiing is great if you live in a small country.
—**STEVEN WRIGHT**

Whenever I feel like exercise, I lie down until the feeling passes.
—**ROBERT HUTCHINS**

I'm not a vegetarian because I love animals. I'm a vegetarian because I hate plants.
—**A. WHITNEY BROWN**

Housework can't kill you, but why take a chance?
—**PHYLLIS DILLER**

QUOTABLE TWEETS

A study found exercise may be bad for your health. Which means I'm not fat, I'm just morbidly over-healthed.
@STEPHENATHOME (STEPHEN COLBERT)

THE PERFECT WORDS TO
BREAK THE ICE

There's a thin line between talking to yourself and arguing with an idiot.
—@FUNNYORDIE

"

Most people hate cell phone use on trains; I love cell phone use on trains. What do you want to do, read that report on your lap, or hear about your neighbor's worst date ever?
—LIZA MUNDY

"

The opposite of talking isn't listening. The opposite of talking is waiting.
—FRAN LEBOWITZ

"

I personally think we developed language because of our deep inner need to complain.
—JANE WAGNER

APRIL FOOLERY

If you love jokes, pranks, and sneaky tricks, get ready for a vocabulary quiz full of words about clowning, foolery, frauds, and cons. For answers, turn to the next page.

1. quip *n.*—A: witty remark. B: magician's box of gear. C: butt of a joke.

2. antic *adj.*—A: like a clown. B: like a thief. C: like a medicine man.

3. wily *adj.*—A: easy to fool. B: overly cautious. C: cleverly deceptive.

4. jape *n.*—A: look of shock and surprise. B: practical joke. C: one dressed in a gorilla suit.

5. deadpan *adj.*—A: caught red-handed. B: showing no emotion. C: hit in head by a skillet.

6. shtick *n.*—A: pie fight. B: comedy routine. C: long, thin object used to stir drinks.

7. ribald *adj.*—A: funny in a coarse way. B: funny in a puzzling way. C: with a shaved, tattooed head.

8. flimflam *n.*—A: audience paid to laugh. B: potion or elixir. C: deception or swindle.

9. lampoon *v.*—A: to mock or riddle in a satire. B: catch in an embarrassing situation. C: remove a lackluster performer from the stage.

10. jocular *adj.*—A: agile and athletic. B: astride a unicycle. C: fooling around and wisecracking.

11. sleight *n.*—A: insulting jab. B: dexterity. C: trick that backfires comically.

12. motley *adj.*—A: old stock of jokes. B: good sense of humor. C: many-colored, as in outfits often worn by clowns.

13. shill *n.*—A: high-pitched laugh. B: stage prop. C: con-game decoy.

14. humbug *n.*—A: lack of any sense of humor. B: tricky impostor. C: nonsense song with a droning chorus.

15. cozen *v.*—A: to hoodwink. B: imitate. C: marry into a neighbor family.

Belly Laughs **167**

"April Foolery" Answers

1. quip—[A] witty remark. Our bowling team captain is always ready with a punchy *quip*.

2. antic—[A] like a clown. If you invite Bozo the Clown to your party, you can only hope your guests will enjoy his *antic* behavior.

3. wily—[C] cleverly deceptive. You just can't trust that *wily* old slyboots.

4. jape—[B] practical joke. An exploding cigar is some people's idea of a funny *jape*.

5. deadpan—[B] showing no emotion. It's hard to remain *deadpan* when chewing a piece of rubber bacon.

6. shtick—[B] comedy routine. A good comedian has a well-honed *shtick*.

7. ribald—[A] funny in a coarse way. The censors weren't too happy about my *ribald* jokes.

8. flimflam—[C] deception or swindle. The agent won't fall for his *flimflam*.

9. lampoon—[A] to mock or ridicule in a satire. On TV, it's common to see comedians *lampoon* our political leaders.

10. jocular—[C] fooling around and wisecracking. That Transylvanian guy in accounting is so funny, we call him Count *Jocular*.

11. sleight—[B] dexterity. A magician will try to fool his audience with *sleight* of hand.

12. motley—[C] many-colored. The king's fool cavorted about the place dressed in a *motley*, patched-together outfit.

13. shill—[C] decoy in a con game. The swindler's partner was just a *shill* pretending to be a customer.

14. humbug—[B] tricky impostor. Better not to take investment advice from that broker, because he's just a *humbug*.

15. cozen—[A] to hoodwink. That's one game designed to *cozen* you out of your paycheck.

WEATHER FACTS

You can't change the weather—but you can at least talk about it sensibly and intelligently. Here's a flurry of useful terms you can try sprinkling into your everyday chitchat. Turn the page for a flood of answers.

1. inclement (in-'kle-ment) *adj.*—A: comfortably warm. B: severe. C: ever-changing.

2. temperate ('tem-pret) *adj.*—A: marked by moderation. B: steamy. C: frigid.

3. aridity (uh-'ri-de-tee) *n.*—A: harshness. B: blazing sunshine. C: drought.

4. nimbus ('nim-bus) *n.*—A: frostbite. B: rain cloud. C: weather vane.

5. doldrums ('dohl-drumz) *n.*—A: sounds of booming thunder. B: stagnation or listlessness. C: weather map lines.

6. inundate ('ih-nen-dayt) *v.*—A: overheat or melt. B: form icicles. C: flood.

7. abate (uh-'bayt) *v.*—A: decrease in force, as rain. B: increase, as wind. C: pile up, as snow.

8. convection (kun-'vek-shen) *n.*—A: cyclonic movement. B: hot air rising. C: meeting of weatherpersons.

9. striated ('striy-ay-ted) *adj.*—A: jagged, as hail. B: banded, as clouds. C: patchy, as fog.

10. hoary ('hor-ee) *adj.*—A: hazy. B: white with frost or age. C: lightly sprinkling.

11. leeward ('lee-werd) *adj.*—A: by the shore. B: out of balance. C: not facing the wind.

12. graupel ('grauw-pel) *n.*—A: snow pellets. B: mudslide. C: warm-water current.

13. insolation (in-soh-'lay-shen) *n.*—A: sunstroke. B: shade. C: winter clothing.

14. permafrost ('per-muh-frost) *n.*—A: dusting of powdery snow. B: stalled front. C: frozen subsoil.

15. prognosticate (prahg-'nahs-ti-kayt) *v.*—A: forecast. B: chill. C: take shelter.

Belly Laughs

"Weather Facts" Answers

1. **inclement**—[B] severe. Today's kite festival has been canceled due to *inclement* weather.

2. **temperate**—[A] marked by moderation. After that cold snap, we could really use some *temperate* conditions.

3. **aridity**—[C] drought. If this *aridity* continues, I swear I'll do my rain dance.

4. **nimbus**—[B] rain cloud. We took one glance at the looming *nimbus* and headed straight for shelter.

5. **doldrums**—[B] stagnation or listlessness. FYI, the everyday use of *doldrums* refers to the area around the equator where prevailing winds are calm.

6. **inundate**—[C] flood. After the storm, our tiny shop was *inundated* with water and debris.

7. **abate**—[A] decrease in force, as rain. "I do believe," said Noah, "that the downpour is about to *abate*."

8. **convection**—[B] hot air rising. Sea breezes are a common weather effect of *convection*.

9. **striated**—[B] banded, as clouds. You could almost climb the ladder suggested by those *striated* cirrus clouds.

10. **hoary**—[B] white with frost or age. Professor Parker's beard was almost as *hoary* as the windshield he was scraping.

11. **leeward**—[C] not facing the wind. We huddled on the *leeward* side of the island, well out of the stiff breeze.

12. **graupel**—[A] snow pellets. As I heaved my shovel in the winter nor'easter, *graupel* stung my cheeks like BBs.

13. **insolation**—[A] sunstroke. *Insolation* is a serious threat during summer football practices.

14. **permafrost**—[C] frozen subsoil. Excavating the *permafrost* in Alaska often requires a jackhammer.

15. **prognosticate**—[A] forecast. We might not always appreciate his opinion, but nobody can *prognosticate* like Punxsutawney Phil.

WEATHER-WISE

Meteorology is the study of weather—so what's that *meteor* doing in there? *Meteor* comes from the Greek *meta*, meaning "over, beyond," plus *aoros*, for "lifted." And the suffix *-ology* means "branch of knowledge, science." So meteorology is literally the science of what's above us (i.e., the *weather*).

ENGLISH RESTORATION

Despite having so many words to choose from—at least a million, by some estimates—we are often at a loss for them. A new website seeks to bring underused but deserving words back into the vocabulary. Here are a few that wordwarriors.wayne.edu is trying to restore to their rightful place. For quiz answers, turn the page.

1. **abecedarian** (ay-bee-see-'der-ee-un) *adj.*—A: rudimentary. B: going on foot. C: in one's 90s.

2. **ebullient** (ih-'bull-yunt) *adj.*—A: countless. B: full of high spirits. C: made of gold.

3. **peckish** *adj.*—A: a little loving. B: a little plump. C: a little hungry.

4. **legerdemain** (leh-jur-duh-'mane) *n.*—A: stock portfolio. B: law of the land. C: sleight of hand.

5. **odium** ('oh-dee-um) *n.*—A: addictive narcotic. B: hatred and contempt. C: Greek theater.

6. **bumbershoot** *n.*—A: umbrella. B: misfiring rifle. C: first growth in spring.

7. **smarmy** ('smar-mee) *adj.*—A: phonily pleasant. B: crawling with ants. C: as slow as molasses.

8. **moot** *adj.*—A: purely academic. B: unable to speak. C: bovine.

9. **tacit** ('tass-it) *adj.*—A: unspoken but understood. B: only temporary. C: firm and binding.

10. **lugubrious** (luh-'goo-bree-us) *adj.*—A: gloomy. B: left-handed. C: in the seat of power.

11. **peccadillo** (peck-uh-'dill-oh) *n.*—A: wild pig. B: slight misdeed. C: pale yellow color.

12. **quixotic** (kwik-'sah-tik) *adj.*—A: tiny, trifling. B: dreamy, impractical. C: fierce, bullying.

13. **uxorious** (uk-'sore-ee-us) *adj.*—A: costing too much. B: doting on one's wife. C: in wild disarray.

14. **bloviate** ('blow-vee-ate) *v.*—A: make unnecessary. B: rupture a blood vessel. C: speak or write wordily.

Belly Laughs

"English Restoration" Answers

1. abecedarian—[A] rudimentary. Archie, with his pipe wrench and his *abecedarian* knowledge of plumbing, has flooded the kitchen.

2. ebullient—[B] full of high spirits. It must be all the coffee that makes Darlene so *ebullient*.

3. peckish—[C] a little hungry. Yes, I did eat the entire pie—I was feeling *peckish*.

4. legerdemain—[C] sleight of hand. Through some last-minute *legerdemain*, Betty Ann, who can't tell a daisy from a dandelion, was voted president of the garden club.

5. odium—[B] hatred and contempt. The outfielder had to endure his teammates' *odium* after he let a pop fly turn into the game-winning home run.

6. bumbershoot—[A] umbrella. A sudden gust swiped Floyd's rain hat and blew his polka-dot *bumbershoot* inside out.

7. smarmy—[A] phonily pleasant. Willard's *smarmy* reply to the boss's e-mail fooled no one but the boss, who promptly promoted him.

8. moot—[A] purely academic. "It's a *moot* point," the meter maid said. "The law's the law."

9. tacit—[A] unspoken but understood. Nate's silence about Grandma's broken Hummel amounted to a *tacit* confession.

10. lugubrious—[A] gloomy. Lugubrious and plodding, Stanley makes every day seem like a rainy Monday.

11. peccadillo—[B] slight misdeed. He claimed that his felony conviction was a boyhood *peccadillo*, but that somehow failed to impress the parole board.

12. quixotic—[B] dreamy, impractical. The ambassador's *quixotic* idea was to invite the warring presidents to an arm-wrestling match.

13. uxorious—[B] doting on one's wife. Our *uxorious* buddy can't play poker—he's taking his wife to the ballet.

14. bloviate—[C] speak or write wordily. While the commencement speaker *bloviated,* the graduates snored.

DEEP ROOTS

Vocabulary—our panoply of words—comes from the Latin *vocare* ("to call") and is directly related to *voice*. Other words from the same root are *vowel*, *vouch* ("to speak up for someone"), *vocation* ("one's calling"), *invoke* ("to call forth"), and *convoke* ("to call together"). *Vocabulary* can also mean "a range of skills" ("a filmmaker with a wide *vocabulary* of techniques").

WHAT THE DICKENS!

When it came to ingeniously descriptive language, Charles Dickens was *lummy* (aka first-rate). Bryan Kozlowski compiles the most colorful terms in his book *What the Dickens?!* You might need some logic to guess the definitions. Turn the page for answers and the words' literary sources.

1. sawbones ('saw-bohnz) *n.*—A: doctor. B: magician. C: old nag.

2. catawampus (kat-uh-'wom-puhs) *adj.*—A: fierce. B: syrupy. C: deep and dark.

3. jog-trotty ('jahg-trah-tee) *adj.*—A: monotonous. B: nervous. C: backward.

4. spoony ('spoo-nee) *adj.*—A: spacious. B: pun-filled. C: lovey-dovey.

5. rantipole ('ran-tih-pohl) *n.*—A: battering ram. B: fishing rod. C: ill-behaved person.

6. gum-tickler ('guhm-tihk-ler) *n.*—A: funny remark. B: strong drink. C: wishbone.

7. stomachic (stuh-'ma-kihk) *n.*—A: winter coat. B: tummy medicine. C: windup toy.

8. sassigassity (sass-ih-'gass-ih-tee) *n.*—A: fancy clothes. B: cheeky attitude. C: gust of hot wind.

9. comfoozled (kuhm-'foo-zuhld) *adj.*—A: on fire. B: pampered. C: exhausted.

10. mud lark ('muhd lark) *n.*—A: scavenging child. B: court judge. C: ancient scribe.

11. plenipotentiary (pleh-nuh-puh-'tehn-shuh-ree) *n.*—A: housewife. B: diplomatic agent. C: bank vault.

12. toadeater ('tohd-ee-ter) *n.*—A: fawning person. B: habitual liar. C: gourmet.

13. slangular ('slang-yuh-luhr) *adj.*—A: oblique. B: using street talk. C: tight around the neck.

14. marplot ('mahr-plot) *n.*—A: flower garden. B: meddler. C: fruit jam.

15. heeltap ('heel-tap) *n.*—A: Irish dance step. B: scoundrel. C: sip of liquor left in a glass.

Belly Laughs

"What the Dickens!" Answers

1. sawbones—[A] doctor. Captain Kirk pulled strings to get his friend McCoy hired as the ship's *sawbones*. (Used in *The Pickwick Papers*)

2. catawampus—[A] fierce. The *catawampus* storm engulfed the tiny village. (*Martin Chuzzlewit*)

3. jog-trotty—[A] monotonous. Will Lauren ever quit that *jog-trotty* data-entry job? (*Bleak House*)

4. spoony—[C] lovey-dovey. Those *spoony* newlyweds just won't stop canoodling! (*David Copperfield*)

5. rantipole—[C] ill-behaved person. A gang of *rantipoles* vandalized the historic building. (*Great Expectations*)

6. gum-tickler—[B] strong drink. Ty downed a few *gum-ticklers* to forget his troubles. (*Our Mutual Friend*)

7. stomachic—[B] tummy medicine. This new organic *stomachic* may be just the thing for your indigestion. (*David Copperfield*)

8. sassigassity—[B] cheeky attitude. No more of your *sassigassity*, young lady! ("A Christmas Tree")

9. comfoozled—[C] exhausted. We were all completely *comfoozled* after the 10K race. (*The Pickwick Papers*)

10. mud lark—[A] scavenging child. Some *mud lark* just snatched my piece of birthday cake! (*Our Mutual Friend*)

11. plenipotentiary—[B] diplomatic agent. Which of those muckety-mucks is the head *plenipotentiary* around here? (*Great Expectations*)

12. toadeater—[A] fawning person. You *toadeaters* will never disagree with your coach! (*Dombey and Son*)

13. slangular—[B] using street talk. Lady Clara was shocked by the *slangular* chatter at high tea. (*Bleak House*)

14. marplot—[B] meddler. The con men were exposed when a *marplot* snitched on them. (*Our Mutual Friend*)

15. heeltap—[C] sip of liquor left in a glass. "I must go," said James Bond, downing the *heeltap* of his martini. (*The Pickwick Papers*)

WHAT'S IN A NAME?

Some Dickens characters have made their way into the lexicon: A *scrooge* is a miser (from stingy Ebenezer Scrooge), and *Pecksniffian* means "hypocritical" (from insincere Seth Pecksniff). It's a coincidence that *dickens*, a euphemism for the devil, is in the dictionary. But *Dickensian*, which refers to living in decrepit conditions, owes its place to his Victorian tales.

TECH TIME

Don't yak away on your cell phone or computer without first testing your knowledge of modern-day telecom terms. For answers, turn the page.

1. avatar *n.*—A: flight-simulation program. B: online dating club. C: virtual representation of a gamer.

2. flame *v.*—A: make prank phone calls. B: be abusive in a chat room. C: lose one's connection.

3. bluesnarfing *n.*—A: despairing over a dead cell phone. B: cursing on a cell in public. C: using Bluetooth to steal info from a wireless device.

4. top up *v.*—A: buy more time for a phone. B: end a chat abruptly. C: be the first to post a message at a site.

5. clamshell *n.*—A: phone that flips open. B: private space for talking. C: silent lurker in a chat room.

6. ROFL *interj.*—A: reply of four letters. B: running out for lunch. C: rolling on floor laughing.

7. faceplate *n.*—A: large cell phone. B: cell phone cover. C: state of being glued to a computer.

8. phish *v.*—A: use a private line. B: con out of private info. C: send musical messages.

9. phreak *v.*—A: lose one's temper. B: tamper with phone systems. C: chat online in a secret language.

10. viral *adj.*—A: fast-spreading on the Web. B: transmitted by cell phone. C: moving hacker to hacker.

11. chatterbot *n.*—A: taped conversation. B: simulation of a person talking. C: constant yakker.

12. digerati *n.*—A: signals transmitted by a modem. B: letters represented as numbers. C: people versed in computer technology.

13. wonky *adj.*—A: not working right. B: highly technical. C: addicted to text messaging.

Belly Laughs

"Tech Time" Answers

1. avatar—[C] virtual representation of a gamer. Like me, my Second Life *avatar* enjoys sitting around all day watching TV.

2. flame—[B] be abusive in a chat room. The online pyromaniacs club hates it when guys from the firefighters group *flame* them.

3. bluesnarfing—[C] using Bluetooth to steal info from a wireless device. Joe got my now ex-girlfriend's number by *bluesnarfing* me.

4. top up—[A] buy more time for a phone. While changing into her bikini, Barb realized she'd forgotten to *top up* her cell for vacation.

5. clamshell—[A] phone that flips open. Nick opted for the *clamshell* because it reminded him of Star Trek.

6. ROFL—[C] rolling on floor laughing. He's a burglar named Joey Lox? *ROFL!*

7. faceplate—[B] cell phone cover. Be brutal—does my new designer *faceplate* make me look fat?

8. phish—[B] con out of private info. Mom, don't give your password to that sleaze; he's just *phishing*.

9. phreak—[B] tamper with phone systems. Jim got free long distance until he was busted for *phreaking*.

10. viral—[A] fast-spreading on the Web. The last thing the senator needed was a *viral* video of the affair.

11. chatterbot—[B] simulation of a person talking. The forum host I was flirting with turned out to be a *chatterbot*. We're going to Circuit City for our first date.

12. digerati—[C] people versed in computer technology. You call yourself one of the *digerati*? Ha! You still use a manual typewriter.

13. wonky—[A] not working right. Ever since I ran over my cell, it's been *wonky*.

DEEP ROOTS

People can get and spread news on a *wiki*, a website created and edited by the users. *Wikipedia* is an example. The word *wiki* is Hawaiian for "quick." And it was a Honolulu airport bus called the *Wiki-Wiki* Shuttle that gave the name its currency.

USE YOUR WORDS, VOLUME 2

MYTHS & MEANING

Like the month of March—which is named for the Roman war god, Mars—the words in this quiz all have their origins in mythology. Muse upon them, then consult the fates for answers (or just turn the page).

1. odyssey ('ah-duh-see) *n.*—A: peculiarity. B: long journey. C: sea monster.

2. nemesis ('neh-muh-sis) *n.*— A: pen name. B: memory loss. C: archenemy.

3. delphic: ('del-fik) *adj.*—A: ambiguous. B: underground. C: greedy.

4. vestal ('veh-stuhl) *adj.*—A: springlike. B: fierce. C: chaste.

5. narcissistic (nar-suh-sih-'stik) *adj.*—A: forgetful. B: generous. C: self-obsessed.

6. mercurial (mer-'kyoor-ee-uhl) *adj.*—A: changeable. B: famished. C: combative.

7. —Aurora: (uh-'roh-ruh) *n.*—A: dawn. B: hearing. C: lions.

8. cornucopia: (kor-nuh-'koh-pee-uh) *n.*—A: abundance. B: madness. C: herd.

9. calliope (kuh-'ly-uh-pee) *n.*—A: echo. B: shooting star. C: steam-whistle organ.

10. —ambrosial (am-'broh-zhuhl) *adj.*—A: delicious. B: of the blood. C: golden.

11. paean ('pee-uhn) *n.*—A: beetle. B: song of praise. C: kinship.

12. venerate ('veh-nuh-rayt) *v.*—A: shine. B: hunt. C: worship.

13. myrmidon ('mer-muh-don) *n.*—A: half dolphin, half man. B: loyal follower. C: huge crowd.

14. lycanthrope ('ly-cuhn-throhp) *n.*—A: sailboat. B: werewolf. C: wine bottle.

15. plutocracy (ploo-'tah-kruh-see) *n.*—A: government by the rich. B: remote solar system. C: chemical reaction.

Belly Laughs

"Myths & Meaning" Answers

1. odyssey [B] long journey. My five-minute errand turned into a day-long *odyssey*.

2. nemesis [C] archenemy. "Ah, my old *nemesis*—we meet again!" the supervillain cackled.

3. delphic [A] ambiguous. Danny was unimpressed by the fortune-teller's *delphic* predictions.

4. vestal [C] chaste. The ancient ritual required *vestal* maidens to dance in a circle around the fire.

5. narcissistic [C] self-obsessed. Does posting five selfies a day make me *narcissistic*?

6. mercurial [A] changeable. "New England weather certainly is *mercurial*," Meg said, peeling off her heavy coat.

7. aurora [A] dawn. The hikers paused to admire the beautiful pink *aurora* before continuing on the mountain trail.

8. cornucopia [A] abundance. "What can I get you? We have a *cornucopia* of craft beers on tap," the bartender said.

9. calliope [C] steam-whistle organ. What's a circus without a *calliope*?

10. ambrosial [A] delicious. An espresso milkshake would taste *ambrosial* about now!

11. paean [B] song of praise. Mom composed a *paean* for us to perform for Dad's birthday.

12. venerate [C] worship. Juliana goes to every single Packers game—she practically *venerates* the team.

13. myrmidon [B] loyal follower. The emperor's *myrmidons* cater to his every whim, no matter how outlandish.

14. lycanthrope [B] werewolf. My boyfriend always disappears when there's a full moon; do you think he's a *lycanthrope*?

15. plutocracy [A] government by the rich. "Only the wealthy can afford to run for mayor—this town has become a *plutocracy*!" Jim complained.

> **MIXED-UP MONTHS**
>
> Though March comes third in our modern calendar, the Roman calendar originally had only ten months, running from March to December. (January and February were added later.) That's why September, October, November, and December are named for the Latin *septem* ("seven"), *octo* ("eight"), *novem* ("nine"), and *decem* ("ten").

THE X FILES

With this quiz, we reach into our lexicon for words beginning or ending with x. For answers, turn the page.

1. hallux ('ha-luhks) *n.*—A: lance-bearing soldier. B: lake carved by a glacier. C: big toe.

2. Xanadu ('zan-uh-doo) *n.*—A: happy, beautiful place. B: evil Greek sorceress. C: treasure sought by Sir Galahad.

3. xeric ('zeer-ik) *adj.*—A: dry, like a desert. B: vast, like an ocean. C: green, like a jungle.

4. onyx ('ah-niks) *n.*—A: long-horned antelope. B: gemstone with colored bands. C: wizard's magic spell.

5. vertex ('vur-teks) *n.*—A: whirling current. B: waistband for a tuxedo. C: highest point.

6. Xanthippe (zan-'thi-pee) *n.*—A: decisive battle. B: giant sea serpent. C: scolding wife.

7. pollex ('pah-leks) *n.*—A: male part of a flower. B: star that guides a traveler. C: thumb.

8. xyloid ('zy-loid) *adj.*—A: robotic. B: resembling wood. C: having the shape of a pyramid.

9. faux ('foh) *adj.*—A: fake or artificial. B: new or original. C: sly or cunning.

10. xanthic ('zan-thik) *adj.*—A: yellowish. B: acting like a clown. C: sticky, as an adhesive.

11. coccyx ('kahk-siks) *n.*—A: female acrobat. B: hub of a spinning wheel. C: tailbone.

12. xenophobic (ze-nuh-'foh-bik) *adj.*—A: fearing loud noises. B: fearing ants or bees. C: fearing foreigners or strangers.

13. vortex ('vor-teks) *n.*—A: whirling current. B: waistband for a tuxedo. C: highest point.

Belly Laughs

"The X Files" Answers

1. hallux—[C] big toe. Dexter wears sandals because his *hallux* is too big for Nikes.

2. Xanadu—[A] happy, beautiful place. Bixby's backyard would be a veritable *Xanadu* if it weren't for the toxic dump next door.

3. xeric—[A] dry, like a desert. Those transplanted Ohioans keep trying to grow phlox here in New Mexico's *xeric* landscape.

4. onyx—[B] gemstone with colored bands. Xavier was hypnotized by the sphinx's *onyx* talisman.

5. vertex—[C] highest point. As he slipped off the rocky crag, Felix was heard exulting, "At last, the *verteeeex!*"

6. Xanthippe—[C] scolding wife (married to Socrates). Xenophon emulated Socrates but drew the line at marrying his own *Xanthippe*.

7. pollex—[C] thumb. Little Jack Bollix stuck in his *pollex* and pulled out a purple plum.

8. xyloid—[B] resembling wood. After Tex failed shop class six years in a row, friends determined that he possessed a *xyloid* head.

9. faux—[A] fake or artificial. Maxine sports fake eyelashes, false teeth, and *faux* pearls.

10. xanthic—[A] yellowish. If you ask me, Xena's roots are more brunette than *xanthic*.

11. coccyx—[C] tailbone. At the rink, Dixie executed a triple axel but landed smack on her *coccyx*.

12. xenophobic—[C] fearing foreigners or strangers. Roxanne is so *xenophobic,* she hid in a closet the entire time she vacationed in France.

13. vortex—[A] whirling current. One untruth led to another until the politician got caught in a *vortex* of lies.

DELISH!

Milk without fat is like nonalcoholic Scotch.
—ANDY ROONEY

You've got bad eating habits if you use a grocery cart in a 7-Eleven, OK?
—DENNIS MILLER

Food, love, mother and career: the four basic guilt groups.
—CATHY GUISEWITE

I don't share blame. I don't share credit. And I don't share desserts.
—BEVERLY SILLS

Everybody likes the guy who offers them a stick of gum.
—STEVE CARRELL AS MICHAEL SCOTT ON *THE OFFICE*

A cookbook is only as good as its poorest recipe.
— JULIA CHILD

LAUGHTER, THE BEST ADVICE

Don't take life too seriously, you'll never get out of it alive.
—ELBERT HUBBARD

"
Never miss a good chance to shut up.
—WILL ROGERS

"
I always advise people never to give advice.
—P.G. WODEHOUSE

"
Always and never are two words you should always remember never to use.
—WENDELL JOHNSON

"
Don't smoke too much, drink too much, eat too much or work too much. We're all on the road to the grave—but there's no need to be in the passing lane.
—ROBERT ORBEN

"
I believe in an open mind, but not so open that your brains fall out.
—ARTHUR HAYS SULZBERGER

A successful man is one who makes more money than his wife can spend. A successful woman is one who can find such a man.

—**LANA TURNER**

"

You should take your job seriously, but not yourself. That is the best combination.

—**DAME JUDI DENCH**

"

If you want to change the world, start off by making your bed.

—**WILLIAM H. MCRAVEN**

"

Don't worry about your heart. It will last as long as you live.

—**W.C. FIELDS**

"

The next time you have a thought . . . let it go.

—**RON WHITE**

"

Any girl can be glamorous. All you have to do is stand still and look stupid.

—**LAURENCE PETER**

> It is easier to build strong children than to repair broken men.
> —FREDERICK DOUGLASS

WIT & WISDOM

Wise men and women offer deep thoughts for us to contemplate our world. As we ponder the wisdom of the past, we can allow wise words to broaden our own horizons and help pave the way forward.

KINDNESS

Whenever you see darkness, there is extraordinary opportunity for the light to burn brighter.
—**BONO**

"

The everyday kindness of the back roads more than makes up for the acts of greed in the headlines.
—**CHARLES KURALT**

"

Resolve to be tender with the young, compassionate with the aged, sympathetic with the striving, and tolerant with the weak and the wrong. Sometime in life you will have been all of these.
—**BOB GODDARD**

"

Life is short and we never have enough time for gladdening the hearts of those who travel the way with us. Oh, be swift to love! Make haste to be kind.
—**HENRI FRÉDÉRIC AMIEL**

I have witnessed the softening
of the hardest of hearts by a simple smile.
—GOLDIE HAWN

If you can't be kind,
at least be vague.
—JUDITH MARTIN

Ask any decent person what he thinks
matters most in human conduct: five to one
his answer will be "kindness."
—KENNETH CLARK

How sweet it is when the strong are also gentle!
—LIBBIE FUDIM

Kindness is never wasted. If it has no effect on
the recipient, at least it benefits the bestower.
—S. H. SIMMONS

GIVING & GRATITUDE

Two important things are to have a genuine interest in people and to be kind to them. Kindness, I've discovered, is everything in life.
—ISAAC BASHEVIS SINGER

"

Always try to be a little kinder than is necessary.
—JAMES M. BARRIE

"

Kindness is more important than wisdom, and the recognition of this is the beginning of wisdom.
—THEODORE ISAAC RUBIN, MD

"

There are three words I like to repeat to myself: glass half full. Just to remind myself to be grateful for everything I have.
—GOLDIE HAWN

"

Giving never happens by accident. It's always intentional.
—AMY GRANT

"

True giving happens when we give from our heart.
—MUHAMMAD ALI

🐦 QUOTABLE TWEETS

The sole source of peace in families, countries and the world is altruism—love and compassion.
@DALAILAMA

> If you give everybody a slice of pie, you will still have more than enough.
> **—JAY LENO**

> Be thankful for what you have—you'll end up having more.
> **—OPRAH**

> I challenge anybody in their darkest moment to write what they're grateful for, even stupid little things like green grass or a friendly conversation with somebody on the elevator. You start to realize how rich you are.
> **—JIM CARREY**

> Outcomes rarely turn on grand gestures or the art of the deal, but on whether you've sent someone a thank-you note.
> **—BERNIE BRILLSTEIN**

Wit & Wisdom

CHARACTER

"When you finally accept that you're a complete dork, your life gets easier. No sense in trying to be cool."
—**REESE WITHERSPOON**

"

The more I like me, the less I want to pretend to be other people.
—**JAMIE LEE CURTIS**

"

When wealth is lost, nothing is lost. When health is lost, something is lost. When character is lost, all is lost.
—**REV. BILLY GRAHAM**

"

To be good, and to do good, is the whole duty of man comprised in a few words.
—**ABIGAIL ADAMS**

"

Discipline equals freedom.
—**JOCKO WILLINK**

FORGIVENESS

The true measure of a man is how he treats someone who can do him absolutely no good.
—**ANN LANDERS**

"

I've never believed in measuring one's worth by the size of his or her bank account. I prefer to look at distance traveled.
—**DAN RATHER**

"

It ain't what people call you. It's what you answer to.
—**TYLER PERRY**

"

Never does the human soul appear so strong and noble as when it forgoes revenge and dares to forgive an injury.
—**E. H. CHAPIN**

"

One of the most lasting pleasures you can experience is the feeling that comes over you when you genuinely forgive an enemy—whether he knows it or not.
—**O. A. BATTISTA**

THE PERFECT WORDS FOR
INTENTIONS

Every child is an artist. The problem is how to remain an artist as we grow up.
—PABLO PICASSO

"

The world is not given by our fathers, but borrowed from our children.
—-WENDELL BERRY

"

The smallest deed is greater than the grandest intention.
—PATTI LABELLE

"

Good intentions are not enough. They've never put an onion in the soup yet.
—SONYA LEVIEN

"

Remember, people will judge you by your actions, not your intentions. You may have a heart of gold, but so does a hard-boiled egg.
—UNKNOWN

DOUBLE ENTENDRE

Many common words have secondary meanings that aren't widely known. Here are 17. Can you identify their other definitions? For answers, turn the page.

1. pen *n.*—A: snowcapped mountain. B: female swan. C: story with a moral.

2. fetch *n.*—A: bosom buddy. B: ghost. C: swamp.

3. rack *v.*—A: run at a fast gait, as a horse. B: print in capital letters. C: meet at right angles.

4. ounce *n.*—A: feeling of well-being. B: short argument. C: snow leopard.

5. burden *n.*—A: refrain of a song. B: footnote. C: reflection in a mirror.

6. troll *v.*—A: walk with a limp. B: travel by canoe. C: sing heartily.

7. poke *n.*—A: tree stump. B: black top hat. C: sack or bag.

8. painter *n.*—A: false compliment. B: drinking song. C: line for mooring a boat.

9. panic *n.*—A: raccoon-like animal. B: kind of grass. C: symbol for 0.

10. shy *v.*—A: con out of money. B: peel the skin of. C: sling or hurl.

11. defile *n.*—A: verse of a poem. B: narrow ravine. C: fishing pole.

12. murder *n.*—A: uphill trail. B: group of crows. C: mindless repetition.

13. patch *n.*—A: fool or clown. B: doctor or nurse. C: copy or clone.

14. bark *v.*—A: lift over one's head. B: turn from back to front. C: bump or scrape.

15. lore *n.*—A: small tropical fruit. B: space between a bird's eye and bill. C: uncharted territory.

16. pulse *n.*—A: insects like hornets and wasps. B: birds like ostriches and emus. C: plants like peas and beans.

17. rote *n.*—A: pang of anxiety. B: sound of the surf. C: thick coat of fur.

Wit & Wisdom

"Double Entendre" Answers

1. pen—[B] female swan. Sitting by the lake, the artist took out her pen and quickly sketched the pair of swans: a cob and a *pen*.

2. fetch—[B] ghost. "Quick! Go fetch an exorcist!" yelled Lenny, running down the stairs. "There's a *fetch* in the attic!"

3. rack—[A] run at a fast gait, as a horse. The two boys *racked* toward the candy rack before their mothers could stop them.

4. ounce—[C] snow leopard. "This spotted Asian *ounce* weighs 100 pounds," said the zoo-keeper, "give or take an ounce."

5. burden—[A] refrain of a song. Janie is constantly burdened by having the *burden* of "It's a Small World" stuck in her head.

6. troll—[C] sing heartily. On YouTube, you can hear a recording of J. R. R. Tolkien *trolling* "Troll Sat Alone on His Seat of Stone."

7. poke—[C] sack or bag. Poking around in her suitcase-size *poke*, Edna found everything but her car keys.

8. painter—[C] line for mooring a boat. Hired to refinish the yacht's deck, the painter failed to tie the *painter* and slid out to sea with the boat.

9. panic—[B] kind of grass. "Don't panic!" the landscaper said to his assistant. "That's not poison sumac—it's just woolly *panic* grass."

10. shy—[C] sling or hurl. Never one to shy from a challenge, George Washington *shied* a silver dollar across the Potomac.

11. defile—[B] narrow ravine. Don't defile the *defile*—use the trash can at the trailhead.

12. murder—[B] group of crows. Perched in the autumn branches, the *murder* of crows, not unlike the ones in Hitchcock's *The Birds*, looked entirely capable of murder.

13. patch—[A] fool or clown. The king's merry *patch* wore patchwork breeches.

14. bark—[C] bump or scrape. Dad *barked* his shin on the coffee table and gave a bark of pain.

15. lore—[B] space between a bird's eye and bill. In ornithological lore, the great egret's *lores* turn a brilliant lime green during breeding season.

16. pulse—[C] plants like peas and beans. Uncle Melvin's pulse quickens whenever he sees a rabbit in his *pulse*.

17. rote—[B] sound of the surf. Listening to the *rote* outside her window, Agnes recited the last ten verses of "The Rime of the Ancient Mariner" by rote.

SHOPTALK

Before you do your next Antiques *Roadshow* impression and start haggling over prices, master this array of market phrases. Done dealing? Answers on the next page.

1. meretricious (mer-eh-'tri-shis) *adj.*—A: falsely or tawdrily attractive. B: eager to sell. C: worth more over time.

2. bodega (bo-'day-gah) *n.*—A: bookstore. B: barbershop. C: wineshop.

3. queue up ('kyu 'up) *v.*—A: add sales tax. B: form a line. C: overspend.

4. haberdasher ('ha-ber-da-sher) *n.*—A: pushy salesman. B: dealer in menswear. C: mender of shoes.

5. caveat emptor ('ka-vee-aht 'emp-ter) *n.*—A: "Let the buyer beware." B: "Everything must go." C: "First come, first served."

6. patronize ('pay-tre-niyz) *v.*—A: visit as a customer. B: put up sale signs. C: argue.

7. mercantile ('mer-ken-tiyl) *adj.*—A: spending freely. B: using false tactics. C: of buying and selling.

8. haute couture ('oht ku-'tur) *n.*—A: pots and pans. B: high fashion. C: bicycle shop.

9. millinery ('mi-le-nar-ee) *n.*—A: women's hats. B: grains and flours. C: paper goods.

10. floorwalker ('flor-wawker) *n.*—A: browser who never buys. B: shoplifter. C: roving sales supervisor.

11. charcuterie (shar-ku-te-'ree) *n.*—A: café curtains. B: hair salon. C: deli specializing in meats.

12. estaminet (e-stah-mee-'nay) *n.*—A: price drop. B: small café. C: shopping spree.

13. chaffer ('cha-fer) *v.*—A: haggle. B: advertise aggressively. C: hoard.

14. defray (di-'fray) *v.*—A: lose value. B: provide payment for. C: offset.

15. monger ('mun- or 'mon-ger) *n.*—A: broker or dealer. B: cheapskate. C: dishonest merchant.

CHECK THIS OUT

If someone gets *cashiered*, he's been fired or dishonorably dismissed. As a verb, *cashier* comes from the Dutch *casseren* ("to cast off") and the French *casser* ("to discharge"); it's also related to *quash* ("to suppress, extinguish"). But a different French root gives us the clerk we call a cashier: *cassier*, which is from *casse*, or "money box."

Wit & Wisdom **195**

"Shoptalk" Answers

1. meretricious—[A] falsely or tawdrily attractive. That skirt is flattering, I suppose, if not a little *meretricious*.

2. bodega—[C] wineshop. Sipping sangria in the *bodega* doorway, June dreamed of Henry's kiss.

3. queue up—[B] form a line. We've got 300 jumpy people *queued up* for just five discount iPads!

4. haberdasher—[B] dealer in menswear. I think Andy gets his suits from the Buster Keaton *haberdasher* on 4th Street.

5. caveat emptor—[A] "Let the buyer beware." At the altar, Pastor Jon should have put a *caveat emptor* sign on my husband!

6. patronize—[A] visit as a customer. One more snide look from that clerk, and I'm going to stop *patronizing* this store.

7. mercantile—[C] of buying and selling. Willie has been in the *mercantile* trade since his first baseball-card swap.

8. haute couture—[B] high fashion. Jan seems to think that flip-flops and bib overalls are *haute couture*.

9. millinery—[A] women's hats. The price tag put an end to Clare's search for a trademark piece of *millinery*.

10. floorwalker—[C] roving sales supervisor. Our new *floorwalker* may as well be a mannequin for all the help he offers.

11. charcuterie—[C] deli specializing in meats. We can't make Dad's five-story hoagie until he gets back from the *charcuterie*.

12. estaminet—[B] small café. Looking for a killer cup of joe? Try the *estaminet* next to the train station.

13. chaffer—[A] haggle. Twenty minutes of *chaffering*, and you got the price reduced by just three cents?

14. defray—[B] provide payment for. For some 15 years, Duke's parents have *defrayed* the cost of his rent.

15. monger—[A] broker or dealer. If you're looking for a good olive oil, try the Italian *monger* downtown.

SOUND SMARTER

When you drastically improve something (say, your job performance, tennis play, or cooking skills), give yourself due credit: You've pulled a *180-degree turnaround,* not a 360-degree one. Logically speaking, 360 degrees would take you back full circle to square one—and right past your newfound success.

SEARCH FOR MEANING

Endings like *-ism* ("belief"), *-mania* ("obsession"), and *-phobia* ("fear") can tell you a lot about a word's meaning. As you navigate this quiz, pay close attention to the suffix of each term for helpful clues. At your wit's end? Turn the page for answers.

1. cryptology (krip-'tah-luh-jee) *n.*—A: raiding of tombs. B: series of puzzles. C: study of codes.

2. empathetic (em-puh-'theh-tik) *adj.*—A: showing understanding or sensitivity. B: sad. C: numb.

3. ovoid ('oh-voyd) *adj.*—A: egg-shaped. B: empty. C: passionate.

4. deify ('dee-uh-fiy) *v.*—A: treat as a god. B: bring back to life. C: disregard.

5. perspicacious (puhr-spuh-'kay-shuhs) *adj.*—A: finicky. B: of acute mental vision. C: fortunate or lucky.

6. indigenous (in-'dih-juh-nuhs) *adj.*—A: poor. B: native. C: mixed.

7. herbicide ('er-buh-siyd) *n.*—A: greenhouse. B: skin lotion. C: agent used to inhibit or kill plant growth.

8. pachyderm ('pa-kih-duhrm) *n.*—A: elephant. B: jellyfish. C: butterfly.

9. Kafkaesque (kahf-kuh-'esk) *adj.*—A: nightmarishly complex. B: gigantic. C: left-wing.

10. atrophy ('a-truh-fee) *v.*—A: waste away. B: win a prize. C: speak out against.

11. knavish ('nay-vish) *adj.*—A: sticky. B: sharply honed. C: deceitful or dishonest.

12. legalese (lee-guh-'leez) *n.*—A: passage of laws. B: strict rules. C: legal language.

13. patriarch ('pay-tree-ark) *n.*—A: Roman vault. B: father figure. C: homeland.

14. obsolescent (ob-soh-'leh-sent) *adj.*—A: teenage. B: quite fat. C: going out of use.

15. solarium (soh-'lar-ee-uhm) *n.*—A: sunroom. B: private nook. C: answer to a problem.

Wit & Wisdom **197**

"Search for Meaning" Answers

1. **cryptology**—[C] study of codes (-ology = "study"). The Enigma code was cracked by aces in *cryptology*.

2. **empathetic**—[A] showing understanding or sensitivity (-pathy = "feeling"). Do you think women are more *empathetic* than men?

3. **ovoid**—[A] egg-shaped (-oid = "resembling"). Jay's *ovoid* physique made him a shoo-in for the role of Falstaff.

4. **deify**—[A] treat as a god (-fy = "make into"). First we *deify* pop stars, then we tear them down.

5. **perspicacious**—[B] of acute mental vision (-acious = "with a quality of"). She's too *perspicacious* to fall for their hoax.

6. **indigenous**—[B] native (-genous = "producing"). The protesters argued that chemical testing would disrupt the island's *indigenous* species.

7. **herbicide**—[C] agent used to inhibit or kill plant growth (-cide = "killing"). Mother Nature is not fond of lawn *herbicides*.

8. **pachyderm**—[A] elephant (-derm = "skin"). Cartoonist Thomas Nast drew the first Republican *pachyderm*.

9. **Kafkaesque**—[A] nightmarishly complex (-esque = "resembling"). Getting my passport back involved a *Kafkaesque* maze of bureaucracies.

10. **atrophy**—[A] waste away (-trophy = "nourishment"). Without rehab, Alison's knee will *atrophy*.

11. **knavish**—[C] deceitful or dishonest (-ish = "like"). OK, who's the *knavish* sneak who swiped my drink?

12. **legalese**—[C] legal language (-ese = "language style"). Please, cut the *legalese* and speak plain English.

13. **patriarch**—[B] father figure (-arch = "chief"). That loudmouth is the *patriarch* of all spin doctors.

14. **obsolescent**—[C] going out of use (-escent = "becoming"). Our landline is now *obsolescent*.

15. **solarium**—[A] sunroom (-arium = "place"). Let us retire to my *solarium* for a little more inspiration.

PSEUDO SUFFIXES

The ending *-gate* is not a natural suffix; it was taken from the Watergate affair and tacked onto new scandals: *deflategate, debategate*. Same with *-athon*, taken from the Greek battle of Marathon, "to make things long": *telethon, walkathon*. Others include *-itis*, for modern maladies (*computeritis*), and *-holic*, for addictions (*shopaholic, tweetaholic*).

TIME OF DAY

While the basics—morning, noon, evening—suffice just fine, this quiz highlights the many ways we can indicate time. Test your knowledge, then see the light of day with the answers on the next page.

1. **per diem** (per 'dee-em) *adv.*—A: daily. B: twice a day. C: every other day.

2. **noctambulist** (nok-'tam-byoo-list) *n.*—A: early riser. B: sleepwalker. C: one who fears the moon.

3. **fortnight** ('fort-niyt) *n.*—A: wee hours. B: two weeks. C: holiday's eve.

4. **soiree** (swah-'ray) *n.*—A: high tea. B: birthday. C: evening party.

5. **circadian** (sir-'kay-dee-en) *adj.*—A: in sunlight. B: in insect season. C: in 24-hour cycles.

6. **ides** ('iydz) *n.*—A: odd hours. B: mid-month days. C: omens at night.

7. **adjourn** (uh-'jurn) *v.*—A: wake up. B: exercise. C: call it a day.

8. **curfew** ('ker-fyoo) *n.*—A: dog day. B: short nap. C: restriction at night.

9. **reveille** ('reh-vuh-lee) *n.*—A: hour-long drill. B: wake-up call. C: noon break.

10. **crepuscular** (kre-'pus-kyuh-ler) *adj.*—A: at twilight. B: of holy hours. C: of morning dew.

11. **repast** (ree-'past) *n.*—A: prior day. B: anniversary. C: time of a meal.

12. **contemporary** (kuhn-'tem-puh-rer-ee) *adj.*—A: part-time. B: on the morrow. C: present-day.

13. **du jour** (doo 'zhur) *adj.*—A: just for today. B: within the hour. C: of legal holidays.

14. **swing shift** ('swing shift) *n.*—A: 4 p.m. to midnight. B: midnight to dawn. C: 9 a.m. to 5 p.m.

15. **advent** ('ad-vent) *n.*—A: commercial holiday. B: day off. C: coming or arrival.

WHERE OUR WEEK COMES FROM

Sunday is literally "day of the sun," and *Monday*, "day of the moon." Most of the remaining days are named for Germanic and Norse gods: *Tuesday* for Tiu or Tyr (war god), *Wednesday* for Woden or Odin (chief god), *Thursday* for Thor (thunder god), and *Friday* for Frigg (Odin's wife). *Saturday* belongs to the Roman agriculture god Saturn, whose festivals in Rome led to *saturnalia* (wild partying).

Wit & Wisdom

"Time of Day" Answers

1. per diem—[A] daily. Your allowance is 75 cents *per diem*.

2. noctambulist—[B] sleepwalker. As a fridge-raiding *noctambulist*, I've wrecked my diet plan.

3. fortnight—[B] two weeks. The roofers will be back in a *fortnight* to add the gutters.

4. soiree—[C] evening party. By coincidence, six different guests brought baked beans to my *soiree*.

5. circadian—[C] in 24-hour cycles. We can't sleep—jet lag has skewed our *circadian* rhythms.

6. ides—[B] mid-month days. The *ides* of March were cold and wet, and the last day was no lamb.

7. adjourn—[C] call it a day. The committee was pooped and had to *adjourn* early.

8. curfew—[C] restriction at night. I can't go out—with the SAT approaching, my parents have imposed a 9 p.m. *curfew*.

9. reveille—[B] wake-up call. Buck's ringtone is a boot camp bugler's *reveille*.

10. crepuscular—[A] at twilight. On the front porch, I swing to the cicadas' *crepuscular* serenade.

11. repast—[C] time of a meal. Though I prefer to eat outside, on busy days, I take my midday *repast* at my desk.

12. contemporary—[C] present-day. "Egad!" and "zounds!" are not exactly *contemporary* expressions.

13. du jour—[A] just for today. The restaurant's soup *du jour* is French onion.

14. swing shift—[A] 4 p.m. to midnight. I feel out of whack after working the *swing shift*.

15. advent—[C] coming or arrival. With the *advent* of the holidays, we'll try to start our shopping early but will probably give in to our tradition of late gift giving!

> ### NAP TIME
> We think of a *siesta* as an afternoon nap, but originally the break was taken at noon. *Siesta* is Spanish and comes from the Latin *sexta,* meaning "the sixth hour." For Romans, noon was the sixth hour after sunrise, a hot time of day in the Mediterranean—and a good time to stop working and get in the shade.

TIEBREAKER

The 2014 Scripps National Spelling Bee was the first to end in a tie since 1962. In honor of the winners, here are tiebreakers from bees past. They're all hard to spell, indeed, but are they easy to define?
Answers on the next page.

1. **fracas** ('fray-kes) *n.*—A: fight. B: winter coat. C: drilling operation.

2. **milieu** (meel-'yer) *n.*—A: huge number. B: environment. C: French chef.

3. **sacrilegious** (sak-ree-'li-jes) *adj.*—A: worthy of worship. B: of all faiths. C: failing to respect.

4. **appoggiatura** (ah-pah-jeh-'tur-uh) *n.*—A: embellishing note. B: statement of regret. C: breakdown.

5. **kamikaze** (kah-meh-'kah-zee) *n.*—A: suicidal crasher. B: stand-up comedian. C: labyrinth.

6. **cerise** (seh-'rees) *adj.*—A: steeply inclined. B: shade of red. C: cool and calm.

7. **vouchsafe** (vowch-'sayf) *v.*—A: swear under oath. B: supply. C: protect.

8. **eczema** ('eg-zeh-muh) *n.*—A: itchy skin condition. B: hasty departure. C: former lover.

9. **semaphore** ('sem-uh-for) *n.*—A: half circle. B: lover of summer. C: signaling with flags.

10. **dulcimer** ('duhl-seh-mur) *n.*—A: stringed instrument. B: period of calm. C: sea monster.

11. **gladiolus** (gla-dee-'oh-les) *n.*—A: street fighter. B: high praise. C: plant.

12. **incisor** (en-'siy-zer) *n.*—A: tooth. B: troublemaker. C: earthworm.

13. **elegiacal** (eh-leh-'jiy-eh-kul) *adj.*—A: approving or complementary. B: menacing. C: lamenting.

14. **deteriorating** (de-'tir-ee-uh-rayt-ing) *v.*—A: stopping. B: growing worse. C: improving slowly.

15. **insouciant** (in-'soo-see-ant) *adj.*—A: uppity. B: nonchalant. C: incomplete.

Wit & Wisdom

"Tiebreaker" Answers

1. **fracas**—[A] fight. Both dugouts emptied as a wild *fracas* erupted at home plate.

2. **milieu**—[B] environment. A sailor's natural *milieu* is the ocean blue.

3. **sacrilegious**—[C] failing to respect. Uncle James considers it *sacrilegious* if you don't eat his homemade salsa.

4. **appoggiatura**—[A] embellishing note. "If you ask me," Karl sniffed after the performance, "the concerto blatantly abused the *appoggiatura*."

5. **kamikaze**—[A] suicidal crasher. Jimmy jumped from the flight of stairs like a *kamikaze* on a mission.

6. **cerise**—[B] shade of red. When Shana gets excited, her face turns a bright *cerise*.

7. **vouchsafe**—[B] supply. Suzie *vouchsafed* her ID but didn't look happy about it.

8. **eczema**—[A] itchy skin condition. Nothing works better than shea butter to soothe my *eczema*.

9. **semaphore**—[C] signaling with flags. Unable to get a word in edgewise at the table, Alison resorted to *semaphore* with napkins.

10. **dulcimer**—[A] stringed instrument. Andy's Appalachian *dulcimer* didn't really fit in with our punk rock band.

11. **gladiolus**—[C] plant. "I'm so sick of the deer eating all my *gladiolus*!" Mom barked.

12. **incisor**—[A] tooth. I think I cracked an *incisor* on your grandmother's biscuits.

13. **elegiacal**—[C] lamenting. The pastor was remarkably sensitive in mixing in humorous recollections during his *elegiacal* speech.

14. **deteriorating**—[B] growing worse. The already tense relations between the North and South are now *deteriorating*.

15. **insouciant**—[B] nonchalant. Taylor's boss noted that she has a decidedly *insouciant* way of attending to her daily priorities.

HISTORY OF "BEE"
The word *bee*, as in *spelling bee*, refers to a group of people gathering to accomplish something specific, usually to help someone. How it came to be associated with spelling isn't entirely clear, but the general meaning of "community" dates back to the 18th century. It is perhaps an alteration of the English *been* or *bean*, meaning "voluntary help given by neighbors."

MADE IN THE SHADE

Colors and patterns are featured in this quiz. Grab a calico crayon or a paisley pencil, and tackle these polychromatic teasers. For answers, turn the page.

1. cerulean (suh-'roo-lee-un) *adj.*—A: as blue as the sky. B: as green as a pea. C: as red as a rose.

2. ecru ('eh-kroo) *n.*—A: pigment from crocus roots. B: fishnet pattern. C: color of raw silk.

3. opaline ('oh-puh-line) *adj.*—A: having a rainbowlike array of colors. B: dyed, as batik. C: displaying a golden aura.

4. stipple ('sti-pull) *v.*—A: mark with spots. B: sprinkle with glitter. C: stripe with different shades of the same color.

5. tattersall ('ta-ter-sawl) *n.*—A: colored lines forming stripes. B: colored lines forming squares. C: colored lines forming a V pattern.

6. aubergine ('oh-ber-zheen) *adj.*—A: white like an eggshell. B: yellow like eggnog. C: purple like an eggplant.

7. skewbald ('skyoo-bawld) *adj.*—A: swirled. B: colorless. C: having brown and white patches.

8. sepia ('see-pee-uh) *n.*—A: silvery sheen of a pearl. B: pale-pink tint. C: brown pigment from cuttlefish ink.

9. incarnadine (in-'car-nuh-dine) *adj.*—A: tinged with yellow. B: blood-red. C: festively multicolored.

10. viridity (vuh-'ri-duh-tee) *n.*—A: translucence, as of glass. B: brightness, as of sunshine. C: greenness, as of grass.

11. alabaster ('al-uh-bas-ter) *n.*—A: white gypsum. B: arabesque diamond pattern. C: green patina on copper.

12. taupe ('tope) *n.*—A: bluish black of a crow. B: yellowish pink of a salmon. C: brownish gray of a mole.

Wit & Wisdom

"Made in the Shade" Answers

1. **cerulean**—[A] as blue as the sky. Looking into her wide, *cerulean* eyes, he could refuse her nothing.

2. **ecru**—[C] color of raw silk. Louise stared at the paint chips for hours, trying to decide between eggshell, French vanilla, and *ecru*.

3. **opaline**—[A] having a rainbowlike array of colors. The famously reclusive actress stepped out of an *opaline* Rolls-Royce.

4. **stipple**—[A] mark with spots. After his business lunch, Wayne realized his necktie was *stippled* with tomato sauce.

5. **tattersall**—[B] colored lines forming squares. Only my brother would wear plaid pants with a *tattersall* shirt.

6. **aubergine**—[C] purple like an eggplant. After the game, an *aubergine* bruise bloomed around the goalie's eye.

7. **skewbald**—[C] having brown and white patches. Nadine may have saved money on the discount dye, but her hair came out *skewbald*.

8. **sepia**—[C] brown pigment from cuttlefish ink. Darren added a *sepia* tone to a picture of himself and told everyone that it was his great-great-grandfather, the Civil War general.

9. **incarnadine**—[B] bloodred. When the cymbal player came in during the pause between movements, the conductor's face became *incarnadine*.

10. **viridity**—[C] greenness, as of grass. The *viridity* of their backyard landscape gave way to the reds and yellows of another autumn.

11. **alabaster**—[A] white gypsum. "An *alabaster* complexion is fine," said Snow White to Doc, "but could it be a symptom of anemia?"

12. **taupe**—[C] brownish gray of a mole. Marian is so dull, she goes out to paint the town *taupe*.

> **DEEP ROOTS**
>
> An artist's use of light and dark shading is called *chiaroscuro* (key-are-a-'skew-row), from the Italian *chiaro* for "light" and *scuro* for "dark." *Chiaroscuro* artwork may be black-and-white or may involve vivid contrasts of light and dark colors.

DREAMS

Dreams come true; without that possibility, nature would not incite us to have them.
—**JOHN UPDIKE**

"

The mind is the limit. As long as the mind can envision something, you can do it.
—**ARNOLD SCHWARZENEGGER**

"

If your world doesn't allow you to dream, move to one where you can.
—**BILLY IDOL**

"

A man who wants to do something will find a way; a man who doesn't will find an excuse.
—**STEPHEN DOLLEY, JR.**

"

You can't build a reputation on what you are going to do.
—**HENRY FORD**

THE PERFECT WORDS FOR
LIFE-CHANGING ADVICE

The most important trip you may take in life is meeting people halfway.
—HENRY BOYE

"
It takes no more time to see the good side of life than to see the bad.
—JIMMY BUFFETT

"
The squeaky wheel may get the most oil, but it's also the first to be replaced.
—MARILYN VOS SAVANT

"
Never tell anyone to go to hell unless you can make 'em go.
—BILL CLINTON

"
Live every day like it's your last, 'cause one day you're gonna be right.
—RAY CHARLES

"
Hunches are not to be sneezed at.
—RICHARD NELSON BOLLES

If you believe you have a foolproof system you have failed to take into consideration the creativity of fools.
—**FRANK W. ABAGNALE**

"

Learn to enjoy your own company. You are the one person you can count on living with for the rest of your life.
—**ANN RICHARDS**

"

One trouble with trouble is that it usually starts out like fun.
—**ANN LANDERS**

"

If you don't get out of the box you've been raised in, you won't understand how much bigger the world is.
—**ANGELINA JOLIE**

"

Kindness consists in loving people more than they deserve.
—**JOSEPH JOUBERT**

"

An eye for an eye only leads to more blindness.
—**MARGARET ATWOOD**